INTERNATIONAL CASES IN THE BUSINESS OF SPORT

Contemporary sport is big business. Major teams, leagues, franchises, merchandisers and retailers are in fierce competition in a dynamic global marketplace. Now in a fully revised and updated second edition, *International Cases in the Business of Sport* presents an unparalleled range of cutting-edge case studies that show how contemporary sport business is done and provides insight into commercial management practice.

Written by a team of international experts, these case studies cover organisations and events as diverse as the NBA, the Americas Cup, the Tour de France, the PGA tour, FC Barcelona and the Australian Open tennis. They explore key contemporary themes in sport business and management, such as broadcast rights, social media, strategic development, ownership models, mega-events, sports retailing, globalisation, corruption and financial problems. Each case study also includes discussion questions, recommended reading and links to useful web resources.

International Cases in the Business of Sport is an essential companion to any sport business or sport management course, and fascinating reading for any sport business professional looking to deepen their understanding of contemporary management.

Simon Chadwick is Professor of Sports Enterprise at Salford University, Manchester, UK, where he is a member of the Centre for Sports Business. He also works as Director of Research at the Josoor Institute in Qatar. His interests are in the areas of sports business strategy, sports marketing, and geo-politics and sport. Chadwick has worked with some of the world's most important sports organisations including FC Barcelona, UEFA, the European Clubs Association and Adidas. His research has been published or covered by outlets ranging from *Sloan Management Review* to

Newsweek, and CNN to the Academy of Marketing Science. *The Times* of London has called him the 'guru of sport management'.

Dave Arthur, in a previous life, was a well-respected and widely published lecturer and researcher who one day saw the light and who now plies his trade as a sought-after consultant and 'pracademic'. As CEO of Sport Business Resources he has undertaken diverse and interesting sport business projects that have seen him work with some of Australia's best professional franchises. His burning entrepreneurial desire has recently seen him set up the Institute of Sport – an online start-up that aims to disrupt tertiary education and equip sport business professionals with the skills to lead and manage sport.

John Beech is an Honorary Research Fellow at Coventry University, UK. He is an International Professor at the Russian International Olympic University in Sochi, Russia, and has held the post of Visiting Professor at FH Kufstein University of Applied Sciences in Austria, and at the Instituto de Empresa Business School in Spain. He currently lectures at universities in Sochi (Russia), Jyväskylä (Finland), Paris (France), Split (Croatia), and Karlsruhe and Salzgitter (Germany). He has published widely, both research articles and textbooks. His research has been reported in national newspapers in the UK and across Europe.

INTERNATIONAL CASES IN THE BUSINESS OF SPORT

SECOND EDITION

EDITED BY SIMON CHADWICK, DAVE ARTHUR AND JOHN BEECH

Routledge
Taylor & Francis Group

LONDON AND NEW YORK

First published 2017
by Routledge
2 Park Square, Milton Park, Abingdon, Oxon OX14 4RN

and by Routledge
711 Third Avenue, New York, NY 10017

Routledge is an imprint of the Taylor & Francis Group, an informa business

British Library Cataloguing in Publication Data
A catalogue record for this book is available from the British Library

Library of Congress Cataloging in Publication Data
Names: Chadwick, Simon, 1964– editor. | Arthur, Dave (Sports management consultant), editor. | Beech, John G., 1947– editor.
Title: International cases in the business of sport / edited by Simon Chadwick, Dave Arthur and John Beech.
Description: Second edition. | Abingdon, Oxon; New York, NY: Routledge, 2016. | Includes bibliographical references and index.
Identifiers: LCCN 2016018724 | ISBN 9781138802445 (hardback) | ISBN 9781138802452 (pbk.) | ISBN 9781315754239 (ebook)
Subjects: LCSH: Sports–Economic aspects–Case studies. | Sports administration–Case studies.
Classification: LCC GV716 .I5725 2016 | DDC 338.4/7796–dc23
LC record available at https://lccn.loc.gov/2016018724

ISBN: 978-1-138-80244-5 (hbk)
ISBN: 978-1-138-80245-2 (pbk)
ISBN: 978-1-315-75423-9 (ebk)

Typeset in Melior
by Out of House Publishing

CONTENTS

FIGURES

TABLES

NOTES ON CONTRIBUTORS

Nola Agha is Assistant Professor in the Sport Management Program at the University of San Francisco. She has experience in international business operations and has provided consultation services to some of the world's largest sporting leagues. To bring a multi-disciplinary approach to her research, she combines her training in economics and management to focus on the economic impacts of teams and stadiums, the efficiency and equity outcomes of stadium subsidies, and a variety of issues related to minor league baseball. Her research can be found in *Journal of Sports Economics*, *Sport Management Review*, *International Journal of Sport Finance* and more.

Kwame J. A. Agyemang is Assistant Professor at Louisiana State University, USA. His research examines the two-way relationship between social change and high profile social actors (e.g., athletes; sport organizations). That is, how social change affects high profile social actors and how these social actors may influence social change. His work draws from and contributes to extant work/theory on social movements and activism, race/ethnicity, social responsibility, and celebrity, among others.

Aila Ahonen at the Senior Lecturer at the JAMK University of Applied Sciences, Finland, teaching sport marketing and sport management in the Sport Business School Finland. She is an organiser of a multicultural Sport Management course and a regular visiting lecturer in many universities abroad. Her research area is focused on sport events management and sport entrepreneurship. She is a member of the Board of the European Association of Sport Management (EASM).

Christos Anagnostopoulos is Associate Professor in Sport Management at Molde University College, Norway and Assistant Professor in Sport Business Management at University of Central Lancashire, Cyprus. He holds a PhD from Coventry University and a Master's in Research in Sport Management and the Business of Football from Birkbeck, University of London. He is a holder of the Early Researcher Award of the

European Association for Sport Management and the Head of the Sports Unit at the Athens Institute for Education and Research. He is notably interested in corporate social responsibility in and through sport, as well as in the management of team sport organisations

Dave Arthur, in a previous life, was a well-respected and widely published lecturer and researcher who one day saw the light and who now plys his trade as a sought-after consultant and 'pracademic'. As CEO of Sport Business Resources he has undertaken diverse and interesting sport business projects that have seen him work with some of Australia's best professional franchises. His burning entrepreneurial desire has recently seen him set up the Institute of Sport – an online start-up that aims to disrupt tertiary education and equip sport business professionals with the skills to lead and manage sport now and into the future.

Emmanuel Bayle has a PhD in management science and is currently Professor in Sports Management at the Institute of Sport Sciences at the University of Lausanne (ISSUL). He has published several books and articles on sports management (great leaders in sport, governance in sport organisations, CSR and sport…) but also on CSR and non-profit management. He is a specialist in governance, management and performance for olympic sport organisations and has experience in executive education in this area. He is currently managing a research project on professionalisation of international sports federations.

Gaye Bebek is a faculty member at the School of Marketing and Management, Coventry University, UK. She holds a PhD and MSc in Marketing from the University of Kent. Her research is focused on ethical consumption, critical and cross-cultural marketing, and contemporary branding and marketing practices. She presented her research at the Academy of Marketing Science, European Association for Sports Management, International Centre for Corporate Social Responsibility Conference at the University of Nottingham, Corporate Responsibility Research Conference at the University of Leeds, and KEDGE Business School. She teaches consumer behaviour and global marketing.

John Beech is Honorary Research Fellow at Coventry University, UK. He is International Professor at the Russian International Olympic University in Sochi, Russia, and has held the post of Visiting Professor at FH Kufstein University of Applied Sciences in Austria, and at the Instituto de Empresa Business School in Spain. He currently lectures at universities in Sochi (Russia), Jyväskylä (Finland), Paris (France), Split (Croatia), and Karlsruhe and Salzgitter (Germany). He has published widely, both research articles and textbooks. His research has been reported in national newspapers in the UK and across Europe.

Johannes Berendt is a PhD student at the German Sports University in Cologne. His research focuses on the element of rivalry and conflict between brands. He holds a diploma in business administration (University of Bielefeld) and worked as a European correspondent for ESPN SportsTicker, the Press Association and NBA.com between 1999 and 2009. He then served four years as Global Head of PR for Team Sauerland, Europe's biggest boxing promoter, before starting his PhD in 2013.

Raymond Boyle is Professor of Communications at the Centre for Cultural Policy Research at the University of Glasgow. He has been researching sport and the media for over twenty years and is the author of a number of books including *Sports Journalism: Context and Issues* (Sage: 2006) and *Power Play: Sport the Media and Popular Culture* (with Richard Haynes, EUP: 2009). He teaches communications, media and public relations on the UEFA Certificate in Football Management course at the University of Lausanne. He sits on the editorial board of the journals *Media, Culture and Society* and *Communication and Sport.*

Aaron Burks is a Sports Industry Entrepreneurial Consultant. He worked with the AC Milan Junior Camp and contributed to their successful first youth camp in New Zealand. He also worked on sponsorships, branding and marketing for other sport-related events. Aaron has played both advisor and client-servicing roles for professional athletes with sports agencies. Aaron's primary focus has been implementing post-career strategies for athletes. Prior to earning his MA in Sport Management from the University of San Francisco, Aaron attended Indiana University on a football scholarship, where he played defensive back for the Hoosiers during the 2006 to 2010 seasons.

Terri Byers joined the University of New Brunswick in July 2014, after nineteen years of teaching and researching in the UK. She has authored a variety of publications including books such as *Key Concepts in Sport Management* (Sage), journal articles in *European Sport Management Quarterly, International Sport Management and Marketing, Corporate Governance* and *Journal of Leisure Research*. She has won over 1 million CAD in funding for her research and currently focuses on how voluntary sport organisations manage declining sport participation.

Charles M. (Chad) Carson is the Associate Dean and Professor of Management at Samford University's Brock School of Business in Birmingham, Alabama. He was named the 'Outstanding Educator' by the Federation of Business Disciplines/Southwest Case Research Association for 2011. Carson is a three-time recipient of the Brock School of Business Research Award, having published over forty peer-reviewed articles in leading academic journals such as *The Journal of Managerial Psychology, Case Research Journal, Educational and Psychological Measurement, Management Decision, Journal of Managerial Issues* and *Human Performance.*

Stephen Castle is Lecturer in Marketing and Entrepreneurship at Northampton University's Business School, UK. He holds a PhD from Sheffield University. Stephen's background is primarily in pharmaceutical/biotech international marketing and business development. Stephen has presented at international conferences on various topics such as risk management, due diligence, partnering and commercialisation of early-stage products. His interests and teaching lie in strategic marketing, corporate reputation and communications. He teaches both undergraduate and postgraduate students in the UK and global partner institutes.

Simon Chadwick is Professor of Sports Enterprise at Salford University, Manchester, UK, where he is a member of the Centre for Sports Business. He also works as Director of Research at the Josoor Institute in Qatar. His interests are in the areas of sports business strategy, sports marketing, and geo-politics and sport. Chadwick has worked with some of the world's most important sports organisations including FC Barcelona, UEFA, the European Clubs Association and Adidas. His research has been published or covered by outlets across the world, ranging from *Sloan Management Review* to *Newsweek,* and from CNN to the Academy of Marketing Science. *The Times* of London has called him the 'guru of sport management'.

Chris Chard is Associate Professor in the Department of Sport Management at Brock University, Canada. His research focuses on the business of sport, including finance as well as sustainability. He has published in various journals such as *Sport Management Review, Case Studies in Sport Management, Journal of Intercollegiate Sport* and *Journal of Management and Sustainability.*

David Cook is Lecturer in Marketing at Coventry University, UK. He holds a Master's in Marketing Management from UCLan, Preston, UK. He is a current PhD candidate, exploring the legacies of sports mega-events. He is notably interested in branding and consumer behaviour in sport, as well as in the management of team sport organisations.

Jonathon Edwards is Assistant Professor in the Faculty of Kinesiology at the University of New Brunswick (UNB), Canada. He teaches courses in sport marketing and sponsorship, and sport delivery systems for the undergraduate and MBA in Sport and Recreation Management programmes at UNB. Jonathon uses Applied Qualitative Research to explore sport delivery systems and athlete pathways through institutional theory, and has published in a variety of journals including the *Journal of Sport Management, Sport Management Review, Canadian Journal of Administrative Sciences* and *Journal of Applied Sport Management.*

Alain Ferrand is Full Professor of Sport Management at the University of Poitiers, France, and Director of the Executive Master in Sport Organisations Management conducted in French (MEMOS). He is an expert in international football and at the National Center for Sports Development (French Ministry of Sports) with regard to major sporting events management and volunteer management. He is a visiting professor at the Catholic University of Louvain-la-Neuve, INEFC Catalunya and 'Scuola Dello Sport' in Rome (Italian Olympic Committee – CONI Servizi).

Aurélien François has a PhD in sports management. Currently, he is lecturer at the University of Rouen, France. He was a member of the Research Center of Sport in Canadian Society at the University of Ottawa, Canada. He is the co-author of one book in French entitled *Sport and CSR: Towards a Responsible Management?* and several book chapters and articles in the sport management and sports economy fields. His topics are focused on CSR practices in sport, public management specifically for sports infrastructures and arenas, and sponsorship.

Leah Gillooly is Lecturer in Marketing at Alliance Manchester Business School, the University of Manchester. Following her PhD, which examined the contribution of sports sponsorship to consumer-based brand equity, Leah has published her research on sponsorship in a range of book chapters and journals including the *Journal of Marketing Management*, *Journal of Marketing Communications and Sport*, *Business & Management: An International Journal*. Leah has also carried out research with a range of sports organisations and is a member of the editorial board for *Sport, Business & Management: An International Journal*.

Michael M. Goldman is Assistant Professor with the University of San Francisco's Sport Management Program. He is also Adjunct Faculty at the University of Pretoria's Gordon Institute of Business Science, and Editor-in-Chief of Emerald's Emerging Markets Case Studies collection. Michael's teaching, research and consulting work is focused on assisting students, managers and clients enhance their competitiveness, especially in terms of acquiring, growing and retaining profitable customers and fans. He has published in *California Management Review*, *International Journal of Sport Marketing & Sponsorship*, *Management Decision*, Ivey Publishing, and others.

Jon Guest is a Principal Teaching Fellow at Warwick Business School. He was awarded a National Teaching Fellowship by the Higher Education Academy in 2011 in recognition of his work in developing teaching methods that promote a more active learning environment in the classroom. Jon is a regular contributor and editor of *Economic Review* and is the co-author of the seventh edition of the textbook *Economics For Business*. He also regularly writes cases on the economics of sport for the 'Sloman in the News' website.

Boris Helleu is Lecturer in Sport Management at the University of Caen, Normandy, France. He has headed the Sport Management programme since 2010. His work looks at the relationship between social media and the fan experience. His recent research deals with digitalisation of sports governing bodies, digital marketing of football clubs, mega-events and social media, and the way football clubs use Twitter. On a daily basis, he shares his international sports marketing and economy press review on his twitter account (@bhelleu). He also runs a blog dedicated to sports marketing (Hell of a Sport).

Maria Hopwood is a highly experienced academic and lecturer in the fields of sport public relations and sport business. Her research interest is in sports public relations and communications, meaning that her work bridges the disciplines of both public relations and sports management. Maria has taught at UCFB Wembley, the University of Northampton, UK, Leeds Beckett University, UK, Bond University, Queensland and Teesside University, UK. Maria has gained extensive experience working with professional sports organisations in both Australia and the UK, has worked with UEFA as an academic consultant and is a published author, accomplished researcher and conference presenter.

Cristina Jönsson is Lecturer in Tourism Management at the University of the West Indies, Barbados. She has extensive knowledge and experience of planning, development and management in the international tourism sector. Cristina has prepared and executed a tourism master plan for a municipal government in Sweden, and has managed and coordinated various projects ranging from sustainable tourism development to regional branding and marketing. She has worked on the development of a sport tourism strategy for Barbados with the Ministry of Tourism and various local stakeholders. Cristina's research interests include tourism foreign direct investment, sport tourism, medical tourism and second home tourism.

Adam Jones is a Senior Lecturer of Strategy and Marketing at the University of Brighton, UK. He is also course leader for the BSc (Hons) in Sport Business Management and MSc in Sport Business Management. Adam has a wealth of marketing knowledge and experience gained from working at a senior strategic level within a FTSE 100 company. His research interests are concerned with the environmental impacts of leisure mobility and mobility and mega sporting events. The basis for the case study in this book was his engagement with Albion in the Community, the charity Foundation arm of Brighton and Hove's football club.

Robert Kaspar has been an International Professor with the Russian International Olympic University in Sochi, Russia, since 2014, where his focus is on sports tourism. Robert lectures on sports and events management at the SKEMA Business School in Sofia Antipolis in France and at various Austrian universities on a wide range of subjects from international sports management to events management. He obtained his Doctorate in International Business Administration at the Vienna University of Economics after having researched and studied in New Zealand, Spain and Sweden. Since 1994 he has served in a number of mega-event companies, ranging from Expos to World Championships. From 2001 to 2003 he held the position of managing director for the Salzburg 2010 Olympic Winter Games and lately acted as coordinator of special projects with the Special Olympics World Winter Games in Austria 2017. Robert has published widely in the field of mega-events in sports and culture and co-edited a textbook on *The Business of Events Management* with Pearson Education in 2014. From 2004 to 2016 Robert headed degree progammes at

Austrian universities of applied sciences on subjects including 'Tourism and Leisure Management', 'Marketing and Communications Management' to 'Sports, Culture and Events Management'.

Courtney Keogh graduated from the MA programme at Department of Sport Management, Brock University, Canada. Her research focuses on environmental sustainability and the sport of golf. She has lectured at Brock University as well as in an international programme in Austria.

Eva Kipnis is Senior Lecturer in marketing at the School of Marketing and Management, Coventry University, UK. She holds a PhD in marketing from Durham University for which she earned the Best Thesis Award. Eva's research interests lie at the intersection of consumer behaviour and branding, comprising three strands: (1) consumer identities and cultural branding in multicultural marketplaces; (2) brands in illicit markets; and (3) political resistance brands and marketplace-mediated consumer resistance. Her work has appeared in *Journal of Business Research*, *Marketing Theory*, *Consumption, Markets & Culture*, *Journal of Public Policy and Marketing*, *Journal of Marketing Management* and others.

Alexey Kirichek has much practical experience in sport business at different senior levels. He currently lectures at the Russian International Olympic University, Sochi, Russia and SYNERGY University in Moscow, Russia. His research interests include sports marketing, sport sponsorship, football management and fan engagement. He works as a consultant in sports marketing for The GAME Agency, where he has been involved in international sports projects including football grass-roots events, sponsorship activations and creating ticketing strategy for the World Combat Games in 2013.

Joerg Koenigstorfer is Professor of Sport & Health Management at Technische Universität München. He received his PhD from Saarland University (2008) and was a postdoc at Pennsylvania State University. His research focus is on consumer behaviour in sports and health. He is a member of the editorial board of the *European Sport Management Quarterly* and has published articles in renowned journals such as *Journal of Sport Management*, *Journal of Marketing Research*, *Journal of Public Policy & Marketing*, *Marketing Letters*, *Appetite*, *Public Health Nutrition* and *Physiology & Behavior*.

Cheryl Mallen is Associate Professor in the Department of Sport Management at Brock University, Canada. Her research involves sport and environmental sustainability, ethics and event management. She is well published, with articles in the *Journal of Sport Management*, *Sport Management Review* and *European Sport Management Quarterly*.

Adel Mansurov graduated from the MA programme at Department of Sport Management, Brock University, Canada. He was a member of the Canadian Olympic

Committee Mission Staff for the 2014 Winter Olympic Games in Sochi, Russia. He is currently completing law school at the University of Ottawa.

Hamish McLean has thirty years' professional experience across a broad range of crisis and risk communication and disaster fields. He has a background in emergency management, journalism and police media, along with operating a consultancy for more than a decade with international clients in the health, aviation, law and allied sectors. His PhD is in media and disasters. He has published widely on political communication during disasters and communication in disaster planning, response and recovery. Dr McLean lectures in crisis communication at Griffith University, Australia.

John Nauright is Professor and Chair, Department of Kinesiology, Health Promotion and Recreation at the University of North Texas in the USA. Until June 2016 he was Professor of Sport and Leisure Management at University of Brighton, UK. He is the author and editor of many books including the award-winning *Making Men: Rugby and Masculine Identity*, *Rugby and the South African Nation* and *Sport Around the World: History, Culture and Practice* in addition to *Making the Rugby World: Race, Gender, Commerce* and *The Rugby World in the Professional Era*. His book *Sporting Entrepreneurs* appears early 2017. He is Honorary Professor of Sport Management at Lomonosov Moscow State University. He is Editor-in-Chief of *SportsWorld: The Journal of Global Sport*.

Gerd Nufer is Professor of Business Administration specialising in Marketing and Sport Management at ESB Business School, Reutlingen University, Germany. He is also Director of the German Institute for Sport Marketing. His teaching, research and consulting specialisations are sport marketing, event management, marketing communications and international market research. He has won awards for both his research and teaching.

Ricard W. Jensen is Associate Professor in the Sports, Events and Tourism Concentration at Montclair State University in Montclair, New Jersey. He has written several journal articles about public relations and marketing issues related to soccer. Many of these articles deal with Hispanic soccer fans in the USA and the reaction of fans in the United States regarding shirt sponsorship in Major League Soccer. Jensen serves on the editorial board of *Soccer and Society* and wrote an article for the journal about the history of national soccer team of the Netherlands. He is now studying the motivations of Hispanics in the USA to attend soccer matches and the atmosphere in soccer stadiums.

Richard E. Oddy is Senior Lecturer in the Department of Management, HR & Enterprise at Birmingham City University, UK. He holds an MBA in Sport Management and is currently undertaking a PhD in Entrepreneurial Marketing in the Golf Industry. Richard is a Senior Fellow of the Higher Education Academy (HEA), with teaching specialisms in sport management, sport marketing and event management. His research focuses on the business and management of golf.

Jiyoon Oh currently works as Sponsorship Sales Head in the PyeongChang Organizing Committee for the 2018 Olympic and Paralympic Winter Games (POCOG). She has worked for the marketing team of the Korean Olympic Committee (KOC) since 2008 and joined POCOG in 2012 as a secondee. She has a PhD and Masters in Sports and Leisure Studies from Yonsei University, an Executive Masters in Sport Organisations Management (MEMOS, organized by the Olympic Solidarity Programme) from the University of Poitiers, France and a Masters in Management from IE (Instituto de Empresa, Spain). She published *Olympic Marketing* (Korean version) with the Professors of MEMOS in Korea.

Adrian Pritchard is Lecturer in Marketing at Coventry University. His interests lie in sports marketing particularly the areas of brand extension and architecture, the adoption of new media and content creation. He has presented his research findings at a number of conferences around the world. His work has been published in a number of textbooks and journals including: *Leisure Studies*, *The International Journal of Sports Marketing and Sponsorship* and *Sport, Business and Management: An International Journal*.

Balwant Samra is Senior Lecturer in Marketing at the School of Marketing and Management, Coventry University, UK. He has over twenty years of experience as practising and consulting marketer in the packaging and retail industry, where he advised on marketing and advertising strategies. His current teaching responsibilities include principles and practice of marketing, retail marketing, global marketing and supervision of dissertations. His research focuses on sports fandom, consumer behaviour, relationship marketing and brand love. He is a guest lecturer at Leuven University and Visiting Lecturer at Infosys (India); Nanjing University, China; PSB, Singapore; Kadhir Has, Turkey.

James Santomier is currently Professor in the Department of Marketing and Sport Management, Jack Welch College of Business, Sacred Heart University, Fairfield, Connecticut, USA. He is also Visiting Professor at the University of Bayreuth, Germany. He received a BA and MA in Physical Education from Montclair State University, and a PhD in Physical Education from the University of Utah. Areas of academic interest include sport management, sport marketing and sponsorship, new media and the psychosocial aspects of sport. Dr Santomier has published in the areas of sport business, sport sponsorship, new media and the sociology of sport.

Nicolas Scelles is Lecturer in Sports Economics at the University of Stirling in Scotland. His PhD defended in 2009 dealt with outcome uncertainty in professional sports leagues. It was awarded by the Grand Prix UCPF (Union of the French

Professional Football Clubs) 2009 in the "Research" category. Nicolas has published scientific articles in several international journals (*Applied Economics*, *Economics Bulletin*, *International Journal of Sport Finance*, *Journal of Sports Economics*). He is a tutor in the IOC (International Olympic Committee) Executive Master in Sport Organisations Management (MEMOS) and member of the I3SAW (International Society for Sports Sciences in the Arab World).

Charlene Shannon-McCallum is a Professor teaching in the Recreation and Sport Studies degree programme in the Faculty of Kinesiology at the University of New Brunswick in Canada. Her research focuses on understanding recreation, leisure and sport behaviour from a social psychological perspective. She has completed studies that have examined peer bullying in youth-serving recreation and sport organisations, youth volunteering, parents' roles in facilitating physically active leisure for their children who are overweight, and factors that influence adolescents' participation in extracurricular activity.

Sten Söderman prepared his doctorate at Oxford University, holds his PhD and earned his docentship at SBS, Stockholm Business School and is now Professor Emeritus of International Business at SBS. Söderman's teaching and research is focused on market strategy development and implementation and on the international expansion of European firms in Asia and vice versa, as well as the global entertainment economy focusing on sport, specifically football. He is a member of editing boards of journals and a columnist at 'Idrottens affärer.se'. Söderman is the author and editor of 20 books, case studies and articles.

Cem Tinaz is the Director of the School of Sport Sciences and Technology at Istanbul Bilgi University, Turkey. Dr Tinaz has published in the areas of sport policy, sport event management and sport sponsorship. He has participated as tournament coordinator, director and marketing manager in many international sport events, including the ATP Istanbul Challenger 2012, 2014, 2015, the Mediterranean Games 2013, the WTA Championships 2013–2012, the Izmir Cup the ATP Challenger 2012–2011–2010, the WTA Istanbul Cup 2010, and the ATP Blackrock Tour of Champions 2008. Additionally, Dr Tinaz has been a board member for the Turkish Tennis Federation since 2009.

Douglas Michele Turco is Senior Research Associate at Sport Business School Finland. Previously, Professor Turco held professorial posts at Drexel University and Illinois State University. Turco was also on faculty at the Rajiv Gandhi Indian Institute of Management, IMC FH-Krems (Austria), and National Taiwan Sport University. He has authored over 50 journal articles on sport and tourism in journals such as *Sport Marketing Quarterly*, *International Journal of Sport Management*, *Journal of Travel Research* and *Journal of Sport and Tourism*. Professor Turco has written several books, including *Sport Tourism* and *Sport and Event Marketing*.

Sebastian Uhrich is Professor of Sport Business Administration at German Sports University's Institute of Sport Economics and Sport Management. His research interests focus on the behaviour of sport consumers and include sport sponsorship, ambush marketing, customer-to-customer interactions and rivalry. Sebastian Uhrich's work has appeared in prestigious journals in the field of sport management as well as in general marketing journals.

Benedikt Wallner obtained his Bachelor of Arts in Business in Sports, Culture and Event Management at the University of Applied Sciences in Kufstein, Tyrol, Austria. Mr Wallner has researched at the University of Applied Sciences in Kufstein with focus on sport and tourism management-related topics. He was also a member of the Organisation Committee of the Winter Olympic Games 2014 in Sochi, Russia.

Darin W. White is Professor of Marketing and founding director of the Sports Marketing programme in the Brock School of Business at Samford University in Birmingham, Alabama. He also serves as Chair of the American Marketing Association's Sport & Sponsorship-Linked Marketing SIG, the leading international scholarly body charged with expanding the knowledge base in the field of sports marketing. In addition, he serves on the board of directors for the Alabama Sports Foundation, Daniel Summit and Youth Sports of the Americas. His research interests include sponsorship-linked marketing and social media in sports. He serves on the editorial review board for two refereed sports business journals and has authored more than fifty journal articles and conference proceedings.

Donna Wong is currently working as Research Fellow in the Centre for Business in Society at Coventry University, UK. Her research interests relate to various social aspects of sport, in particular sports events in Southeast Asia. To this end, she has researched on the inaugural Youth Olympic Games, which took place in Singapore in 2010. As her ongoing interest is mediated sport, she has also looked at media sport development in Japan and Singapore. Dr Wong has disseminated her works widely in books, chapters and international journals. She is an active reviewer for a number of international journals and book publishers.

ACKNOWLEDGEMENTS

Simon Chadwick would like to thank his wife Barbara, son Tom and everybody else who supports, helps, encourages and challenges him to think differently on a daily basis.

John Beech would like to acknowledge the unceasing support of his wife Sue.

Dave Arthur would like to deeply acknowledge the never-ending support of his wife Selena in all his sane and less sane endeavours!

INTRODUCTION

Over the last two decades, sports across the world have undergone some radical and fundamental changes. From the commercialisation of leagues such as the NBA, to the branding of athletes such as David Beckham; from governance challenges in sports including cycling, to the growth of new markets in countries from China to Qatar, sport has become an industry characterised by exciting opportunities and complex managerial issues.

The industry is currently estimated to be worth $145 billion (PriceWaterhouse Coopers, 2011), although China has recently announced a state plan that is intended to lead to the creation of a domestic sport industry worth $850 billion by 2025 (Chadwick, 2015). This means that the industry's growth is not going to level out in the short term. Indeed, with nations around the world actively engaged in promoting the industrial development of sport, it seems likely that the coming two decades will see further change and growth.

For the last half a century, North American sport has been a trailblazer in the business and management of sport. So much so that almost 50 per cent of the global sport industry is now accounted for by this part of the world. Hence, North America is a mature marketplace from which many of us can learn a great deal and has led the way in the development of both practice and academic study in the fields of, for example, sponsorship, television rights and venue management. Cases presented here in this book adopt such practices as a focus in order to assist readers in understanding what has been happening in what is still the world's biggest sport economy.

More recently, the European sport industry has grown in maturity and, while not yet of the size or the strength of the North American industry, it is nevertheless a reference point for sport business and management practitioners and academics

1

across the world. The continent plays host to some of the biggest competitions (such as UEFA's Champions League), the most famous brands (like Real Madrid) and the most important governing bodies (the International Olympic Committee being one example) in the world.

As such, Europe has set some important benchmarks for the global sport industry, perhaps most notably the overseas commercial development of its properties. The European industry is, however, rather different to that in North America; the former tends to organise its sports based on free market principles, with little central intervention. In the latter's case, there is much greater intervention in sport via franchise awards, salary caps and draft systems. This means one gets a very distinctive model of sport in Europe and therefore a distinctive approach to sport management. We believe that the cases presented in this book encapsulate some of the most pertinent issues.

One must not forget also the role that Australia and New Zealand play in the world of sport business and management. Their industries are similarly mature to the European industry, reflecting an intense passion for sports in the region, and there is an established competence in fields such as event management and sponsorship. We therefore include several cases in this book from this part of the world.

But there are new industries, new markets and new competitors now growing in prominence across the world of sport. From having hosted the Olympic Games in 1988, China is now pursuing a vision of creating a domestic sport economy worth $850 billion by 2025. The Chinese have thus invested in sports properties, facilities and stars ranging from a brand new F1 circuit in Shanghai to a 13 per cent stake in Premier League club Manchester City. With a state-led sporting model allied to healthy entrepreneurial support, China seems to be creating a model of sport that will help define the industry in new ways as the twenty-first century progresses. Yet China is not alone; indeed, several other countries, including Qatar, India and Azerbaijan, are currently tilting the balance of power in world sport.

This means the theory and practice of sport management will continue to evolve over the coming decades, a development that is likely to have a distinctly Asian dimension to it. At the same time, such countries are looking towards the mature sports markets of the world for inspiration and in order to benchmark their managerial activities. As such, we anticipate this book being of relevance beyond what one might call the old industrial heartlands of sport. We therefore look forward to contributing to research and practice within these emerging markets and to cases from such countries taking greater precedence in potential future editions of our cases books.

Given the rapid development of the global sport industry, we therefore believe that this second edition of *International Cases in the Business of Sport* is a timely addition to work on the business and management of sport. We believe that the cases selected are interesting and relevant, and will enable both academics and practitioners to consider the most important issues facing sport in the second decade of the century. In the cases that appear here, we have aimed to present challenging, changing or complex situations that have required strong management and leadership or creative solutions.

With this in mind, we anticipate this book and the cases within it serving one of three purposes:

- It can be an accompaniment to a core text and readings;
- It can be used as the basis for seminar activities;
- It can be used in conjunction with reading or analysing a journal article.

Alternatively, the book can be used as part of a case-based approach to teaching either a module or a programme. The book might also be used as part of a dissertation or work placement. Readers should note that cases vary in length, thus enabling each of the cases to be used for different purposes.

Each of the cases presented here is organised into a standard format, which is as follows:

- Learning outcomes;
- Overview of the case;
- Case study;
- Questions;
- Conclusions;
- Recommended reading.

We hope the book serves the purposes of those reading it, but we implore readers to use the book pragmatically and flexibly. For example, although we provide questions for users to consider, for the purposes of a seminar readers are encouraged to formulate and consider their own questions. To aid in this, we hope that the recommended readings provide helpful insights. Otherwise, we would like to make you aware that we are all active on social media and can be contacted via our respective Twitter accounts:

- Professor Simon Chadwick @Prof_Chadwick
- Dr John Beech @JohnBeech
- Dr Dave Arthur @drsportbiz

We hope you enjoy reading this book!

REFERENCES

Chadwick, S. (2015). 'Global brands follow football's silk road to China', The Conversation, available at: https://theconversation.com/global-brands-follow-footballs-silk-road-to-china-16087 (accessed 7 March 2016).

PriceWaterhouseCoopers (2011). 'Changing the game – outlook for the global sports market to 2015', report, available at: www.pwc.com/gx/en/hospitality-leisure/pdf/changing-the-game-outlook-for-the-global-sports-market-to-2015.pdf (accessed 7 March 2016).

CASE 1

BRINGING THE NATIONAL FOOTBALL LEAGUE'S SUPER BOWL TO THE BIG STAGE: THE MARKETING AND BUSINESS ASPECTS OF SUPER BOWL XLVII

RICARD W. JENSEN

LEARNING OUTCOMES

Upon completion of this case study, the reader should be able to:

- understand the domestic and international spectator interest in the National Football League (NFL) Super Bowl;
- know why companies want to sponsor sports mega-events;
- comprehend the extent to which sports spectacles can bring tourists to a destination;
- learn about the various resources a community needs to be able to host sports mega-events.

OVERVIEW OF THE CASE

This case examines the sports business aspects associated with the hosting of the Super Bowl by New York and New Jersey in February 2014. Materials in the case cover such topics as bidding, planning, sponsorship, advertising, tourism, and economic impact. The 2014 Super Bowl is unique because it was one of the first events in this series hosted in a region that typically has cold weather and snow during the time of year when the event is held, and because it was the first instance in which this mega-event was hosted by New York City, which is the largest media market and financial center in the USA.

5

CASE STUDY

In the United States, the National Football League's annual championship, the Super Bowl, is viewed as the nation's ultimate sports event, drawing huge television ratings and creating a scene in popular culture that is so pervasive it has been compared to a national holiday (Hinckley, 2014). Across the world, the Super Bowl has a smaller following than the FIFA World Cup, the Olympic Games, and Formula One racing (Martin and Reeves, 2010). The Super Bowl attracts more than 108 million television viewers in the USA as well as a larger global audience (Schultz, 2013), and the cost of buying a 30-second Super Bowl television advert is about $4 million, more than the cost of purchasing any other television programming (Smith, 2013). Advertising during the Super Bowl does not just garner television viewers for sponsors of the stadium and the event. Crupi (2012) points out that when Metlife purchased the naming rights for the stadium that hosted Super Bowl XLVII, it gained more brand impressions than many other sports properties. Super Bowl advertising and sponsorship also sparks social media conversations that build buzz around the brands (Lee and Fixmer, 2013). The projected economic impact of Super Bowl XLVII was estimated at more than $600 million, a figure similar to previous Super Bowls (Schlossberg, 2013). Hosting a Super Bowl is thought to increase expenditure by fans; not only will this spectacle increase tourism (Newman, 2013), but it will also spur fans to purchase a variety of items (Rishe, 2013), including tickets to the game, food and beverages, legal and illegal betting (Traina, 2014), and merchandise (Lefton, 2013a).

In February 2014 the Super Bowl was held for the first time by the adjoining states of New York and New Jersey (even though both NFL teams in the region are named the New York Jets and the New York Giants, the actually play their home games at nearby MetLife Stadium in East Rutherford, New Jersey). The decision to have the New York City region host one of the most important sports events in the nation's biggest economic and marketing mecca was a strategic decision by the National Football League and its business partners, including its sponsors. Several factors had a major influence in giving the game to New York and New Jersey, including the fact that in 2010 the teams had built a new stadium that they share (MetLife), the idea that the region had already hosted every major sports event in the United States except the Super Bowl, the idea that so many corporations and financial firms are headquartered in the region, and the notion that this could be a novel event (Cimini, 2010). Woody Johnson, the owner of the Jets, had been campaigning to have the region host the Super Bowl for years; NFL commissioner Roger Goodell explained that the League awarded the game to the region because "New York is a unique market. It's the No. 1 market in our country and in many cases around the world. It will be a great experience for our fans and a great experience for the NFL" (Battista, 2010). Al Kelley, the chairman of the New York/New Jersey Super Bowl Committee, explained the NFL's choice to host the game in the region by saying, "It's the biggest sporting event in North America. It's only right that it gets on the biggest stage in the world" (Politi, 2013). Local politicians in New York and New Jersey said they anticipated that hosting the event would bring "glory" and heightened exposure to the region (Dopp and Matuszewski, 2013).

In considering which city a Super Bowl will be awarded to, determining factors include: whether it is a warm-weather venue, the extent to which the stadium is modern and adequate, and the capability of the region to have sufficient infrastructure to cover many factors, including security (Myers, 2013), airports, highways, hotel rooms (Haddon, 2013), and mass transit (Hinds, 2013). The winning bid submitted by the New York and New Jersey Super Bowl Host Committee specified that the stadium and all parking would be made available rent-free to the NFL (which controls 100 percent of all tickets and luxury suites), that a host committee with a full-time director and a staff of event and marketing professionals would be formed, and that there was the ability to raise $18 million or more to fund and manage major events. The cost of the bid totalled more than $70 million (Sherman, 2014).

The NFL awarded this mega-event to New York City and New Jersey, despite knowing that winters in this region are typically cold, and ice and snow a distinct possibility; there were significant concerns that cold weather would keep fans away and might even make it impossible to stage a half-time entertainment show starring Bruno Mars on the middle of the field (Margolin, 2013). A unique aspect of the marketing of Super Bowl XLVIII is the way in which the NFL facilitated relationships to engage fans with corporate sponsors. In most previous Super Bowls, the League hosted The NFL Fan Experience within a large convention; this event allows tourists and fans to engage with sponsors by taking part in events like throwing or kicking a football, having their photo taken near football-themed memorabilia, meeting star athletes, and so on. However, in the case of New York City, the only major convention center in the city (The Javitts Center) is not big enough to house this event and it was already booked for another engagement (Lefton, 2013b). As a result, the Super Bowl XLVII Host Committee developed an unusual alternative for fans to become involved with sponsors: they were able to close off Broadway Avenue (where major plays and musicals are performed) for 15 city blocks for a period of about a week before the game was played, and this area was temporarily renamed "Super Bowl Boulevard" (Goldman, 2013). The length of Super Bowl Boulevard was filled with corporate-sponsored events, including (among others) a six-story toboggan run on which guests could ride, a museum that allowed tourists to see Super Bowl trophies, opportunities to have oneself videotaped while acting the role of a star of concerts or commercials, and giveaways and discounted purchases of food, beverages, and merchandise. Twenty-nine major corporations in such diverse sectors as financial firms and banks, real estate, television, digital content, newspapers, beer, soft drinks, petroleum products, energy, high-tech, technology and manufacturing, telecommunications, insurance, jewellery, business aviation, men's apparel, car rental, and golf equipment, each paid $1 million or more to become a sponsor of the Host Committee (Caulderwood, 2013).

The Super Bowl was a success on several levels. Fox Television, which broadcast the game, reported that more than 111 million viewers watched at least part of the telecast, even though the game was not competitive with Seattle winning decisively by a score of 43–8 (Cox, 2014). The co-owner of the New York Giants, John Mara, said after the game that he was optimistic the event would return to New York City because it had been such an economic success (Myers, 2013). Many economists estimated the Super Bowl would bring in more than $600 million to the New York and New Jersey region (Belzer, 2014). The New York and New Jersey Host Committee, which led the efforts to bring the game to the region, reported that the game raised more than $100 million in revenue, although a comprehensive analysis of the actual impact of the event on business and tourism has not yet been published (Sherman, 2014).

QUESTIONS

1. To what extent might the NFL Super Bowl provide marketing opportunities for global companies? How should a global firm consider investing in Super Bowl-related marketing compared to other events like the FIFA World Cup, the Olympics, or Formula One?
2. From a marketing, branding, and sponsorship perspective, what are the main characteristics that need to be considered when sites are chosen to host mega sports events? How important are such factors as location, weather, facilities (convention centers, etc.), and the size of the media market?
3. How might you respond as a marketing or sponsorship professional if conventional means of activating brands and engaging with fans are not available? Is the NFL's example of creating Super Bowl Boulevard something you might want to develop? What are the pros and cons to this approach? What other alternatives might you consider?

CONCLUSIONS

The 2014 Super Bowl represented a major departure from the manner in which the National Football League decided to stage this huge mega-event. First, it proved that a mega-event can be hosted in a city or region that is often negatively affected by cold weather; on the day in February that this Super Bowl game was played, the temperatures were surprisingly warmer than they had been for weeks. Second, it showed that there are significant economic advantages in hosting a mega-event in an internationally well-known major city instead of a smaller or lesser-known site (e.g. compare the advantages of hosting the Olympics in London versus Sochi). Third, even when traditional preferred circumstances are not available to activate sponsorships, innovative alternatives can be found that can be successful; for example, the lack of a convention center did not prevent New York City from hosting the event.

RECOMMENDED READING

To begin with, students might find it helpful to read an introductory text on the business of sports such as *Managing Sports Business* (Trenberth and Hassan, 2012) or an introduction to sports tourism such as *International Sports Events* (Shipway and Fyall, 2012). Students who want to learn more about the business of the Super Bowl may want to read *The Billion Dollar Game* (St. John, 2010) or *Entertaining from Ancient Rome to the Super Bowl* (Adamson and Segan, 2008).

REFERENCES

Adamson, M. W. and Segan, F. (2008). *Entertaining from Ancient Rome to the Super Bowl*. Greenwood Press, Westport, CT.

Battista, J. (2010). "Jets owner instrumental in luring Super Bowl." May 25. *New York Times*. Available at www.nytimes.com/2010/05/26/sports/football/26nfl.html.

Belzer, J. (2014). "New York's Super Bowl XLVIII: the ultimate sports marketing case study." January 27. *Forbes*. Available at www.forbes.com/sites/jasonbelzer/2014/01/27/new-yorks-super-bowl-xlviii-the-ultimate-sports-marketing-case-study/.

Caulderwood, K. (2013). "Nearly half of Super Bowl 2014 sponsors are Wall Street firms." *IBI Times*. Available at www.ibtimes.com/nearly-half-super-bowl-2014-sponsors-are-wall-street-firms-1436572

Cimini, R. (2010). "NY/NJ has it down cold as XLVIII host." May 26. ESPN. Available at http://sports.espn.go.com/nfl/news/story?id=5219486.

Cox, K. (2014). "Super Bowl 2014 ratings set new record." February 3. CBS Sports. Available at www.cbsnews.com/news/super-bowl-2014-ratings-set-new-record/.

Crupi, A. (2012). "What does an insurance company need with a stadium?" *Advertising Age*. January 30. Available from www.adweek.com/news/advertising-branding/what-does-insurance-company-need-stadium-137795.

Dopp, T. and Matuszewski, E. (2013). "Super Bowl brings NYC glory even as New Jersey plays game host." Bloomberg. November 25. Available from www.bloomberg.com/news/articles/2013-11-23/n-j-towns-finding-super-bowl-less-of-a-boon-than-hoped-for.

Goldman, H. (2013). "New York's Broadway to become 'Super Bowl Boulevard' in 2014." January 24. Bloomberg. Available from www.bloomberg.com/news/articles/2013-01-24/new-york-s-broadway-to-become-super-bowl-boulevard-in-2014.

Haddon, H. (2013). "The game before Super Bowl." *Wall Street Journal*. May 22. Available from www.wsj.com/articles/SB10001424127887323475304578499493046953974.

Hinckley, D. (2014). "The Super Bowl is the biggest show of the year, but football is only part of it." *New York Daily News*. February 2. Available at www.nydailynews.com/entertainment/tv-movies/football-part-super-bowl-article-1.1597013.

Hinds, T. (2013). "The First Mass Transit Super Bowl?" Transportation Nation. April 19. Available from www.wnyc.org/section/transportationnation/.

Lee, A. and Fixmer, A. (2013). "Super Bowl sponsors justify record rates with online hits." *Bloomberg*. January 29. Available from www.bloomberg.com/news/articles/2013-01-29/super-bowl-sponsors-justify-record-rates-with-online-hits.

Lefton, T. (2013a). "Expect early arrival for Super Bowl licensed merchandise." *Sports Business Daily*. March 11. Available from www.sportsbusinessdaily.com/Journal/Issues/2013/03/11/Marketing-and-Sponsorship/The-Lefton-Report.aspx.

Lefton, T. (2013b). "NFL Experience will bow out to Broadway." *Sports Business Daily*. February 11. Available from www.sportsbusinessdaily.com/Journal/Issues/2013/02/11/Events-and-Attractions/NFL-Experience.aspx?hl=NFL%20Experience%20will%20bow%20out%20to%20Broadway&sc=0.

Margolin, J. (2013). "Next year's NY-NJ Super Bowl could be too cold for halftime musical act." *New York Post*. February 4. Available from http://nypost.com/2013/02/04/next-years-ny-nj-super-bowl-could-be-too-cold-for-halftime-musical-act/.

Martin, C. and Reeves, J. (2010). "The whole world isn't watching: the Super Bowl and U.S. Solipsism." In D. Wiggins (ed.), *Sport in America, Volume II*. Human Kinetics: Champaign, IL, pp. 421–43.

Myers, G. (2013). "NFL prepared to keep New York City safe for Super Bowl XLVIII at MetLife Stadium." May 20. *New York Daily News*. Available from www.nydailynews.com/sports/football/nfl-defense-security-super-concern-boston-attacks-article-1.1348793.

Newman, R. (2013). "2014 Super Bowl hotel rooms already scarce and pricey." *The Bergen County Record*. February 10. Available from www.northjersey.com/news/2014-super-bowl-hotel-rooms-already-scarce-and-pricey-1.549175?page=all.

Politi, S. (2013). "New York area on the clock for history-making Super Bowl." CNN. February 8. Available from http://edition.cnn.com/2013/02/08/us/superbowl-in-nj-2014/.

Rishe, P. (2013). "Super Bowl XLVIII pricing: A lesson in demand elasticity." *Forbes*. Available from www.forbes.com/sites/prishe/2013/09/19/super-bowl-xlviii-pricing-a-lesson-in-demand-elasticity/#61d088d96b23

Schlossberg, D. (2013). "Super Bowl preparations." *New Jersey Business*. February. Available from http://digital.njbmagazine.com/article/Super+Bowl+Preparations/1293764/143760/article.html.

Schultz, E. (2013). "Under review: Is Super Bowl worth $4 Million?" *Advertising Age*. November 4. Available from http://adage.com/article/special-report-super-bowl/game-time-decision-super-bowl-worth-4-million/245091/.

Sherman, T. (2014). "How MetLife Stadium scored Super Bowl 2014, bringing the big game to New Jersey." *The Newark Star-Ledger*. January 19. Available from www.nj.com/super-bowl/index.ssf/2014/01/how_metlife_stadium_scored_super_bowl_2014_bringing_the_big_game_to_nj.html.

Shipway, R. and Fyall, A. (2012). *International Sports Events*. Routledge, London.

Smith, A. (2013). "Super Bowl ad price hits record $4 million." CNN. January 3. Available from http://money.cnn.com/2013/01/03/news/companies/cbs-super-bowl/.

St. John, A. (2010). *The Billion Dollar Game*. Anchor Books, New York.

Traina, J. (2014). "Super Bowl 48 betting expected to be bigger than ever." Fox Sports. January 27. Available from www.foxsports.com/nfl/story/super-bowl-48-betting-expected-to-be-bigger-than-ever-012714.

Trenberth, L. and Hassan, D. (2012). *Managing Sports Business: An Introduction*. Routledge, London.

RECOMMENDED WEBSITES

Sports Business Daily: www.sportsbusinessdaily.com
The Business of Sports: www.thebusinessofsports.com
Forbes: www.forbes.com

CASE 2

RIVALRY IN THE GERMAN BUNDESLIGA: OPPORTUNITIES FOR AND THREATS TO MARKETING FOOTBALL

SEBASTIAN UHRICH, JOHANNES BERENDT AND
JOERG KOENIGSTORFER

LEARNING OUTCOMES

Upon completion of this case study, the reader should be able to:

- define the concept of rivalry;
- describe the special features of rivalry in sports;
- describe the ambivalent character of rivalry in a sporting context;
- discuss the opportunities and threats deriving from rivalry from the marketing perspective.

OVERVIEW OF THE CASE

This case addresses the concept of rivalry – a key phenomenon in the world of sports. Rivalry is a double-edged sword. On the positive side, it increases fan attention and demand (via gate attendance and the number of spectators in the media), enhances the enjoyment of sports consumption, helps develop fan identification and contributes to the attractiveness of the sport to different stakeholders. On the downside, rivalry may provoke unethical behaviour in fans, ranging from milder forms such as *Schadenfreude* about the rival's defeat to severe cases of violence. Negative effects may also occur for sponsors that get caught in the crossfire of rivalries. Presenting examples from the German Bundesliga, one of the most popular football leagues on the globe, this case study discusses opportunities and threats that sports marketing managers face when dealing with rivalry.

CASE STUDY

The concept of rivalry

Whether it is Real Madrid vs. FC Barcelona in Spain, Arsenal vs. Tottenham Hotspur in England or Borussia Dortmund vs. FC Schalke 04 in Germany, some football games seem to be more important than others. These opponents share a special relationship, which is called 'rivalry' (sometimes referred to as arch-rivalry). Rivalries are a highly prevalent phenomenon in the world of sports and can be observed across different countries, leagues and sports. In its most basic form, rivalry occurs on the pitch between the opposing teams or athletes. However, rivalry also transcends the sidelines and spills over to the stands directly into the minds of the spectators. The fans of sports teams (or individual athletes) have largely contributed to cultivating and nurturing the rivalry with other teams (or athletes) and their fans. These clashes between rivals are considered by many as the highlight of the season. From the perspective of fans, players and coaches, rivalries are a double-edged sword as they make victories sweeter and losses hurt more. The characterization of rivalries from the marketing perspective is similarly ambivalent, because rivalry comes along with a number of positive and negative facets that translate into opportunities and threats.

Rivalry can be defined as 'a subjective competitive relationship that an actor has with another actor that entails increased psychological involvement and perceived stakes of competition for the focal actor, independent of the objective characteristics of the situation' (Kilduff *et al.*, 2010: 945). Outside the sports context, the concept of rivalry is often negatively connoted. Rivalry has been described as a destructive competition that shares many characteristics with hostility (Vogler, 2011). Some authors have argued that envy and jealousy are subcategories of rivalry (Rost and Schulz, 1994). This may also be true in sports, because thinking and talking about a rival team hardly ever elicits positive associations. Highly identified fans often denigrate and insult rival teams and their supporters. This can lead to aggression, violence and riots. However, a closer look reveals that there is more to rivalry in sports than aggressive or violent behaviour. In what follows next, we provide a sport-specific definition of rivalry and present key reasons why rivalry may be evaluated positively from the marketing perspective, despite the downsides of unethical behaviours mentioned before.

Sports rivalry is defined as 'a fluctuating adversarial relationship existing between two teams, players or groups of fans, gaining significance through on-field competition, on-field or off-field incidents, proximity, demographic make-up, and/or historical occurrence(s)' (Havard *et al.*, 2013: 51). This definition includes potential reasons why rivalries develop in sports. An important determinant of rivalry is similarity between teams with regard to factors such as cultural values, distribution of talented players, geographical location of the teams and sporting competitions (Kilduff *et al.*, 2010). However, low similarity between teams with regard to other variables, such as when teams represent different religions or cultures, can also contribute to rivalry. In sport sociology there have been attempts to categorize rivalry in terms of power inequalities (e.g. rich vs. poor), submerged nationhoods (Croatian teams in Austria), playing style (e.g. modern vs. traditional) or local differences (civility vs. backwardness) (Giulianotti and Armstrong, 2001). These factors can be classified along two dimensions, that is the geographical (e.g. territory and origin) and the ethnic (e.g. nationality, ethnic identity, language, religion) dimensions (Dmowski, 2013). This case focuses on rivalries in German football from the perspective of marketing. The next section describes team rivalries in the German football league (Bundesliga).

Rivalry in the German Bundesliga

The Bundesliga is one of the most popular team sports leagues in Europe. There are numerous rivalries within this league, which therefore represents a fertile ground for discussion of this topic. Most rivalries in the Bundesliga have regional roots, such as those between Borussia Dortmund and FC Schalke 04 (Ruhr Valley), between Hamburger SV and SV Werder Bremen (North), or between Hannover 96 and Eintracht Braunschweig (Lower Saxony). Other rivalries are performance-based, for instance that between Borussia Dortmund and FC Bayern München (Munich), which are the only two teams to have won the national championship between 2011 and 2016. The following descriptions highlight the special character of rival games in the Bundesliga and point out the fan perceptions and fan behaviours that manifest the phenomenon.

One characteristic of rivalries is the special choreography that fan communities typically perform before and during rival games. Sometimes large groups of fans meet hours before a rival game to march to the stadium together. These practices add to a more heated atmosphere in the stadium (Uhrich and Benkenstein, 2010). For example, during a 2013/14 season game between rivals Hannover 96 and Eintracht Braunschweig, the stadium was full of blue-and-yellow flags (i.e. the colours of Braunschweig), signs with lions (i.e. the mascot of Braunschweig) and confetti. Another example is a banner with the slogan 'A feeling, deeper than hate!' that Dortmund fans rolled out during a 2013/14 season game between Borussia Dortmund and FC Schalke 04. Other activities include intense discussions in online forums that start earlier, before clashes between rivals take place, and that last longer after the completion of the game compared to games against non-rival teams.

Rivalries can provoke negative emotions in fans, which may in turn increase aggressiveness and insults or even cause violent behaviour. Highly identified fans typically derive pleasure from seeing the rival team suffer (or lose), a phenomenon referred to as *Schadenfreude* (Leach *et al.*, 2003). Many more light-hearted pranks often occur around clashes between rivals. In 2010, a Dortmund fan managed to hoist a Dortmund flag on Schalke's stadium roof. This incident received national media attention – just like the Dortmund fan who took a picture of himself and then

Schalke head coach Mirko Slomka, who was unknowingly holding a scarf that said '(expletive) Schalke'. Such activities represent rather harmless forms of animosity. However, fan creativity can quickly turn into criminal acts. Incidents of smearing the rival's team bus are common. Hamburger SV fans once painted an underpass near Werder Bremen's stadium in Hamburger SV club colours, as did FC Bayern München fans inside the stadium of city rival TSV 1860 München.

More recently, the rivalry between Hannover 96 and Eintracht Braunschweig caught the public's attention – for all the wrong reasons. Separated by some 60 kilometres, the two rivals had not faced each other in the top flight for 37 years. Yet their fans managed to preserve their mutual hatred. Club officials and authorities were concerned about an escalation of violence, fearing hooligans would use the derby to fight each other. Up to 700 policemen were deployed on game night. Upon arriving at Hannover central station on a chartered train, Braunschweig fans covered the tracks with animal innards and pig heads. They also set off fireworks, injuring five policemen. Fearing an escalation of violence, no less than 3,200 policemen were brought in for the second derby in April 2014. With a sell-out crowd of 22,687 fans in attendance, this resulted in a 1:7 ratio of policemen and fans. The overall costs for the police operation amounted to 2 million euros, adding fuel to the ongoing discussion about whether it is the clubs or the state who should cover such expenditure (HAZ, 2014).

Case diagnosis

This section discusses both opportunities and threats arising from rivalries from the perspective of sports marketing. In terms of opportunities, rivalries increase demand (via enhancement of many of the enjoyable aspects of team sports consumption), offer fans opportunities to build and reinforce a positive self-concept via their commitment to the team and contribute to the attractiveness of leagues. The major threats include detrimental effects on the image of individual teams (or the entire league and the brands associated with it, including sponsors) through incidents of aggression and violence.

Opportunities for marketing football

High demand due to increased enjoyment of team sports consumption

Clashes between rival teams usually receive high fan attention. The more exciting football games are and the higher the importance of a certain game is (games against rivals are typically among the most important games), the more positively fans evaluate the consumption experience of following the game, in particular when their favourite team wins (Bizman and Yinon, 2002; Wann and Dolan, 1994). Fans enjoy the atmosphere at the stadium even more than usual when their team plays against rivals, or engage in particularly heated debates on the game in and outside the stadium.

Uhrich (2014) refers to this as 'intensifying', because many activities inside and outside the stadium are more enjoyable around fixtures between rival teams than for regular games. Also, the fans' engagement as co-producers of the event increases. For example, fans contribute more to producing the special atmosphere in the stadium. High fan attention is positively associated with turnover, because fans have a higher willingness to pay for attending or watching these games (thereby influencing ticket prices, broadcasting revenues and sponsorship revenues – the latter via an indirect pathway). The demand for gate attendance therefore increases. Also, there is higher media demand. For example, the Ruhr rivalry between Borussia Dortmund and FC Schalke 04 has set a number of viewing records in the past (DWDL, 2014). Other rivalries also set new records, as in January 2013 when the north derby (Hamburger SV vs. SV Werder Bremen) and the south derby (FC Bayern München vs. VfB Stuttgart) combined attracted almost 2 million pay-TV viewers in Germany – a new record for a Sunday match day. Fans may also spend more on merchandise because it allows them to stand against their rivals. This brings us to the concept of team identification.

Building and reinforcing identification

Many team sports consumers develop strong ties to a particular team in order to develop a positive self-concept. Social Identity Theory (Tajfel and Turner, 1979) provides a conceptual substantiation of this phenomenon. Associating oneself with a particular group and dissociating from other groups helps people to reinforce and strengthen their own social identity. Individuals strive for positive distinctiveness, which can be achieved through competition between their own group and other groups. Rivalry offers rich opportunities to develop a positive social identity because the rival team and its supporters represent a particularly relevant out-group (Berendt and Uhrich, 2016). Any evidence of superiority over the out-group, such as scoring a goal, winning a game or finishing the season higher up in the league table, contributes to distinctiveness. Highly identified fans in particular often 'bask in reflected glory' and demonstrate to others that they stand behind their club (Cialdini *et al.*, 1976), which also increases their loyalty to the team. Of course, losing a game against the rival represents an equally important threat to one's self-concept. However, even losses can make highly identified fans stick to their team, similar to a romantic partnership in which partners weather good times and bad times (Uhrich and Koenigstorfer, 2009).

Enhanced attractiveness of leagues

The more rivalries there are in a league, the more attractive the league is as a whole. This is because the league profits from high fan and media attention (see above), and because the associations that are linked to rivalries between teams may transfer to the league as a whole (e.g. 'competitive', 'exciting' and 'thrilling'). Two types of rivalries in particular may contribute to the attractiveness of a league: (1) fierce competitors who score equally as regards performance but differ in some other factors (e.g. teams that have similar success and player talent, but differ with regard to personality attributes); (2) underdog versus star club scenarios, where there is some likelihood of the underdogs beating the star club (Koenigstorfer *et al.*, 2010).

Threats affecting the marketing of football

Violence

Violence threatens the image of individual teams or the league as a whole. Aggression and violence decrease enjoyment and intention to attend games for most fans. For example, families may avoid rival games because they have concerns about their safety in and around the stadium. This is problematic because opportunities to build team identification, which is often formed in childhood and lasts for a lifetime, are reduced. The increased violence calls for new public relations and communication strategies, with a need for officials to remain reasonable (e.g. avoiding excessive exploitation of rivalry). A key task for team sports marketers is managing rivalries in a way that reduces this threat while maintaining the positive aspects. Marketers also have to make sure that they (in collaboration with the police) deal with crowd control and aspects that are related to traffic (Wood *et al.*, 2011).

Detrimental effects on sponsors

Different target groups (here: fans of the favourite team vs. fans of the rival team) perceive sponsorship differently. The bigger the rivalry with a club is, the more negative the fans' attitude is towards the sponsors of the rival team (Bauer *et al.*, 2012). This is particularly true for highly identified fans (Bee and Dalakas, 2013). Brands should therefore assess in detail whether they should make use of the special features of rivalries to activate or leverage their sponsorship. This sponsorship may be subject to critique as perceived by fans of the rival team and produce a backlash effect (e.g. consumer reaction or responses that harm the brand in social media).

QUESTIONS

1. How can sports marketing managers exploit the marketing potential that goes along with rivalries?
2. What are suitable strategies for limiting the threats arising from rivalries?
3. What are the challenges of creating new leagues such as the European Nations League in light of rivalries?
4. Beside fan rivalries, there are fan friendships, that is fan communities that support each other. What are the potential threats and opportunities to be found in fan friendships?

CONCLUSIONS

Due to its diverse effects, rivalry in team sports is a double-edged sword from the perspective of team sports marketing. While sometimes it seems that you can't live with rivals, you can't live without them either. The key challenge for sports marketing managers is to exploit rivalry's marketing potential and avoid its threats simultaneously. Mastering this challenge is not only a task for individual teams (or athletes) but also needs to be addressed at the league (or event) level. Besides individual teams (or athletes) and representatives of the league (or event), the management of rivalry also requires the involvement of other key stakeholders of sports such as fans, the media, sponsors and security authorities.

RECOMMENDED READING

To begin with, students might find it helpful to read an introductory text on psychology – specifically chapters on social groups, emotions and interactions with others. Thereafter, students should consider looking at journal articles in this area of psychology in sports (for example, Bizman and Yinon, 2002). Next, reading texts on rivalry (for example, Kilduff *et al.*, 2010) is a good way to find out about the causes and effects of rivalry in sports. These have appeared both in sports journals (for example, in the *Journal of Sport Behavior* – Havard *et al.*, 2013) and in general marketing literature (for example, in *Marketing Review St. Gallen* – Bauer *et al.*, 2012, and in the *Journal of Consumer Research* – Wood *et al.*, 2011).

REFERENCES

Bauer, H. H., Hattula, S., Grimm, A. and Ebertin, C. (2012). Die dunkle Seite des Sponsoring – Unliebsame Effekte von Rivalität auf die Sponsorenmarke [The dark side of sponsorship – Undesired effects of rivalry on the sponsor's brand]. *Marketing Review St. Gallen*, 29(1), 54–60.

Bee, C. and Dalakas, V. (2013). Rivalries and sponsor affiliation: Examining the effects of social identity and argument strength on responses to sponsorship-related advertising messages. *Journal of Marketing Communications*, 21(6), 408–24.

Berendt, J. and Uhrich, S. (2016). Enemies with benefits: The dual role of rivalry in shaping sports fans' identity. *European Sport Management Quarterly*, 16(5), 613–34.

Bizman, A. and Yinon, Y. (2002). Engaging in distancing tactics among sport fans: Effects on self-esteem and emotional responses. *Journal of Social Psychology*, 142(3), 381–92.

Cialdini, R. B. *et al.* (1976). Basking in reflected glory: Three (football) field studies. *Journal of Personality and Social Psychology*, 34(3), 366–75.

Dmowski, S. (2013). Geographical typology of European football rivalries. *Soccer & Society*, 14(3), 331–43.

Giulianotti, R. and Armstrong, G. (2001). Constructing social identities: Exploring the structured relations of football rivalries, in G. Armstrong and R. Giulianotti (eds), *Fear and Loathing in World Football*. Berg, Oxford, 267–79.

Havard, C. T., Gray, D. P., Gould, J., Sharp, L. A. and Schaffer, J. J. (2013). Development and validation of the sport rivalry fan perception scale (SRFPS). *Journal of Sport Behavior*, 36(1), 45–65.

Kilduff, G. J., Elfenbein, H. A. and Staw, B. M. (2010). The psychology of rivalry: A relationally dependent analysis of competition. *Academy of Management Journal*, 53(5), 943–69.

Koenigstorfer, J., Groeppel-Klein, A. and Kunkel, T. (2010). Attractiveness of national and international football leagues – Perspectives of fans of 'star clubs' and 'underdogs'. *European Sport Management Quarterly*, 10(2), 127–63.

Leach, C. W., Spears, R., Branscombe, N. R. and Doosje, B. (2003). Malicious pleasure: Schadenfreude at the suffering of another group. *Journal of Personality and Social Psychology*, 84(5), 932–43.

Rost, W. and Schulz, A. (1994). *Rivalität. Über Konkurrenz, Neid und Eifersucht* [Rivalry. On Competition, Envy and Jealousy]. Springer Verlag, Berlin.

Tajfel, H. and Turner, J. C. (1979). An integrative theory of intergroup conflict, in W. G. Austin and S. Worchel (eds), *The Social Psychology of Intergroup Relations*, Brooks/Cole, Monterey, CA, 33–47.

Uhrich, S. (2014). Exploring customer-to-customer value co-creation platforms and practices in team sports. *European Sport Management Quarterly*, 14(1), 25–49.

Uhrich, S. and Benkenstein, M. (2010). Sport stadium atmosphere: Formative and reflective indicators for operationalizing the construct. *Journal of Sport Management*, (24)2, 211–37.

Uhrich, S. and Koenigstorfer, J. (2009). Atmosphere at major sports events – A perspective from environmental psychology. *International Journal of Sports Marketing and Sponsorship*, 10(4), 325–44.

Vogler, J. (2011). *Theorie der Konkurrenz. Rivalität und Wettbewerb in den internationalen Beziehungen* [The Theory of Competition. Rivalry and Competition in International Relationships]. Metropolis-Verlag, Marburg.

Wann, D. and Dolan, T. (1994). Spectators' evaluations of rival and fellow fans. *The Psychological Record*, 44(3), 351–8.

Wood, S., McInnes, M. and Norton, D. A. (2011). The bad thing about good games: The relationship between close sporting events and game-day traffic fatalities. *Journal of Consumer Research*, 38(4), 611–21.

RECOMMENDED WEBSITES

DWDL (2014). Revierderby beschert Sky neuen Quotenrekord [Ruhr derby sets new viewing rate records for Sky], accessed 17 August 2015 from www.dwdl.de/zahlenzentrale/33796/revierderby_beschert_sky_neuen_quotenrekord/.

HAZ (2014). Derbyeinsatz kostete zwei Millionen Euro [Police operation at derby cost two million Euro] 2014, accessed 17 August 2015 from www.haz.de/Hannover/Aus-der-Stadt/Uebersicht/Derbyeinsatz-kostete-zwei-Millionen-Euro.

Meedia (2013). Nord- und Süd-Derbys bescheren Sky Rekord [Derbies between Northern and Southern teams set new records for Sky], accessed 17 August 2015 from http://meedia.de/2013/01/28/nord-und-sud-derbys-bescheren-sky-rekord.

CASE 3

IF THE QUENELLE IS RACIST, THEN 'ALL PRIESTS ARE PAEDOPHILES' AND PINEAPPLES WILL BE BANNED[1]

GAYE BEBEK, STEPHEN CASTLE AND EVA KIPNIS

LEARNING OUTCOMES

Upon completion of this case study, the reader should be able to:

■ identify and explain the detrimental effects of racism on football and for sport in general;
■ evaluate alternative means of penalizing clubs, individuals and authorities when racism is shown to occur;
■ assess what impact racism has or could have on clubs;
■ critically evaluate how clubs themselves and the football authorities can eradicate racism from the field and terraces. What can business do?

OVERVIEW OF THE CASE

This case looks at the long history of racism on and off the football pitch. Although this case focuses on UK football, the issue does not exist solely within the UK – it is found in many countries and even threatens to disrupt the 2018 World Cup in Russia.

The case highlights the poor attempts by clubs and by football (and other) authorities to stamp out racism. The examples demonstrate the lack of consistency in dealing with the problem and the apparent unwillingness of people at the top to deal with this issue. Perhaps business needs to be drawn into the furore to ensure action – hit racists where it hurts (and we are not talking footballs here). Umbro's withdrawal of sponsorship of John Terry is a start; Zoopla's withdrawal of their West Bromwich Albion shirt sponsorship another – let's have some bigger action off the pitch.

CASE STUDY

Everton FC player Dixie Dean walked off from a game at half time after being offended by racist comments. That was in the 1930s (FTB, 2012). More than half a century later one would like to hope that racism is no longer an issue, especially in sports. Sadly, with the lack of real monetary punishment, it is a case of game over ethics for clubs. The 1980s in particular was a rough time, especially in the UK, regarding issues around racism, and football brought the tension to the playing fields. What is interesting is that the fan groups (and clubs) who used racial abuse as a way to upset or damage an opponent in the 1980s have not changed much in the 2010s.

Chelsea's first black player, Paul Canoville, was subject to continuous racial abuse during his early career in the club. During his debut with Chelsea in 1982 he was offended by none other than his own club's fans. He later told *The Telegraph* how he remembers that day: 'As I ran down the line, I heard the abuse for the first time: "you black ****, you golliwog", "go back home you n*****". I expected it on the street, but not in a professional stadium' (*The Telegraph*, 2008).

That was not the only time that Chelsea has been involved with racial abuse. In 2008 Chelsea's Israeli manager Avram Grant received offensive anti-Semitic comments and death threats from Chelsea fans (BBC, 2008a). Chairman Bruce Buck said at the time: 'It unfairly smears the reputation of the vast majority of the Chelsea fans who rightly do not want to be associated with such activity' (BBC, 2008b). But some saw Chelsea's inability to prevent such offence by their fans as acceptance or even approval of the offence. More recently, offensive behaviour by Chelsea fans turned to involve the players as well. In 2011 Queens Park Rangers player Anton Ferdinand claimed to have been racially abused by the Chelsea captain John Terry (*The Guardian*, 2011b). Terry fully denied the claims, and Chelsea manager André Villas-Boas declared that the club supported the team captain and described the matter as 'blown out of proportion' (BBC, 2011a). The issue was taken up by the Metropolitan Police and in 2012 Terry was found guilty, fined £220,000 and banned for four games (BBC, 2011b, 2012a). However, most importantly Terry lost a sponsorship deal worth nearly £4 million with Umbro (TopNews, 2012). Umbro had said that Terry's deal would remain in place, but in September 2012 the deal was not renewed (Footy Boots, 2012). As for Chelsea, they were hit only with the captain's four-game ban. Chelsea's club sponsors, Samsung, stated that they do not endorse individual players: 'Samsung Electronics enjoys this commercial partnership with the club only. It does not extend to any members of the playing staff at Chelsea FC' (*The Telegraph*, 2012). There was no monetary punishment for the club itself, and hence no real measures were subsequently taken by Chelsea.

Chelsea's inaction towards racist offence either by the players or the fans could have been regarded as a 'green light' by fans, as similar offences continued to be seen on the terraces. Only in 2012 when a Chelsea fan made a monkey gesture to Didier Drogba did Chelsea decide to take action (BBC, 2012b). The fan was pictured while hurling the abuse at Drogba, and was banned for life from attending any football game in the UK or abroad. A Chelsea spokesman later stated: 'Chelsea Football Club and the overwhelming majority of our fans abhor all forms of discrimination and believe they have no place in our club or our communities' (BBC, 2012c). This punishment and statement can be regarded as Chelsea's baby steps towards repairing their image. Yet it cannot be said to be anywhere near effective, as in September 2013 it was Chelsea fans again who were chanting anti-Semitic comments towards the Tottenham terraces. The incident, however, was never followed up (Channel 4, 2014).

Newcastle United has also been cited on more than one occasion in relation to racial abuse. Cyrille Regis was abused by Newcastle fans whilst playing for West Bromwich Albion in the 1980s. He was known as Big Cyrille, or the 'Gentle Giant', and was admired by West Brom and Coventry supporters. Later he said that the 1980s was a tough time to be a black player in England. He had to endure monkey chants and bananas being thrown at him. The abuse became serious when he was called to play for the England squad. Regis was sent a bullet in the mail (SJA, 2010). Then in 2007 Newcastle United fans used Islamophobic chants to taunt Middlesbrough's Egyptian player Mido (*Daily Mail*, 2007). Unfortunately, the issue was quickly overlooked. Later on Middlesbrough boss Gareth Southgate said: 'I always find it strange that 3,000 people can abuse one person and nothing is done' (*Daily Mail*, 2007). But it was not just the Newcastle *fans* who were guilty! In 2008 Newcastle's Turkish player Emre Belezoglu was accused of using racially abusive comments on several occasions: first in 2006 to Everton players, then to Bolton Wanderers player Diouf in 2007. However, Diouf never pursued the case and Emre was cleared of charges from the Everton game as well (BBC, 2007a, 2007b). No one would know what went on in private between Newcastle's management and Emre at the time, but the club's press release in 2007 gave no impression that they took a stance against racism. The club said that the press articles were inaccurate and prejudicial and that they reduced 'the chances of the player receiving a fair hearing'. On such sensitive issues, particularly when the player or the club is accused more than once, one would think that clubs would wish to take more responsibility and respond to allegations of racism to show that they take the matter sertiously; yet with a lack of 'cost' to the clubs, inaction continues.

West Ham fans are another example of a racially abusive group. Similar to Newcastle fans, West Ham fans also used offensive language towards Mido in 2005. He was targeted by chants such as 'Your mum's a terrorist' and 'Shoe, shoe, shoe bomber', in reference to Londoner Richard Reid who was arrested in 2003 for attempting a terrorist attack on an aircraft in flight from France to America. However, only one fan was arrested for racist chanting (BBC, 2012c). West Ham fans were also involved in anti-Semitic chanting towards Tottenham Hotspur. Yet this time strict measures were taken; West Ham cooperated with Spurs to file charges and they issued their first lifetime ban to a fan (*The Independent*, 2012). West Ham took

22

the correct measure in this instance, and they continue to regulate tension on the terraces. In 2013 they issued a warning before the game with Spurs, saying the club would not tolerate anti-Semitic chanting (*Daily Mail*, 2013).

This raises the question whether there is an actual penalty for racist behaviour. The clubs seem to take the approach that the 'game must go on'. Viv Andersen relates that in the mid-1970s, when he was playing for Nottingham Forest, bananas were thrown at him, and when he retreated to the touchline, he was told off by his coach Brian Clough, who said 'Well get your ******* arse back out there then and fetch me two pears and a banana!' (*Daily Mail*, 2010). If the football is good and there is no monetary punishment involved, then bad behaviour is ignored. Without the risk of a financial punishment, clubs expect the players to focus on the game and get over it.

Unfortunately, there are many other examples that show that racism is still prevalent in UK football. In 2011 Liverpool's Luis Suárez was said to have racially abused Manchester United's Patrice Evra by using the N-word. He publicly apologized and was banned for eight matches. Liverpool's statement later on underlined the club's stance against racism, but also declared their belief that it was a misunderstanding (*The Guardian*, 2011a). Liverpool fans, on the other hand, wore T-shirts to support their player.

Another recent issue was West Bromwich Albion's player Anelka making the 'quenelle' gesture in the match against West Ham in 2014. Anelka argued it was not intended in an offensive way and that he made the gesture to show his support for the controversial comedian Dieudonné M'bala M'bala. The Football Association did not show mercy and Anelka was given a five-match ban. However, Anelka remains unrepentant (hence the title of this case study). Interestingly, there was a corporate backlash against the club with Zoopla announcing that they would not renew their £3 million shirt deal with West Brom in the light of Nicolas Anelka's 'anti-Semitic' celebration (Sky, 2014).

However, it is not just in the UK that racism is an issue, as a quick look at Wikipedia shows. CNN (2014) poses the question 'Is racism endemic in Spanish football?', exemplified by Atlético Madrid fans abusing Real Madrid's Marcelo *and* his five-year-old son (WorldSoccer, 2014), or a banana being thrown at Dani Alves (BBC, 2014a). In the latter incident the fan was arrested, had his season ticket withdrawn and was given a lifetime ban (BBC, 2014b) – and the club? Villareal was fined €12,000 by the Spanish football federation (*The Guardian*, 2014).

Other examples can be found in Eastern Europe, with Nazi flags being unfurled by Spartak Moscow fans in October 2013 (ESPN, 2013). In the same month CSKA Moscow was punished for racist chants (BBC, 2013c) and then again in February 2014 (BBC, 2014c). The 'punishment' for the October 2013 incident was a partial closure of one part of the stadium for one game (BBC, 2013c), whilst a €50,000 (£41,200) fine together with one game to be played behind closed gates was handed down for the February 2014 incident (BBC, 2014c). This demonstrates UEFA's position on racism by fans – first incident: partial closure for one game; second incident: full closure for one game, plus €50,000 fine. Yaya Touré has suggested players could boycott the 2018 World Cup over racism (*The Guardian*, 2013).

In Italy racial abuse of players still continued in the lead-up to the 2014 World Cup (*The Telegraph*, 2014), following on from comments in the press that there was 'nothing black and white about football and racism' (CNN, 2013) or 'Racism [is] still rife in Italian football' (BBC, 2010).

FIFA President Sepp Blatter stated in October 2013 that clubs should lose points if their fans were to act in a racist manner, criticizing the current punishment of fining the clubs (BBC, 2013a). Yet FIFA have been known to fine a 'late show' to games more harshly than racially abusive acts (*The Guardian*, 2012). In 2013 Roma was fined £42,000 for racist chanting towards AC Milan (BBC, 2013b), and Serbia and Roma were fined £65,000 and £30,000 respectively in different games (*The Telegraph*, 2013). In contrast, Denmark striker Nicklas Bendtner was fined £80,000 for revealing a sponsor's logo on his underpants during Euro 2012 (BBC, 2013e).

These fines would not be nearly as effective as the loss of a lucrative sponsorship deal, however. Will the Anelka incident be the only time that racism is penalized in a way that matters to a club? Is racism good for a club's bottom line? If this were extended to involve other corporate sponsors, there might be a change for the better. Have we reached decision time?

Should there be any room for misunderstanding when it comes to racism? Surely not. As a parliamentary report in 2012 concluded, racism is still a significant problem in football in the UK (CNN, 2012). Sport is war without the killing, but regardless of whether it is a 'defensive mechanism', as Spurs suggest (BBC, 2013d) or unintentional, racism just does not fit in with the beautiful game that is football. In May 2013 FIFA suggested that 'racism measures could see teams expelled or relegated' (BBC, 2013e). In contrast, in April 2014 Sepp Blatter (FIFA President) was still suggesting that point deductions is the way forward (BBC, 2014d).

Conversely, can the players do more to stamp out racism, as exemplified by Dani Alves in April 2014? Or was this just a great marketing gimmick (Eurosport, 2014)? And will it, in fact, make things worse?

QUESTIONS

1. Do you think a football club only has responsibility towards its fans? What other bodies or groups have an interest in a football club, and as such does the club have a responsibility towards them?
2. What impact could racism have on a club? Consider this in its widest context.
3. What factors contribute to racism in football, as opposed to other sports?
4. Compare racism with hooliganism, another blight on 'the beautiful game'.

24

5. Do you think FIFA, clubs and other authorities – as well as players – are doing enough to stamp out racism? What more could be done? Is it any different with hooliganism?

CONCLUSIONS

Racism in sport has been with us for many years; it takes different forms and is used to show superiority or power. The various sporting authorities seem to approach racism with scant regard to what is actually happening in society at large. Consider what would happen to BP or a leading political party if such displays of racism were allowed to continue. Yet the clubs and the racists do not get penalized. Although, for many, racist acts are abhorrent, are they actually bad for the clubs? Or are they good? If racism was bad, surely the clubs would do more to combat it? So if it is not bad for business …

RECOMMENDED READING

To begin with, students might find it helpful to read supporting texts on sport racism such as Garvie (1991), Back *et al.* (2001) and Farrington *et al.* (2012). Thereafter, students should consider looking at texts on reputation management and communications such as Roper and Fill (2012) or Cornelissen (2014). An introductory text on marketing might be useful, Solomon *et al.* (2009) is one example.

NOTE

1 Quote from Nicholas Anelka (Mirror, 2014).

BIBLIOGRAPHY AND RECOMMENDED WEBSITES

Back, L., Crabbe, T., Solomos, J. (2001). *The Changing Face of Football: Racism, Identity and Multiculture in the English Game.* Oxford: Berg.

BBC (2007a). Newcastle's Emre denies FA charge, accessed 4 April 2014 from http://news.bbc.co.uk/sport1/hi/football/teams/n/newcastle_united/6256787.stm.

BBC (2007b). Emre faces new racism allegation, accessed 4 April 2014 from http://news.bbc.co.uk/sport1/hi/football/teams/n/newcastle_united/6407915.stm.

BBC (2008a). Chelsea boss gets death threats, accessed 4 April 2014 from http://news.bbc.co.uk/1/hi/uk/7254547.stm.

BBC (2008b). Chelsea angry at Grant barracking, accessed 4 April 2014 from http://news.bbc.co.uk/sport1/hi/football/teams/c/chelsea/7020854.stm.

BBC (2010). Racism still rife in Italian football, accessed 26 August 2016 from http://news.bbc.co.uk/1/hi/world/europe/8511106.stm

BBC (2011a). Chelsea manager Andre Villas-Boas says John Terry race row is over, accessed 4 April 2014 from www.bbc.co.uk/sport/0/football/15449070.

BBC (2011b). John Terry to face police investigation over race allegations, accessed 4 April 2014 from www.bbc.co.uk/sport/0/football/15548056.

BBC (2012a). John Terry banned and fined by FA over Anton Ferdinand incident, accessed 4 April 2014 from www.bbc.co.uk/sport/0/football/19723020.

BBC (2012b). Chelsea v Manchester United: 'Monkey gesture' fan banned, accessed 4 April 2014 from www.bbc.co.uk/sport/0/football/20234878.

BBC (2012c). Chelsea fan banned over racist abuse of Didier Drogba, accessed 4 April 2014 from www.bbc.co.uk/news/uk-england-london-17933326.

BBC (2013a). Should football teams lose points for racist fans, accessed 4th April 2014 from www.bbc.co.uk/newsround/24691031.

BBC (2013b). Roma fined £42,000 for racist chants in game at AC Milan, accessed 4 April 2014 from www.bbc.co.uk/sport/0/football/22513780.

BBC (2013c). Yaya Toure: CSKA Moscow punished for racist chants, accessed 4 April 2014 from www.bbc.co.uk/sport/0/football/24749146.

BBC (2013d). Tottenham to issue questionnaire over anti-Semitic term, accessed 4 April 2014 from www.bbc.co.uk/sport/0/football/24102318.

BBC (2013e). Fifa racism measures could see teams expelled or relegated, accessed 4 April 2014 from www.bbc.co.uk/sport/0/football/22728162.

BBC (2014a). Dani Alves: Barcelona defender eats banana after it lands on pitch, accessed 4 April 2014 from www.bbc.co.uk/sport/0/football/27183851.

BBC (2014b). Spanish police arrest Dani Alves banana thrower suspect, accessed 4 April 2014 from www.bbc.co.uk/news/world-europe-27222240.

BBC (2014c). CSKA Moscow: Russian side punished again for racist abuse, accessed 4 April 2014 from www.bbc.co.uk/sport/0/football/26243455.

BBC (2014d). Sepp Blatter wants points deductions to help fight racism, accessed 4 April 2014 from www.bbc.co.uk/sport/0/football/27070453.

Channel 4 (2014). Channel 4 Dispatches on racism in football, accessed 4 April 2014 from www.channel4.com/info/press/news/channel-4-dispatches-on-racism-in-football#.

CNN (2012). Racism remains 'significant' problem in English football, accessed 4 April 2014 from http://edition.cnn.com/2012/09/19/sport/football/football-racism-england-report/index.html.

CNN (2013). For Italy's 'ultras', nothing black and white about football and racism, accessed 4 April 2014 from http://edition.cnn.com/2013/02/21/sport/football/italian-football-racism-milan/.

CNN (2014). Bananas and monkey chants: Is racism endemic in Spanish football, accessed 4 April 2014 from http://edition.cnn.com/2014/05/05/sport/football/diop-monkey-chants-racism-football-atletico-madrid/.

Cornelissen, J. (2014). *Corporate Communication: A Guide to Theory and Practice.* London: Sage.

Daily Mail (2007). I just wanted to silence the drunkards, says Mido, accessed 4 April 2014 from www.dailymail.co.uk/sport/football/article-478140/I-just-wanted-silence-drunkards-says-Mido.html.

Daily Mail (2010). Viv Anderson Exclusive: Racists were raining down fruit. Brian Clough just said 'get me two pears and a banana', accessed 4 April 2014 from www.dailymail.co.uk/sport/football/article-1269285/Viv-Anderson-Exclusive-Racists-raining-fruit-Brian-Clough-just-said-pears-banana.html#ixzz2zp91PkqT.

Daily Mail (2013). West Ham warn fans about racist chants ahead of Tottenham clash, accessed 4 April 2014 from www.dailymail.co.uk/sport/football/article-2284185/West-Ham-warning-racist-chants-v-Tottenham.html.

ESPN (2013). Russia shame as Spartak fans unfurl Nazi banner, accessed 4 April 2014 from www.espn.co.uk/football/sport/story/253309.html.

Eurosport (2014). The shock secret you need to know about the banana anti-racism campaign, accessed 4 April 2014 from https://uk.eurosport.yahoo.com/blogs/pitchside-europe/anti-racism-banana-movement-revealed-cleverly-planned-marketing-104501574.html.

Farrington, N., Kilvington, D., Price, J., Saeed, A. (2012). *Race, Racism and Sports Journalism*. Abingdon: Routledge.

Footy Boots (2012). John Terry dropped by Umbro, accessed 4 April 2014 from www.footy-boots.com/john-terry-umbro-football-boot-deal-20811/.

FTB (2012). Is racism being a part of football, accessed 4 April 2014 from www.ftbpro.com/posts/joel.parker/39005/is-racism-being-part-of-football#/posts/joel.parker.

Garvie, G. (ed.) (1991). *Sport Racism and Ethnicity*. Abingdon: Routledge.

The Guardian (2011a). Liverpool furious as Luis Suárez banned in Patrice Evra racism row, accessed 26 August 2016 from www.theguardian.com/football/2011/dec/20/liverpool-luis-suarez-patrice-evra.

The Guardian (2011b). John Terry to learn fate after alleged racial slur of Anton Ferdinand, accessed 4 April 2014 from www.theguardian.com/football/2011/oct/24/john-terry-anton-ferdinand-chelsea-qpr.

The Guardian (2012). Manchester City fined more for being late than Porto fans for racism, accessed 4 April 2014 from www.theguardian.com/football/2012/apr/11/manchester-city-fined-porto-racism.

The Guardian (2013). Yaya Touré: players could boycott 2018 World Cup in Russia over racism, accessed 4 April 2014 from www.theguardian.com/football/2013/oct/24/yaya-toure-boycott-world-cup-russia.

The Guardian (2014). Villarreal fined €12,000 for banana thrown at Barcelona's Dani Alves, accessed 4 April 2014 from www.theguardian.com/football/2014/may/07/dani-alves-villarreal-barcelona-racism-banana.

Mirror (2014). Nicholas Anelka: If the quenelle is racist then 'all priests are paedophiles' and pineapples will be BANNED, accessed 4 April 2014 from www.mirror.co.uk/sport/football/news/nicolas-anelka-quenelle-its-racist-3364651#ixzz2znZ4jk2u.

Roper, S., Fill, C. (2012). *Managing Corporate Reputation*. Harlow: Pearson.

SJA (2010). Regis on Big Ron, racism and death threats sent with a bullet, accessed 4 April 2014 from www.sportsjournalists.co.uk/other-bodies/football-writers/regis-on-big-ron-racism-and-death-threats-wrapped-in-a-bullet/.

Sky (2014). Zoopla ends West Brom deal over Anelka salute, accessed 4 April 2014 from http://news.sky.com/story/1198031/zoopla-ends-west-brom-deal-over-anelka-salute.

Solomon, R. *et al.* (2009). *Update to Marketing: Real People, Real Choices*, 8th Edition. Old Tappan, NJ: Pearson Higher Education.

The Telegraph (2008). Top 10: Football hate figures, accessed 4 April 2014 from www.telegraph.co.uk/sport/football/teams/england/3202229/Top-10-Football-hate-figures-Football.html.

The Telegraph (2012). John Terry racism trial: Chelsea captain faces tense wait to hear verdict on Friday after court adjourns, accessed 4 April 2014 from www.telegraph.co.uk/sport/football/teams/chelsea/9395097/John-Terry-racism-trial-Chelsea-captain-faces-tense-wait-to-hear-verdict-on-Friday-after-court-adjourns.html.

The Telegraph (2013). Anti-racism group reports England to Fifa after fans sang abusive songs during World Cup qualifier in San Marino, accessed 4 April 2014 from www.telegraph.co.uk/sport/football/teams/england/9960531/Anti-racism-group-reports-England-to-Fifa-after-fans-sang-abusive-songs-during-World-Cup-qualifier-in-San-Marino.html.

The Telegraph (2014). Mario Balotelli racially abused by Italy fans during training camp for World Cup in Brazil, accessed 4 April 2014 from www.telegraph.co.uk/sport/football/teams/italy/10846231/Mario-Balotelli-racially-abused-by-Italy-fans-during-training-camp-for-World-Cup-in-Brazil.html.

Top News (2012). Racial trial star Terry gets 'boot' from football 'boot' sponsor Umbro, accessed 4 April 2014 from http://topnews.in/sports/racial-trial-star-terry-gets-boot-football-boot-sponsor-umbro-226317.

WorldSoccer (2014). Marcelo racially abused by Atletico Madrid fans, accessed 4 April 2014 from www.worldsoccer.com/news/marcelo#pwJdJLMTc7QPGgM5.99.

CASE 4

THE SOCHI WINTER OLYMPIC GAMES AND THEIR SPORTS TOURISM AND EVENTS MANAGEMENT POTENTIAL FOR THE RUSSIAN FEDERATION

ROBERT KASPAR AND BENEDIKT WALLNER

LEARNING OUTCOMES

Upon completion of this case study, the reader should be able to:

- understand the complexity of hosting Olympic Winter Games;
- discuss the infrastructural needs of a global mobile event;
- scope the dimensions of winter sports infrastructure required for an outdoor snow sports and indoor ice sports event;
- reflect the challenges of post-event use of sports events infrastructure;
- preview implications for a wider Russian events and sports tourism strategy.

OVERVIEW OF THE CASE

This case study will discuss the elements of the events strategy developed and launched by the Russian Federation in sports as different as snow and ice sports, football, swimming and athletics. While a focus is given to the Olympic Winter Games and both their destination and sports infrastructure, the post-event developments and their wider implications for tourism are also considered.

CASE STUDY

The Russian Federation has decided to launch an integrated events strategy that results in bidding for and hosting a variety of winter and summer sports events. Not many countries around the globe have endeavoured to develop such an events strategy. While tremendous financial resources are needed, there is the advantage of transferring knowledge between the events and also contributing to the development of both sports participation and elite sports in Russia. A key challenge nevertheless remains: the long-term utilization of the created infrastructure for tourism, events and sports training.

As a promising start to Russia's event strategy, the IAAF World Championships in Athletics were hosted in Moscow in 2013. With around 1,970 participants from 206 countries, it was the biggest mobile single sports event of that year worldwide (Kaspar, 2014: 18). Russia topped the medals table for the first time since 2001 with seven gold medals. Furthermore, the IAAF World Championships attracted a total of 261,792 spectators during eight evening sessions. As a sports venue, the vast 1980 Summer Olympic stadium, which normally holds more than 80,000 spectators, was reconfigured to a capacity of 50,000 seats. Moreover, the Luzhniki Stadium was selected as the 2018 FIFA World Cup final venue, and hosted the Champions League final in 2009. Through the reconfiguration of the Stadium to a smaller capacity, it can be demonstrated that the main venue of the 1980 Olympic Summer Games has been in use for 38 years as the nation's key sports venue.

By staging the Formula One Grand Prix as a place event (Kaspar, 2014: 18) in the years 2014 to 2020, Russia is clearly endeavouring to identify the southern Black Sea resort of Sochi as an international sports destination by attracting sport event clientele in the off-peak season. The Sochi circuit is the first purpose-built Formula One facility in Russia and is unquestionably one of the most outstanding circuits in the world. The 55,000-seat venue is integrated into the unique Olympic Park infrastructure and located close to the Olympic railway and Sochi International Airport.

After a complex bidding process, Russia was awarded the right to host FIFA's showpiece event, the World Cup, in 2018, receiving an absolute majority of votes from the FIFA Executive Board. The World Cup 2018 provides opportunities not only in one geographic region, but also across a wide area of the Russian Federation. Hosting the mega-event will be used as a catalyst for modernization; for example, transport links will be upgraded and appropriate infrastructure will be constructed. Therefore, the hosting concept is designed as four major venue clusters: the central region with Moscow, Northern, Volga River and Southern, including the city of Sochi as one of the 11 host cities.

The City of Kazan will not only be one of the host cities during the FIFA World Cup 2018, but was also host to the FINA World Swimming Championships in 2015. Kazan has now developed one of the most advanced sporting infrastructures in Russia and has one of the most advanced aquatic facilities in the world. These facilities have already been used for the 2013 Summer Universiade, a multi-sports student event, which was seen as a rehearsal for upcoming large-scale projects. It was hoped that hosting this international event would create an aquatic sports legacy and the opportunity to elevate sport to a higher level of prominence within the nation.

The IIHF World Ice Hockey Championships 2016 was staged in state-of-the-art venues in Moscow and St Petersburg, and it is seen as a prestigious international event, coinciding with the 70th anniversary of ice hockey in Russia. It follows the success of the Kontinental Hockey League (KHL), which was created in 2008 in order to promote and market the successful development of ice hockey, primarily in Russia, in a new format. It currently comprises 28 member clubs based in Belarus, Croatia, Finland, Kazakhstan, Latvia, Russia, Slovenia and Slovakia and it intends to expand to more countries. It is already the premier professional ice hockey league in Eurasia and second in the world behind the National Hockey League of the USA and Canada.

Russia also bid for the right to host the World Games 2021 in the city of Ufa. Furthermore, the Zenit Arena in St Petersburg was selected to be one of the 13 host cities for the UEFA European Football Championships 2020.

Among a wide range of diverse sports events taking place in the near future, which will reinforce the image of Russia as a capable host nation, the developed event strategy contains similar international cultural events, such as the Manifesta in St Petersburg. For this, the State Hermitage Museum was selected to stage the European Biennial of Contemporary Art in 2014.

From the business events perspective, in 2015 Sochi hosted the SportAccord Convention, the world's premier annual event in the sports service area, bringing together more than 100 international sports federations and other key stakeholders.

The Sochi Olympic Winter Games have so far been the first winter sports mobile mega-event in the Russian Federation that has been hosted to a premium quality. While there were considerable concerns before the event, the Olympic Winter Games were widely described by athletes as very well organized at all levels.

For the first time in Winter Olympic history the 2014 Winter Olympics and Paralympics sports venues were divided in two distinct 'clusters'. With the coastal cluster, located in the Adler city district of Sochi on the shores of the Black Sea, comprising the impressive and futuristic Olympic Park facilities, these Games are seen as the most compact in Olympic history so far. The Olympic Park was designed so that all the completely newly built sports venues, training facilities, the Olympic Village (designed for 3,000 people and divided in 47 buildings) and the international broadcasting centre are accessible, within walking distance of each other and are gathered around the Medal Plaza. The Olympic Park complex included the newly constructed 40,000-seat Fisht Olympic Stadium (scene of the Opening and Closing Ceremonies), the oval-shaped Adler Arena (the speed skating competitions venue), the 3,000 seat Ice Cube curling centre, the 7,000-seat ice hockey competition venue the Shayba Arena (the design of which was based on a snowdrift), the main ice hockey venue the Bolshoi Ice Dome (with its eye-catching construction and a capacity of 12,000) and the Iceberg Skating Palace, which hosted figure skating, short track competitions, with stands for 12,000 spectators. The medal ceremonies were held in the Olympic Park.

Nevertheless, it has to be noted that while the ice venues were all in one compact cluster, they were quite far away from downtown Sochi, thus depriving the city centre of its potential Olympic atmosphere.

Situated 50 kilometres inland, the mountain village of Krasnaya Polyana formed the Mountain Cluster, including all snow sports venues and an additional Mountain Olympic Village.

The newly constructed Rosa Khutor Alpine Centre, which incorporates 20 kilometres of competition tracks with tribunes for 7,000 spectators, hosted all alpine skiing disciplines. In addition, a new resort, including a number of luxury hotels and resembling a ski resort in the central Alps, was designed and built. The adjacent Rosa Khutor Extreme Park was home to freestyle skiing and snowboarding competitions, with spectator capacities ranging from 4,000 to 6,250. The ultra-modern Sanki Sliding Centre hosted all bobsleigh, luge and skeleton events. The 1.5km track features 18 corners, and has a permanent seating of 500 (and during the Olympic Games an extra temporary seating of 500).

Situated in the village of Esto-Sadok, the 7,500-seat jumping centre RusSki Gorki, now owned by Russian bank Sberbank, hosted all ski jumping and Nordic combined disciplines. The Laura Cross Country Ski & Biathlon Center, currently owned by Gazprom, is another facility purpose-built for the sport mega-event. The complex is unique on the world circuit as it comprises two separate stadiums and separate sets of tracks for cross-country skiing and biathlon.

As well as the construction of all sports venues and facilities, Sochi was undergoing significant and extensive expansion and renovation of its infrastructure, resulting in new accommodation and transport facilities. Electrical infrastructure and sewage treatment facilities were enlarged, and the creation of an advanced technological infrastructure in the form of media centres was necessary. Additionally, an enormous railway network with state-of-the-art rail stations was constructed. One 50-kilometre route connects the Olympic Park beside the Black Sea with the mountain venues and resorts.

Nevertheless, the key concern is the use after the Games of the infrastructure created both in Sochi and in the other destinations. While there is general agreement that the infrastructure ranging from the airport to railways and roads will be beneficial, the utilization of hotels in Sochi and Krasnaya Polyana and the sports venues remains a complex challenge.

Before hosting the Olympic Winter Games, Russia had already drawn up a legacy plan, comprising a post-event use for Sochi's array of new venues as well as other long-term benefits for the region. The Olympic Park is already part of the Formula One circuit and hosts a F1 Grand Prix race annually. According to official plans, the Fisht Olympia Stadium will be used as a training centre by the Russian national football team and will host a series of matches before being used during the 2017 Confederations Cup and the 2018 World Cup. The Bolshoi Ice Dome will serve as a multi-purpose sports centre and is the home of the newly formed local ice hockey club HC Sochi, which is participating in the Kontinental Hockey League. The Adler Arena has a designated legacy use as an exhibition centre and has already hosted international tennis matches. Both the Iceberg Skating Palace and the Ice Cube Curling Centre will be used as multifunctional sport and entertainment centres for the local public. Meanwhile, Shayba Arena can be dismantled and it had been thought that it would be moved to Stavropol, but this did not happen. The Mountain Cluster complexes, primarily around Krasnaya Polyana and Rosa Khutor, should attract national as well as international winter sports tourists and turn it into a high standard winter sport destination in the near future. Moreover, it was envisaged that the ski jumping centre RuSki Gorki would be used as a further training centre for national athletes, assuming it is added to the official venues for the FIS Ski Jumping World Cup. The post-use prospects for Sanki Sliding Centre were promising. The venue had already been awarded the right to host both the 2015 FIL European Championships in Luge and the 2017 Bobsleigh and Skeleton World Championships, just for being part of regularly running World Cup events. Nevertheless, both the financial as well as sports management success of all the venues concerned can only be judged from 2020 onwards when sufficient data is available. Finally, the Russian International Olympic University has entered its fourth year of student intake in 2017, offering a Master of Sports Administration (MSA) with international appeal.

QUESTIONS

1. Which events should Russia host on an annual basis?
2. Has Russia bid for the right events and thus selected an ideal portfolio?
3. Which future events should Russia bid for?
4. Do you believe that Sochi can be a successful winter sports destination?
5. What are the infrastructural implications of the 2018 FIFA World Cup?

CONCLUSIONS

It will take time to assess the acceptance of Sochi as a winter sports tourism destination and training centre and/or an international congress destination. In any case, the development of Sochi has added to the knowledge bank needed for future developments of this type.

For the Russian Federation, sports events are a key strategic element in the development of the nation's sports potential. Nevertheless, the long-term benefits to Russian sporting organisations, athletes and the citizens of the destinations concerned remain to be critically assessed.

RECOMMENDED READING

Students first of all need an understanding of events management from a broader perspective. Common text books on events management include *The Business of Events Management* (Beech *et al.*, 2014, Bowdin *et al.*, 2012). Thereafter, students should consider looking at more specific texts on sports events management, for example *Strategic Sport Event Management* (Masterman, 2014). The Russian International Olympic University in Sochi, as one of the key legacy projects, has a sound archive of works on the Sochi Olympic Winter Games.

REFERENCES

Bowdin, G. *et al.* (2012). *Events Management*. Oxford: Butterworth-Heinemann.

Kaspar, Robert (2014). The dimensions of events management. In: J. Beech, S. Kaiser, R. Kaspar (eds), *The Business of Events Management*. Harlow: Pearson, pp. 15–29.

Masterman, G. (2014). *Strategic Sports Event Management: An International Approach*. Amsterdam: Elsevier Butterworth-Heinemann.

RECOMMENDED WEBSITES

2018 FIFA World Cup Russia: www.fifa.com/worldcup/russia2018
FINA World Championships Kazan Russia 2015: www.kazan2015.com
International Biathlon Union: www.biathlonworld.com
International Bobsleigh & Skeleton Federation: www.ibsf.com
International Ice Hockey Federation: www.iihf.com
International Luge Federation: www.fil-luge.org
International Ski Federation: www.fis-ski.com
International Swimming Federation: www.fina.org
Kontinental Hockey League: en.khl.ru
Russian International Olympic University: www.olympicuniversity.ru
Olympic Games: www.olympic.org
Sochi 2014: www.sochi2014.com
SportAccord: www.sportaccordconvention.com

CASE 5

SUPER LEAGUE MAGIC WEEKEND: USING EVENTS TO ENGAGE RUGBY LEAGUE FANS NEW AND OLD

LEAH GILLOOLY

LEARNING OUTCOMES

Upon completion of this case study, the reader should be able to:

- examine the challenges facing sports events when trying to meet the needs of different groups of consumers;
- discuss event and experience design elements used by sports events to enhance the spectator/fan experience;
- appraise relevant marketing activities in the context of professional sports events and their target customers;
- formulate appropriate recommendations to inform future strategy for sports leagues and events in engaging multiple fan groups.

OVERVIEW OF THE CASE

This case study explores how the Super League Magic Weekend is used as a tool to engage and reward rugby league fans whilst also seeking to attract new fans to the sport. In particular, the case explores how the Magic Weekend event seeks to satisfy the needs of these different sport consumer groups and assesses the marketing actions undertaken in reaching these two target markets.

Notable within the case is the tension that sports marketers can experience when trying to appeal to a sport's core fans whilst also trying to attract new spectators to the sport. This case also identifies the growing importance of event marketing to sports marketers looking for new ways to connect with fans.

CASE STUDY

Sports organizations, including teams, leagues and events, increasingly compete in the entertainment industry and can no longer rely on the quality of the sporting competition or event to attract and engage fans (Jowdy and McDonald, 2003). Therefore, like many governing bodies, the Rugby Football League (RFL) has employed a range of initiatives to engage fans, one of which is Magic Weekend. Launched in 2007, Magic Weekend is a two-day event held over a weekend in May, at which all 14 Super League teams play a complete round of fixtures at one venue. The Magic Weekend fixtures act as a '27th round' of the Super League in that they are additional to the regular season fixtures of each team playing each other home and away. Therefore, no teams lose out on a home fixture as a result. At the time of writing, Magic Weekend is unique in sport as the only single venue event hosting a complete round of fixtures for a league and as such can be seen as a unique selling point for the sport (Björner and Berg, 2012).

Fitting in with wider shifts in the marketing environment which have seen consumers increasingly desire experiences over goods and services (Pine and Gilmore, 1998), Magic Weekend was designed to create a celebratory event for fans of all Super League teams. Magic Weekend sits in the UK rugby league calendar alongside two other premier events: the Challenge Cup Final and the Grand Final. However, not every team will get the chance to play in one of these premier events, so the idea behind Magic Weekend was to engage and build long-term relationships with fans (Crowther and Donlan, 2011; Jowdy and McDonald, 2003; Schwarz *et al.*, 2013) by creating a 'big' event that fans of all teams could enjoy. In its early years Magic Weekend moved around, being hosted in Cardiff, Wales in 2007 and 2008, Edinburgh, Scotland in 2009 and 2010, and back to Cardiff in 2011, before arriving in Manchester, England in 2012. In the three years from 2012 to 2014, Magic Weekend was held at the Etihad Stadium in Manchester (home of Manchester City Football Club). Due to building work taking place at the Etihad Stadium, Magic Weekend 2015 was held at St James' Park, Newcastle. This case study relates to Magic Weekend 2014. Historically, Magic Weekend has taken place over the Spring Bank Holiday weekend at the end of May; however, in 2014 the event was held on the regular weekend of 17/18 May. Key to the success of the event has been the support, from the outset, of all of the Super League teams and the main broadcaster, Sky. Without the cooperation of these main stakeholders, the RFL would have faced a stiff challenge in attracting fans and building the event into the spectacle it is today.

Magic Weekend ticket pricing

Consistent with the objective of creating an event to engage and offer something different to fans of all 14 clubs, season ticket holders receive a 50 per cent discount on tickets for Magic Weekend. The prices for Magic Weekend 2014 are shown in Table 5.1.

L. Gillooly

Table 5.1 Magic Weekend 2014 ticket prices (The RFL, 2014)

Category		Reserved Seating		Unreserved Seating		Reserved Seating (North/South Stand)	
		Adult	*Concession*	*Adult*	*Concession*	*Adult*	*Concession*
Daily	Regular	£45.00	£22.50	£30.00	£15.00	£25.00	£12.50
	Season Ticket	£22.50	£11.25	£15.00	£7.50	£12.50	£6.25
Weekend	Regular	£60.00	£30.00	£45.00	£22.50	£40.00	£20.00
	Season Ticket	£30.00	£15.00	£22.50	£11.25	£20.00	£10.00

In addition to discounts for season ticket holders, an early bird pricing offer was in place for Magic Weekend 2014, allowing fans who purchased tickets before 5 March to get a 40 per cent discount on a £45 reserved ticket or a 20 per cent discount on a £25 reserved ticket. The majority of tickets sold are for the unreserved seating, which allows fans to move around during the day(s). Therefore, the use of early bird ticketing offers on reserved seating is an attempt to entice fans into these less popular seating categories.

Tickets can be purchased either directly from the RFL (via their website: www. rugbyleaguetickets.co.uk/) or from each of the Super League clubs. Prices are kept consistent across the different selling outlets, but there is a strong incentive for the clubs to promote Magic Weekend tickets because they get to keep all ticket revenue that they generate. As such, many of the clubs will develop promotional campaigns to encourage fans to purchase Magic Weekend tickets through them, often offering additional services such as transport. Despite its success, the pricing of Magic Weekend tickets poses some degree of challenge to the RFL, as it tries to balance pricing the event appropriately to reflect its premier status in the rugby league calendar with the fact that it is another 'created' event which is targeting the same fans, and is thus asking the same consumers to spend more money on watching the sport and their favourite team. Rugby league remains a predominantly working class sport and there is concern among some clubs that even though fans enjoy and appreciate Magic Weekend, they may eventually say 'enough is enough' and 'we can't afford to keep spending more money to watch our team', particularly in difficult economic times. Even though the RFL believes ticket prices to be very reasonable, the cost of attending for a family, when tickets, transport, food and drink have been taken into account, is still significant. This could be particularly pertinent given that Magic Weekend is broadcast in its entirety on Sky Sports, offering fans an alternative way of following the event without paying to attend in person. While it is the experiential quality of the event which represents the unique selling point of Magic Weekend (as discussed below), Sky has taken the opportunity of the reduced set-up costs of having seven fixtures across two days in one venue to employ new technological innovations, such as ref cam (where the referees wear a small camera on their head, allowing a referee's eye view for TV spectators) and an aerial camera, which offers a closer view of the action on all areas of the pitch. Therefore, it is possible that as the TV viewing experience improves, this may pose a threat to the ability of Magic Weekend to attract fans to the venue. Realising that attending the event in person will entail both time and monetary costs places a great emphasis on the organizers to create a superlative event experience (Crowther and Donlan, 2011), in order to provide fans with a compelling reason to attend. The following section will explore in more detail the fan experience of attending Magic Weekend.

The Magic Weekend fan experience

Events allow sports organizations such as the RFL the opportunity to engage fans and to raise their level of involvement with the sport (Close *et al.*, 2006), but the creation of effective events requires creativity, imagination and a firm understanding of fans' needs (Wohlfeil and Whelan, 2007). Consistent with this, and unsurprising given the event's success, Magic Weekend offers fans something that they cannot get anywhere else. Indeed, feedback from fans is that they very much enjoy the event because it provides them with an experience that cannot be obtained from any other sport. Magic Weekend is therefore firmly positioned as a unique experience, giving fans the opportunity not only to watch seven matches over the course of the weekend, but also much more as part of the whole event experience. In addition to the rugby matches, there is live music at the stadium, a fan village where fans can socialize, have some food and drink and follow the matches on a big screen, and a host of interactive and experiential sponsor activations from brands including Heinz, Foxy Bingo and Irn Bru. Examples of sponsor/partner activations in recent years have included a climbing wall, competitions to win a VIP trip to the Super League Grand Final, the chance to have your photograph taken with the Rugby League World Cup trophy and free gift giveaways.

These sponsor activations play a significant role in enhancing the overall entertainment experience for fans, and sponsors have bought into the event concept as it allows them to reach a very large number of fans in one venue. As such, the RFL ensures that the event meets sponsor as well as fan objectives (Jowdy and McDonald, 2003), working closely with the sponsors to ensure that their activations enhance the experience of fans attending Magic Weekend. To a large extent, many of the experience elements of Magic Weekend are enhanced by the modern and conducive surroundings of the Etihad Stadium, which has a ready-made fan village with outside bars and spacious concourses and is well served by public transport.

Spectators are free to come and go throughout the event and, when combined with the flexibility of unreserved seating, fans can create their own experience, combining some or all of the event attractions, depending on their needs and wants. As such, two fans can attend Magic Weekend and have a completely different experience: for example, one fan might stay in the stadium and watch three or four matches, while another might watch his or her team's match and combine this with sampling the sponsor activations, spending time in the fan village bar and mingling with fans from other clubs. Some fans will stay for the whole day (or two days), while others will arrive just in time for their team's match and leave afterwards. Work on effective event design highlights the importance of creating events that have personal relevance to attendees (Poulsson and Kale, 2004) and which nurture a sense of community (Crowther and Donlan, 2011). Therefore, this flexibility can be seen as a great strength of the event, in that it allows the RFL to meet the needs of a range of different fan groups and enhances the event atmosphere by allowing fans of all teams to mix together in the stadium and in the wider event arena, taking from the event what is relevant to them. Similarly, effective event design principles emphasize the importance of interactivity (Kale *et al.*, 2010). Both the clubs and the RFL itself promote Magic Weekend through social media, asking fans to post their 'Magic Moments'. Some of these are then put onto large screens and perimeter boards at the event, again reinforcing the connection between fans and the event/sport and facilitating direct interaction between fans and event organizers. However, the flexibility which enhances the attendee experience has contributed to a significant negative perception of the event: that it appears not to be well attended.

Those matches perceived as 'bigger' within the Magic Weekend fixture list are scheduled later in the day. This can result in the stadium being quite empty early in the day as many fans have not yet arrived, particularly if their team is not playing until later. In addition to this, the transient nature of the crowd, facilitated by the ability to arrive and leave whenever they want as well as the unreserved seating, and the desire of many fans to sample aspects of Magic Weekend other than just the rugby action, means that the stadium never looks full. The total number of tickets sold for the days will not reflect the number of people actually in the stadium at any one time; therefore, while ticket sales have continued to be strong over the years, there remains the outward perception, particularly to those watching the event on television, that it is not well supported. Clearly, the unreserved seating aids the fan experience, in that throughout the day fans can watch from different angles, sit in or avoid the sun and move to sit near other fans of their club. Fans at the event appreciate that spectators come and go throughout the event. However, this could be perceived as a hindrance to the RFL's hopes that television viewers will see how great the event is and want to attend the following year.

In terms of the fixtures themselves, since the inception of Magic Weekend in 2007 the RFL has tried a range of different approaches, including a random draw of opponents and selecting the matches based on local/historical rivalries (derby matches). Based on feedback from fans, who said that they prefer watching derby matches, or at least matches between teams that have a strong rivalry, the current format is to select the fixtures for Magic Weekend on these bases. However, the ties do vary year by year to avoid the event becoming stale and to introduce some element of novelty to give the fans what they want. Having Magic Weekend made up predominantly of derby matches also aids the sense of the event being a big, celebratory occasion, which was how it was originally conceived by the RFL. However, some critics argue that some teams can play their derby opponents multiple times within the regular season (including league, cup and playoff matches) and that introducing another derby match between the same teams at Magic Weekend devalues what fans perceive as a premium fixture. Equally, some teams do not have logical derby opponents and their fans can perceive that they receive less attractive fixtures at Magic Weekend as a result. The fact that Magic Weekend introduces an additional (27th) round of fixtures into the regular league calendar has also been a cause for concern among some fans and club officials, who note that there will be one team that each other team has to play three times. The perceived level of difficulty of this fixture is put forward as an argument, suggesting that some teams might have an 'easier' match at Magic Weekend than others, and this may prove crucial at the end of the season in terms of league placing. As such, there is concern that the selection or 'fixing' of fixtures at Magic Weekend could harm the integrity of the league. Despite these issues, the clubs are broadly happy with the Magic Weekend concept and agree that overall it provides a fantastic event to engage fans and showcase the sport of rugby league.

Changing priorities for Magic Weekend

While Magic Weekend continues to serve the function of offering a celebratory occasion to fans of all 14 Super League clubs, the RFL is now also using the event as a catalyst to grow the sport in the Manchester region. While many clubs are based geographically close to Manchester, the city itself does not traditionally have a strong rugby league following, and as such the RFL (and several of the clubs) see this as an opportunity to target a new segment of potential fans. The design and set-up of Magic Weekend lends itself naturally to allowing newcomers to rugby league to dip in and out of watching the sport, while taking in all of the other event attractions, such as the fan village and sponsor activations. It is unlikely that a first-time visitor will sit and watch four matches of a new sport in one day, so Magic Weekend's flexibility should be ideal as a first taste of rugby league. Representatives from the clubs and the RFL are confident that new fans will enjoy the experience when they are there, but the challenge of attracting new fans to the event in the first place remains.

When developing their marketing strategies and tactics, sports organizations have a range of market-targeting approaches open to them, including differentiated and niche marketing. One such option is focused marketing (Jobber and Ellis-Chadwick, 2013), which involves developing different marketing mixes for different target market segments. With Magic Weekend now being used as a tool to reach both existing fans (clients) and new fans (prospects) (Ferrand and McCarthy, 2009), the RFL needs to consider the appropriateness of its marketing activities in relation to the event. Key to developing appropriate marketing strategies and tactics is a comprehensive understanding of the motivations of the different target markets for attending the event. Wann *et al.* (2008) identify eight motivations for sport consumption: escape, economic, eustress, self-esteem, group affiliation, entertainment, family and aesthetics, while James and Ross (2004) propose ten motivations: empathy, social interaction, family, team effort, team affiliation, achievement, entertainment, skill, drama and escape. While existing fans might have motivations around team affiliation, group affiliation and skill, the motivations of the newcomer to rugby league may centre more around entertainment and escape. However, these motivations may also be relevant to existing fans, and as such it is advisable for the RFL to play on these shared motivations in promoting Magic Weekend. At present, Magic Weekend is promoted through the existing Extraordinary Rugby campaign (The Rugby League of the Extraordinary, 2012), which emphasizes the skill, speed and physicality of the sport; these attributes fit very well with existing fans' motivations for attending Magic Weekend, but perhaps resonate less with newcomers to the sport. Therefore, despite having two target markets, Magic Weekend appears very much at present to adopt a single marketing mix, which is tailored more to the needs of one target consumer (fan) group than the other. The challenge then remains for the RFL to balance the more entertainment-focused message needed to attract new fans to the sport with the message used to attract existing fans year after year.

In order to grow the sport of rugby league in Manchester, in addition to the showcase event of Magic Weekend (and the Super League Grand Final, which is held at Old Trafford, Manchester), more engagement is needed with the local communities through work with schools and universities. Given its geographic proximity to Manchester, Magic Weekend also offers opportunities for clubs to work with local communities to build the sport and their own fan bases among the Manchester population. Magic Weekend 2013 did achieve more sales from the Manchester area than ever before, so there is evidence that the event is starting to reap rewards in terms of attracting new fans. In order to achieve sustained success in using Magic Weekend to grow the sport's fan base, it is crucial for the event to remain in Manchester for a period of several years, giving the community outreach work time to filter into more new fans attending Magic Weekend and other matches.

One area in which the marketing mix is varied between existing and new fans is in the use of differential pricing (Dibb *et al.*, 2012), with season ticket holders getting a 50 per cent discount on Magic Weekend tickets. Again, as discussed above, this is very successful in encouraging attendance among existing fans, but could represent a challenge to the achievement of the new fan acquisition objective. New fans may be put off by the higher prices they face and they may be unwilling to spend such an amount of money to sample a sport they have never watched before. While a headline price of £25–£45 might be seen to represent good value in that it allows a spectator to watch up to four matches in a day, the tickets cannot be sold on this basis because a new fan may not want to watch four matches in a row. Therefore, the regular ticket prices may not be cheap enough to attract new fans to the sport. On the other hand, offering season ticket holder discounts is an integral part of the strategy of engaging existing fans. There is, consequently, a tension between meeting the needs of the different target markets in terms of the marketing proposition of Magic Weekend. All sporting events and experiences need continually to look to evolve and change or add elements to keep the event offering new and interesting (Pine and Gilmore, 2000) and thus to keep attracting fans (new and old) year in and year out. Therefore, while Magic Weekend is undoubtedly a success at achieving many of its objectives, the RFL still faces considerable challenges in balancing the needs of different groups of fans and truly using it as a vehicle to grow the sport outside of its traditional heartland areas.

QUESTIONS

1. What do you think are the advantages and disadvantages of Magic Weekend to both the RFL (and the wider sport of rugby league) and to the fans of the sport?
2. To what extent do you think enhancing the television coverage of Magic Weekend helps or hinders the promotion of Magic Weekend and the sport of rugby league?
3. Wood and Masterman (2007) identify seven event attributes that enhance the event experience: involvement with the event, interaction, immersion of all senses, intensity, individuality of experience, innovation and integrity. Assess the extent to which Magic Weekend addresses these seven attributes in its event design and delivery.
4. Assume you have been appointed by the RFL as a consultant to advise them on the future marketing strategy for Magic Weekend. Outline and justify appropriate marketing strategies and tactics that you think they should employ to continue the pursuit of their dual goals of fan engagement and new fan recruitment.
5. What other marketing strategies and tactics could the RFL employ to grow the sport of rugby league and engage existing fans if it were not to continue with Magic Weekend? Provide an appraisal of whether it is in the best interests of the sport to continue with Magic Weekend or spend the marketing budget in other ways to achieve the same objectives.

CONCLUSIONS

Rugby league's Magic Weekend has worked and continues to work very well at providing a celebratory event for fans of all 14 Super League teams. The event experience is considered to be excellent, with positive feedback from fans attending the event. As the event's objectives have shifted over recent years to a greater focus on growing the sport in Manchester, so has the RFL faced challenges in

adapting the event (and associated marketing) offering to the needs of both existing and new fans of the sport. Magic Weekend currently works very well at reaching and satisfying existing rugby league fans, so in the future a significant focus
needs to be on using the event to bring new fans to the sport, whilst continuing
to serve the loyal fans, who have grown to love the unique Magic Weekend event
experience.

RECOMMENDED READING

Students looking for a very good overview of literature on sport consumer motivations which impact on sport consumer behaviour are advised to look at James and
Ross (2004). This article also provides a discussion of the differing motivations for
consuming different sports, which highlights the importance of understanding sport
consumers in context. Extending this, Wann *et al.* (2008) identifies motivational profiles for fans of different sports, that sports organizations can use to inform their
target marketing activities. For students interested in the events aspect of this case,
Pine and Gilmore (1998) is one of the earliest, but most important articles that sets
out the shift in marketing orientation towards what the authors call the experience
economy. Therefore, it provides valuable context regarding the growth of experiential marketing. Bringing application of literature on experiential marketing and
events into a sports context, Jowdy and McDonald (2003) is a very readable article
that addresses the contemporary phenomenon of fan festivals as a way of engaging
sports fans. The case study in their article provides an insightful look at how interactive fan festivals can be employed and is therefore a useful resource for anyone
looking at the use of experiential marketing in sport.

BIBLIOGRAPHY

Björner, E. and Berg, P. O. (2012). Strategic creation of experiences at Shanghai World Expo: a
    practice of communification. *International Journal of Event and Festival Management*,
    3(1), 30–45.
Close, A. G., Finney, R. Z., Lacey, R. Z. and Sneath, J. Z. (2006). Engaging the consumer through
    event marketing: linking attendees with the sponsor, community, and brand. *Journal of
    Advertising Research*, 46(4), 420–33.
Crowther, P. and Donlan, L. (2011). Value-creation space: the role of events in a service-
    dominant marketing paradigm. *Journal of Marketing Management*, 27(13/14), 1444–63.
Dibb, S., Simkin, L., Pride, W. M. and Ferrell, O. C. (2012). *Marketing Concepts and Strategies*,
    6th edition. Cengage, Andover.
Ferrand, A. and McCarthy, S. (2009). *Marketing the Sports Organisation*. Routledge, Abingdon.
James, J. D. and Ross, S. D. (2004). Comparing sport consumer motivations across multiple
    sports. *Sport Marketing Quarterly*, 13(1), 17–25.
Jobber, D. and Ellis-Chadwick, F. (2013). *Principles and Practice of Marketing*. 7th edition.
    McGraw-Hill, Maidenhead.

Jowdy, E. and McDonald, M. (2003). Relationship marketing and interactive fan festivals: The Women's United Soccer Association's 'Soccer Sensation'. *International Journal of Sports Marketing and Sponsorship*, 4(4), 295–311.

Kale, S. H., Pentecost, R. D. and Zlatevska, N. (2010). Designing and delivering compelling experiences: Insights from the 2008 Democratic National Convention. *International Journal of Event and Festival Management*, 1(2), 148–59.

Pine, B. J. and Gilmore, J. H. (1998). Welcome to the experience economy. *Harvard Business Review*, 76(4), 97–105.

Pine, B. J. and Gilmore, J. H. (2000) Satisfaction, sacrifice, surprise: three small steps create one giant leap into the experience economy. *Strategy & Leadership*, 28(1), 18–23.

Poulsson, S. H. G. and Kale, S. H. (2004). The experience economy and commercial experiences. *The Marketing Review*, 4(3), 267–77.

Schwarz, E. C., Hunter, J. D. and LaFleur, A. (2013). *Advanced Theory and Practice in Sports Marketing*, 2nd edition. Routledge, Abingdon.

The Rugby Football League (2014). Rugby League Tickets. Available at: www.rugbyleaguetickets.co.uk/ (accessed 24/02/14).

The Rugby League of the Extraordinary (2012). Watch. Available at www.youtube.com/watch?v=L2N3mFn5Pd0 (accessed 26/08/16).

Wann, D. L., Grieve, F. G., Zapalac, R. K. and Pease, D. G. (2008). Motivational profiles of sport fans of different sports. *Sport Marketing Quarterly*, 17(1), 6–19.

Wohlfeil, M. and Whelan, S. (2007). Like being a drop in a freshly-poured Guinness pint: consumer motivations to participate in the 'Guinness Storehouse'. *The Marketing Review*, 7(3), 283–300.

Wood, E. H., and Masterman, G. (2007). Event marketing: Experience and exploitation. Paper presented at the Extraordinary Experiences Conference: Managing the Consumer Experience in Hospitality, Leisure, Sport, Tourism, Retail and Events, Bournemouth University, 3–4 September 2007.

RECOMMENDED WEBSITES

The Rugby Football League (2014). Rugby League Tickets. Available at: www.rugbyleaguetickets.co.uk/ (accessed 24/02/14)

The Rugby Football League (2014). RFL. Available at: www.therfl.co.uk/ (accessed 24/02/14)

The Rugby Football League (n.d.). Facebook Page. Available at: www.facebook.com/rugbyfootballleague (accessed 24/02/14)

The Rugby Football League (n.d.). Twitter feed. Available at: https://twitter.com/TheRFL (accessed 24/02/14)

The Rugby Football League (n.d.). YouTube Channel. Available at: www.youtube.com/user/ukrugbyleague (accessed 24/02/14)

The Rugby League of the Extraordinary (2012). Watch. Available at www.youtube.com/watch?v=L2N3mFn5Pd0 (accessed 26/08/16)

CASE 6

PARIS SAINT-GERMAIN: A NEW BRAND TO DREAM EVEN BIGGER

BORIS HELLEU AND NICOLAS SCELLES

LEARNING OUTCOMES

Upon completion of this case study, the reader should be able to:

- recognise that a football club is also a brand;
- understand how a professional sports team can build brand equity;
- design the global strategy of a sports brand.

OVERVIEW OF THE CASE

This case examines the branding strategy of Paris Saint-Germain. If 'Dream bigger' became the club slogan in 2012, when business matters, the club has greater goals. Not only has the richest French football club purchased famous and skilful football players but it has also designed a new brand strategy. This case enables us to understand how a well-known team at a national/continental level is becoming a global brand.

CASE STUDY

Paris Saint-Germain (PSG) is a professional football club established in 1970. It was bought by the TV channel Canal + in 1991 to improve its TV supply. In 2006 the club came into the ownership of Colony Capital (an American investment fund specialising in real estate) who were interested in the renovation of the stadium. In 2011 PSG was sold again, and this time bought by Qatar Sports Investments (QSI, Qatar's sovereign investment fund) as an important element of its soft/sport power strategy. Provided with huge financial means, the club's ambition is to become not only one of the best in Europe but also a global sports brand. For the season 2014–2015, 36,000 season tickets were sold (75 per cent of the stadium capacity). At the end of the season 2012–2013 (when PSG won its first title since 1994) the club announced that it had sold 400,000 shirts (an increase of 60 per cent compared to the previous season).

In 2014 the club made a strong entry into the Deloitte Football Money League ranking. With €398.8 million of revenue (including €254.7 million of commercial revenue), the Parisian club was ranked fifth, ahead of AC Milan (€263.5 million), Juventus (€272.4 million), Chelsea (€303.4 million) and Manchester City (€316.2 million). By contrast, Forbes has estimated the club value at $634 million (€555.8 million), placing it twelfth in the Forbes ranking, well behind Real Madrid ($3.2 billion/€2.8 billion).

Nevertheless, the club is not a new 'idle rich' one. It applies itself to redefining its marketing strategy. As Frédéric Longuépée (Assistant Managing Director) explains:

> one of the main stakes for Paris-Saint-Germain is to develop an internationally recognised brand, a sports franchise in the Anglo-Saxon meaning of the word. We are not here only to pilot a sports project. Sport remains the priority, but around that we have authority to develop a brand [that is] internationally recognised like Ferrari, Roland Garros tournament or Manchester United. It is often related to history, but it can also be related to a proactive approach which capitalises on great assets such as Paris, media and social media, which did not exist at the time of these major sports brands and have grown over time.
>
> (Longuépée, 2014)

The club marketing strategy relies on the following pillars:

- **Players:** Zlatan Ibrahimovic, David Luis, Thiago Silva and Edinson Cavani strengthen brand equity through their star power. They also ensure the brand spreads in strategic markets. During his few months spent in the French capital, David Beckham was not only a football player but also a major PSG advocate, in particular in the Asian and North American markets.
- **Management:** The most important club recruit is not a player. Jean-Claude Blanc joined the club in 2011 as Managing Director. A graduate of Harvard, he has

worked on the 1992 Winter Olympic Games, the Tour de France, the Roland Garros French Open and with Juventus. As a strategist of the new PSG, he explains:

Our ambition is to make Paris-Saint-Germain a worldwide brand in sport. We want to join the Top 10 of brands such as Real Madrid, FC Barcelona, Manchester United, Ferrari or the All Blacks. In sport, there are some clubs that, regardless of their talent, cannot reach targets beyond a city or a country. A team like Dortmund is excellent, but its media potential is naturally limited. Our chance is that we can rely on the Paris brand. We can associate the popularity of football with the aura of Paris.

(Blanc, 2013)

- **Identity:** The club has applied itself to highlighting 'Paris' in its brand equity. At the beginning of 2013 it suggested a new logo. So as not to upset the historical sensitivity of fans, the visual identity kept its original attributes but the word 'Paris' took an important place on the crest. A golden fleur-de-lys under the Eiffel Tower strengthens the luxurious and international positioning.
- **Digital strategy:** International development is ensured by a strong presence in social media. PSG takes advantage of the most important digital fan base in France: 3.92 million followers on Twitter, 25.5 million fans on Facebook, 6.8 million subscriptions on Instagram (data recorded on 7 November 2016) and a presence in Chinese social media. In its report Red Card 2014, Mailman agency ranked PSG as the thirteenth most effective European club in Chinese social media.
- **Stadium:** Parc des Princes (which belongs to the city of Paris) is the historical base of the club. The new agreement between PSG and the municipality plans an annual rent worth more than €1 million and a variable payment based on revenues. Later, a capacity increase or a naming contract could be envisaged. The club will invest €75 million in stadium renovation so as to improve the matchday experience. It plans to increase the capacity of business seats by 10 per cent so that they represent 45 per cent of matchday revenues.

QUESTIONS

1. What are the main strengths and weaknesses of Paris Saint-Germain?
2. When it comes to becoming one of the greatest sports brands, is it better to invest in football talent or to pay a marketing manager?
3. Could QSI have conducted the same project with the same goals in a different city from Paris?
4. Can a sports team become a global brand without winning a major title?

CONCLUSIONS

According to the managers, the club had had the potential for a fan base of 12 million, with 80 per cent of them overseas. However, before PSG's purchase by QSI, it only had 500,000 fans. Thus the sudden enrichment of the club has been accompanied by a new marketing strategy which seems to have worked. In three years the club has become rich, is performing well, and is renowned and appreciated. This should be considered a success, since not so long ago, due to problems of violence in and around the stadium, it suffered from a very bad reputation. Even so, the club has not won the prestigious Champions League yet so as to establish itself in the Top 10 of the major sports brands. For this, PSG still has to invest in players, and thus make even higher revenues. With this in mind, it would be necessary to persuade UEFA to apply its Financial Fair Play protocol with more flexibility.

RECOMMENDED READING

Marketing and Football (2006), edited by Michel Desbordes, is a good introductory book on the marketing of football. Also recommended are *Global Sport Marketing, Contemporary Issues and Practice* (2012) by Desbordes and Richelieu, and more specifically Chapter 1: Building sports brands and Chapter 2: The internationalization of sports teams as brands.

BIBLIOGRAPHY

Apostolopoulou, A. (2002). Brand extensions by U.S. professional sport teams: Motivations and keys to success. *Sport Marketing Quarterly*, 4(11), 205–14.

Bekdikhan, S. (2014), personal communication.

Blanc, J.-C. (2013). Le Paris Saint-Germain peut devenir une marque mondiale / Paris Saint-Germain can become a worldwide brand, www.lesechos.fr/industrie-services/dossiers/0202178927188/0203192894418-jean-claude-blanc-jean-claude-blanc-le-paris-saint-germain-peut-devenir-une-marque-mondiale-637522.php, 16 December.

Bodet, G. and Chanavat, N. (2010). Building global football brand equity: Lessons from the Chinese market. *Asia Pacific Journal of Marketing and Logistics*, 22, 55–66.

Couvelaere, V. and Richelieu, A. (2005). Brand strategy in professional sports: The case of French soccer teams. *European Sport Management Quarterly*, 5(1), 23–46.

Desbordes, M. (ed.) (2006). *Marketing and Football: An International Perspective*. Elsevier, Oxford.

Desbordes, M. and A. Richelieu (eds) (2012). *Global Sport Marketing. Contemporary Issues and Practice*. Routledge, London and New York.

Gladden, J. M. and Milne, G. R. (1999). Examining the importance of brand equity in professional sports. *Sport Marketing Quarterly*, 8(1), 21–9.

Hill, J. S. and Vincent, J. (2006). Globalisation and sports branding: The case of Manchester United. *International Journal of Sports Marketing and Sponsorship*, 7(3), 213–30.

Longuépée, F. (2014). Devenir une marque internationale / Becoming an international brand, *L'Equipe*, 27 July.

Ozerdim, B. (2012). Personal communication.

Richelieu, A., Lopez, S. and Desbordes, M. (2008). The internationalization of a sports team brand: The case of European soccer teams. *International Journal of Sports Marketing and Sponsorship*, 9(4), 29–44.

Richelieu, A. and Pons, F. (2006). Toronto Maple Leafs vs. FC Barcelona: How two legendary sports teams built their brand equity. *International Journal of Sports Marketing and Sponsorship*, 7(3), 231–50.

Ross, S. D. (2006). A conceptual framework for understanding spectator-based brand equity. *Journal of Sport Management*, 20, 22–38.

Yang, Y., Shi , M. and Goldfarb, A. (2009). Estimating the value of brand alliances in professional team sports. *Marketing Science,* 28(6), 1095–111.

RECOMMENDED WEBSITES

Brand Finance (2015). The Brand Finance Football 50 2015, accessed 26 August 2015 from http://brandirectory.com/league_tables/table/top-50-football-club-brands-2015

Deloitte (2015). Deloitte Football Money League 2015, accessed 26 August 2015 from www2.deloitte.com/uk/en/pages/sports-business-group/articles/deloitte-football-money-league.html

Forbes (2014). Soccer team valuations, Paris Saint-Germain, accessed 26 August 2015 from www.forbes.com/teams/paris-saint-germain/

Forbes (2014). The soccer teams that score the most with social media, accessed 26 August 2015 from www.forbes.com/sites/mikeozanian/2014/05/09/the-soccer-teams-that-score-the-most-with-social-media/

Forbes (2015). Paris Saint-Germain Club, Hublot Unveil Big Bang Unico Bi-Retrograde Watch atop Rockefeller Center, accessed 26 August 2015 from www.forbes.com/sites/robertanaas/2015/07/23/paris-saint-germain-club-hublot-unveil-big-bang-unico-bi-retrograde-watch-atop-rockefeller-center/

Mailman Group (2015). Red Card 2015 – China Digital Football Index, accessed 26 August 2015 from www.mailmangroup.com/red-card-2015/

The New York Times (2012). Qatar Is Becoming a Player in French Sports, accessed 26 August 2015 from www.nytimes.com/2012/10/27/sports/soccer/with-paris-saint-germain-qatar-is-a-player-in-french-sports.html?_r=0

The New York Times (2013). Qatari Hopes for Paris Saint-Germain Meet Reality, accessed 26 August 2015 from www.nytimes.com/2013/05/25/world/europe/25iht-letter25.html

The New York Times (2014). Money Is No Object for Paris Saint-Germain, accessed 26 August 2015 from www.nytimes.com/2014/03/14/sports/soccer/money-is-no-object-for-paris-saint-germain.html

Sport Business Daily/Global Journal (2015). Paris St. Germain Aims to Become One of World's Most Famous Sports Franchises, accessed 26 August 2015 from www.sportsbusinessdaily.com/Global/Issues/2015/07/29/Franchises/PSG.aspx

The Wall Street Journal (2014). Soccer's Financial Fair Play to Test UEFA's Platini, accessed 26 August 2015 from www.wsj.com/articles/SB10001424052702303939404579527453188192022

The Wall Street Journal (2015). How Europe Roots for the Champions League, accessed 26 August 2015 from www.wsj.com/articles/how-europe-roots-for-the-champions-league-1424721670

CASE 7

"CELEBRIFICATION": A CASE STUDY OF LOLO JONES

KWAME J. A. AGYEMANG

LEARNING OUTCOMES

Upon completion of this case study, the reader should be able to:

- recognize the process of "celebrification";
- highlight the features of celebrity;
- understand the role of media (old and new) in creating celebrity;
- identify dilemmas pertaining to the "celebrification" process;
- assess best practices on how to manage one's celebrity.

OVERVIEW OF THE CASE

This case examines the manner in which an athlete can generate high levels of public attention, thereby creating their celebrity. In particular, the case centers on U.S. 100-meter hurdler Lolo Jones in the buildup to the 2012 Olympic Games in London. This process is referred to as "celebrification".

The present example is notable given Lolo Jones competes in a less recognizable sport as compared to sports such as basketball, football, or even tennis, just to name a few. So the tactics she used to generate her celebrity are especially noteworthy. Furthermore, the case is also notable when studying the response to Lolo Jones's tactics.

CASE STUDY

As the 2008 Olympic Games in Beijing approached, Lolo Jones was regarded as one of the frontrunners to win the women's 100-meter hurdles. After all, she not only had the fastest time in the world at the time, but the top five times as well. Yet Jones's likeness and image were not displayed on popular products, nor did she feature in advertisements. One can imagine her bewilderment and frustration given her athletic exploits.

Fast-forward to the two years leading up to the 2012 Olympic Games in London. Jones had struggled with injuries and even underwent a procedure for a spinal condition in August 2011. As a result, her performance was inconsistent, and given her times, she was not among the favorites to make the U.S. Olympic team for the 100-meter hurdles. However, she persevered and placed third in the U.S. trials, earning the last qualification spot.

Even though she was still considered one of the best competitors in the 100-meter hurdles, Jones did not possess a major Olympic sponsor. One would think that given her successes through the years, sponsors would have been at her doorstep, seeking her likeness and image for their products.

Jones soon realized acquiring such deals was not solely about performance, because if it were, sponsors most certainly would have been at her beck and call (especially in 2008). Jones's issue was that, despite her good past performances, she was relatively unknown to both U.S. and international audiences.

Jones started to conduct her own research into how she could become more relevant. "Who is getting the top sponsorships? What are those athletes doing that I am not?", she asked (Ewing and Grady, 2013).

Her initial task was to drive action and create a "buzz" on the internet, specifically on social networking sites such as Twitter and Facebook. She discovered that the number of Twitter and Instagram followers one has, in addition to the number of "likes" on one's Facebook profile, plays an integral role in receiving endorsement deals from prominent sponsors.

With this newfound knowledge, Jones set out to prioritize how she utilized social media. This consisted of sharing information via video footage and pictures, among other strategies, and gave observers an "inside look" at the life of Lolo Jones.

Through most certainly purposeful and calculated action on her part, Jones had commenced the "celebrification" process. But how exactly did she do it? What information did she share?

One strategy she made use of was aligning herself with other well-known sport celebrities, such as members of the U.S. men's basketball team. Given the NBA is a global brand, it was definitely a smart move on her part to be seen with such stars. Mentioning these athletes in her tweets and other posts, to which the basketball players then responded, drove curiosity as to who Lolo Jones was.

What also endeared her to fans and sponsors is that she demonstrated her sense of humor. In one instance she posed for a picture with New Orleans Pelicans star

Anthony Davis, then alluding to the height discrepancy between the two in the picture. She asked, "Can we retake this photo @antdavis23? Let me stand on the stairs…" (Davis is one foot – approximately 0.30 meters – taller than Jones).

Finally, and equally as important, Lolo also showcased her dedication to her sport. Jones provided footage of her training regimen in preparation for the London Olympics.

As a result of her efforts, fans and sponsors gravitated toward Jones. There was now a sense of connection that did not previously exist; fans felt as if they truly knew her as a result of the access she granted them. Sponsors then capitalized on this. She was now a household name and companies such as McDonald's, Procter & Gamble, Asics, Red Bull, and British Petroleum became personal sponsors as the London Olympics approached.

There was, however, a distinct and obvious anti-Jones sentiment, as some had grown tired of Jones's celebrification. This included two of her teammates, Dawn Harper and Kellie Wells, who eventually won silver and bronze, respectively, in London. Harper and Wells felt as if the attention Jones garnered was unjustified, and that they should have received more attention considering they medalled, while Jones did not (she placed fourth in 100-meter hurdles). They even went as far as discussing their displeasure on nationally broadcast interviews.

Then there was a scathing *New York Times* article written by Jeré Longman, which essentially accused Jones of being an "attention grabber" and a contradiction. For instance, Longman cites Jones's willingness to use sex appeal (i.e., posing nude for ESPN the Magazine) to produce publicity, while also noting that Jones has spoken candidly about her Christian faith and being a virgin.

Soon after the London Olympic Games finished, Jones addressed her detractors.

In response to the criticisms from Harper and Wells, Jones said that the reason for her receiving attention might have been as simple as having a marketing agent and being purposeful about her personal brand.

In an interview with espnW's Kate Fagan, Jones drew attention to Longman's reproach: "There's definitely a whole double standard," she said. "I don't understand it. A guy can be sexy and good-looking, and it totally just enhances his credibility as an athlete" (espnW, 2012).

A successful celebrification? One would venture to say yes. However, there was also some backlash, and reports after the Games suggested that Jones had yet to speak to her teammates who criticized her.

QUESTIONS

1. What is "celebrification"?
2. What is unique about track and field (i.e., athletics) when it comes to the celebrification process?

3. What can be learned from Lolo Jones's case and be applied to other aspiring sport celebrities?
4. From the perspective of a brand management team, what are some strategies for avoiding potential negative reactions toward an athlete?
5. Discuss some of the benefits and detriments of celebrity.
6. Consider a current athlete who you think has the potential to become a global sport celebrity. What is your initial assessment of the athlete and what strategies would you employ to "celebrify" him or her?

CONCLUSIONS

A number of present-day athletes are not content with just being known for their athletic prowess. Nor are they satisfied with solely being associated with the club/ team they compete for or the sport they play. Instead, they desire to be global icons, appearing on the most coveted products and in television broadcasts and movies, among other things. As such, more athletes will attempt to "celebrify" themselves. Moreover, with such a cluttered marketplace, it is difficult to keep potential consumers' attention. Thus one could assume that the strategies used will only grow in the years to come. As these athletes attempt to become global icons, they will have to consider emerging markets in Africa and Asia. How might their strategy in these markets differ from the one employed in their local market? Furthermore, how (if at all) will an athlete becoming a celebrity impact the team, club, or league they compete in? Needless to say, there are some intriguing issues and questions to be answered.

RECOMMENDED READING

Each of the following works provides interesting insight on celebrity creation. For instance, Elberse's (2013) *Blockbusters: Hit Making, Risk-Taking, and the Big Business of Entertainment* offers understanding on how superstars such as LeBron James and Maria Sharapova use their celebrity. Though not in the sport context (focusing rather on Jay-Z and Lady Gaga), students may also be interested in a chapter in which Elberse discusses the future of blockbuster strategies. Furthermore, students should consider looking at texts that consider building an emotional attachment in a saturated market. One example is *The Global Brand: How to Create and Develop a Lasting Brand Value in the World Market* (Hollis, 2010). Lastly, Berger's (2013) text *Contagious: Why Things Catch On* answers the question "What makes things popular?", while Agyemang and Williams' 2013 paper offers insight on the use of "brandpression" management in this process.

BIBLIOGRAPHY

Agyemang, K. J. A. and Williams, A. S. (2013). Creating revenue via organisational 'brand-pression' management (OBpM): A marriage of brand management and impression management in professional sport. *International Journal of Revenue Management*, 7(2), 171–81.

Berger, J. (2013). *Contagious: Why Things Catch On*. New York: Simon & Schuster.

Carlson, B. D. and Donavan, D. T. (2013). Human brands in sport: Athlete brand personality and identification. *Journal of Sport Management*, 27(3), 193–206.

Chung, K. Y. C., Derdenger, T. P. and Srinivasan, K. (2013). Economic value of celebrity endorsements: Tiger Woods' impact on sales of Nike golf balls. *Marketing Science*, 32(2), 271–93.

Elberse, A. (2013). *Blockbusters: Hit-making, Risk-taking, and the Big Business of Entertainment*. New York: Henry Holt and Co.

Ewing, H. and Grady, R. (Directors). (2013). 'Branded' [Television series episode]. In R. Roberts and J. Rosenthal (Producers), *Nine for IX*. Bristol, CT.

Hollis, N. (2010). *The Global Brand: How to Create and Develop Lasting Brand Value in the World Market*. New York: Palgrave Macmillan.

Thomson, M. (2006). Human brands: Investigating antecedents to consumers' strong attachments to celebrities. *Journal of Marketing*, 70(3), 104–19.

RECOMMENDED WEBSITES

ESPN (2012). Jones earned every marketing dollar, accessed 7 July 2015 from http://espn.go.com/olympics/summer/2012/espnw/story/_/id/8249477/espnw-lolo-jones-worked-create-image-sells

ESPN (2012). *Nine for IX*: Exclusive clip from 'Branded', accessed 7 July 2015 from http://espn.go.com/video/clip?id=9601851

espnW (2012). Lolo Jones' saga in London part of bigger story, accessed 7 July 2015 from http://espn.go.com/espnw/news-commentary/article/8296143/espnw-takeaway-lolo-jones-saga-london

New York Times (2012). For Lolo Jones, everything is image, accessed 7 July 2015 from www.nytimes.com/2012/08/05/sports/olympics/olympian-lolo-jones-draws-attention-to-beauty-not-achievement.html?_r=1

Slate (2012), The *New York Times* goes after hurdler Lolo Jones and gets Olympic sexism wrong, accessed 7 July 2015 from www.slate.com/blogs/five_ring_circus/2012/08/06/lolo_jones_2012_olympics_the_new_york_times_goes_after_the_olympic_hurdler_and_gets_olympic_sexism_wrong_.html

Sports Business Daily (2012). Has Lolo Jones become a star because of athleticism or market-ability?, accessed 7 July 2015 from www.sportsbusinessdaily.com/Daily/Issues/2012/08/07/Olympics/Lolo.aspx

The Daily Beast (2012). New York Times attack on Olympic athlete Lolo Jones unfounded and unfair, accessed 7 July 2015 from www.thedailybeast.com/articles/2012/08/07/new-york-times-attack-on-olympic-athlete-lolo-jones-unfounded-and-unfair.html

CASE 8

END OF THE ROAD: WHY THE ISTANBUL F1 GRAND PRIX CAME TO A SCREECHING HALT

CEM TINAZ, DOUGLAS MICHELE TURCO AND JAMES SANTOMIER

LEARNING OUTCOMES

Upon completion of this case study, the reader should be able to:

- identify the goals of Formula One in selecting Istanbul as a host city;
- define Istanbul's goals in hosting Formula One races;
- distinguish the problems that Formula One faced in Istanbul before and after the construction of the track;
- determine to what extent the lack of a grass-roots sports culture played a role in the failure of the Istanbul Formula One race;
- relate the local sports culture to the success or failure of an international sporting event.

OVERVIEW OF THE CASE

This case study explores the series of strategic decisions taken by event organizers and Formula One Management that ultimately drove Formula One's Istanbul Grand Prix to a dead end. The Istanbul Grand Prix required high levels of subsidy from the Turkish government and private investors, yet ended before realizing the expected goals. Findings reveal several factors that contributed to the discontinuation of Istanbul's Formula One Grand Prix, including a misunderstanding of the Turkish market, high costs, low spectator interest, and increased competition from other cities. This case provides a model that other cities considering hosting a major inter-national motorsport event should take into account.

Formula One has had the reputation of being the top organization for motorsport for over half a century, and the brand itself conveys an elite status to the hosts of the Formula One auto racing events. In recent years Formula One has attempted to expand beyond the traditional European and North American markets. This desire to expand brought Formula One to Istanbul, Turkey. However, a lack of market analysis and inadequate planning caused Formula One to shutter its event after only seven years. In order to understand the failure of Formula One in Istanbul completely, it is necessary to focus on the goals of the Formula One organization as well as the goals of the Turkish government. Ultimately, the relationship foundered because each entity could not meet the needs of the other.

With total revenues expected to reach almost US$3.3 billion in 2016, Formula One is one of the major sport enterprises worldwide (Baldwin, 2011). The sport's commercial rights alone annually produce US$1.5 billion, and its top teams, backed by some of the largest global corporations, have budgets of over US$400 million (Mehrotra and MacAskill, 2011). The money that flows through Formula One makes it attractive to cities that earn the rights to host Formula One events: the economic gains purportedly boost everything from infrastructure to tourism.

Not surprisingly, several studies have focused on the economic impact of Grand Prix events in host cities. One of the most comprehensive event analyses ever completed was a 1986 study of the Adelaide Grand Prix, which was published as a book. Burns, Hatch, and Mules (1986) scrutinized the economic, social, cultural, and environmental impact of the Grand Prix. This book constitutes a guide for communities and their governments regarding special sporting events, and provides detailed information about motorsport-related issues, such as noise pollution, property damage, disruption to normal services, and effects of the race on South Australian entrepreneurship. According to the authors' cost–benefit analysis, the 'psychic income' reached AUS$25 million. From a sponsorship perspective, Donahay and Rosenberger (2007) determined that Formula One team sponsorship can cost up to US$50 million annually. Perhaps the most important benefit Formula One events can bestow is to enhance the image of host cities. Liu and Gratton (2010) explored the impact of the 2008 Shanghai Formula One Grand Prix on that city's image. Their findings indicated that in order to achieve the most effective impact on spectators, event organizers must give priority to improving service quality and spectator satisfaction.

Although the benefits of hosting Formula One events in cities are numerous, Formula One CEO Bernie Ecclestone has demonstrated a willingness to cancel or reschedule events at short notice. The Grand Prix in Indianapolis was cancelled in 2007 after an eight-year run due to disagreements between race organizers and Formula One Management over the terms of the race (Olson, 2010). On the other hand, in March 2010 Ecclestone announced his plans to bring a Formula One race to New York City for the 2012 season. Although this race did not come to fruition, rather than leave the US entirely, Ecclestone made agreements to move the race to another American city. In May 2010 Austin, Texas, was awarded a ten-year contract starting in 2012 (Formula1.com, 2010). In 2011 the Bahrain Grand Prix was cancelled for one year after the Arab Spring uprisings (Weaver, 2012). The race returned to Bahrain in 2012. In October 2011 the inaugural Delhi Grand Prix took place without government subsidy. Mehrotra and MacAskill (2011) reported that billionaire Jaiprakash Gaur spent US$450 million to build the track and then paid an additional US$200 million in royalties over five years to the Fédération Internationale de l'Automobile (FIA). However, Ecclestone announced in early 2013 that the 2014 Indian Grand Prix would have to be dropped to allow modifications to the racing calendar. Reportedly, he could not agree on dates with the Indian organizers (Rao, 2013). The most recent race to be dropped from the list was the Korean Grand Prix. This race ended primarily because it was not profitable. The location of the track discouraged spectators from attending, and when the Korean organizers attempted to renegotiate with Formula One to lower the costs, they were rebuffed. In the end the Korean Grand Prix was removed from the race schedule (Davies, 2013). The long list of cancelled races is evidence of Formula One's instability in new markets, even in developed countries. The high construction and operation costs and short operating time make hosting Formula One races a risky investment for governments or private investors.

The Istanbul Grand Prix is a prime case of Formula One's transformational financial and marketing models in the new Formula One era. In Formula One's haste to expand and the Turkish government's haste to host a prestigious event, both failed to analyse the market and plan for the long-term success of the event. After building a track and surrounding infrastructure and hosting several races, the Istanbul Grand Prix was cancelled after seven years, with announcement of the cancellation being made on 30 July 2011 (BBC News, 2011). One of the main reasons given for the cancellation was that Ecclestone had doubled the Istanbul race licensing fee from 8 million GBP to 16 million GBP, an amount the Turkish government was unwilling to underwrite. However, other contributing factors included an inadequate sport consumer market, a poorly designed track, a lack of marketing, and ultimately increased competition from other host cities.

Complexity theory

Several sport scholars have attempted to describe and explain sport organizational behaviours, change management, and decision-making, including Smith (2004), Slack (1997), Cousens, (1997), and Westerbeek et al. (1995). Smith's application of complexity theory provides an enlightened view on the dynamics of sport, sport governance, and sport management. He synthesizes three distinguishing characteristics of complexity theory as follows:

1. Complexly structured, non-additive behaviour emerges out of the organization's interactive networks;
2. Complex systems exhibit nonlinear behaviour that is unpredictably related to input; and
3. Complex behaviour is somewhere between predictability and non-predictability, a position sometimes described as the 'edge of chaos' (Peters, 1992). This is the point at which there is enough chaos or unpredictability to ensure that consistency and predictability is lost, 'but also enough order or predictability for consistency and patterns to endure' (Peters, 1992: 72).

As Smith (2004: 70) notes, 'some sophisticated change and innovation occurs at the planned instigation of senior management, but not all that occurs.' He posits the potential benefits of complexity theory for managing or understanding how organizations are managed: 'If complexity theory and the principle of emergence are useful constructs for explaining certain murky but advantageous changes, the possibility for such change to be deliberately harnessed and incorporated into strategic efforts may be improved' (2004: 70). For this case study, complexity theory offers a perspective for interpreting the behaviour of the Istanbul Formula One management team. With the awareness that the collective activity of the units is not fully explained by their sum, and that they may produce emergent properties, these properties feature spontaneous, unpredictable and self-organized patterns, behaviours, and outcomes (Smith, 2004).

The case study analysis has two elements. The first element is to discuss the rationale for hosting the Istanbul Formula One Grand Prix, identifying key decisions for track placement, track and event financing, and responsibilities of management entities. The second is to discuss the organization of the race and related managerial issues leading to the discontinuation of the event. Beech and Chadwick (2004) identified three interactive environments that directly impact a sport organization's success. These are the global environment (macro-environment), the industry environment (micro-environment), and the organizational environment. For this case study the micro-environment, organizational environment, and managerial decisions regarding the Istanbul Formula One Grand Prix are examined and discussed.

Early plans

Some global economists consider Turkey to be the 'rising star' of the Middle East (Champion and Parkinson, 2011). Turkey attracted 37.5 million visitors in 2012 and ranked sixth worldwide as a tourism destination (Tourism Highlights, 2013). Without question, Istanbul, with a population of 13.4 million, is the most visited and globally recognized city in Turkey. Marcuse (2008: 29) has defined mega-cities as 'the products of their own positions within the world of globalization, with its thread of colonization, uneven development, competition, division of labor, and exploitation'. One could argue that Istanbul has risen to the level of a 'mega-city'.

It is understandable on a number of levels why the city of Istanbul (the municipality, governorship, and other institutions) wanted to host a Formula One event. Politicians and persons of influence wanted to elevate Istanbul's position to that of a 'world-class city'. Derudder and Witlox (2008: 11) define a world-class city as 'at least entailing the presence of well-connected international airports, major hotel chains, and a climate that is somehow conducive to inviting and redirecting globalised capital'. Istanbul's attempt to achieve international acclaim through Formula One, as well as through a bid for the 2020 Olympics, reveals the city's aspirations to join the world of elite sport.

As a result of lobbying efforts, Bernie Ecclestone visited Turkey in March 2002. He stated in his press meeting that:

> Turkey is a hidden geography. We should use it. Your demand for hosting a Formula One race in Turkey is now serious ... There are lots of advantages and I don't see any disadvantage. We should first construct a proper track. Then you can consider hosting the race ... I expect that the interest will be higher than in Malaysia.
>
> (Turkiyef1.com, 2002)

During the ground-breaking ceremony for the track in 2005 Ecclestone added: 'We have been working for 10 years to have a race in Turkey. I am very happy for achieving our goal. Thank you very much to the Prime Minister and other authorities for their efforts. Tens of thousands of people will visit Turkey because of the race. There will be great effects on your tourism' (Ntvmsnbc.com, 2003). However, bringing Formula One to Turkey was actually a long and often tedious process.

The marketing manager of Formula One indicated that the most important objective for bringing Formula One to Istanbul was to enhance the international prestige of Turkey (Ozerdim, 2012). Istanbul was emerging as a global destination in the early 2000s, and hosting Formula One was deemed to be a suitable and timely way to implement the city's international strategy. However, hasty decisions related to acquiring global recognition and reputation precluded extensive market research, and because of this, the viability of Formula One in Istanbul was immediately disadvantaged. Formula One's marketing manager further stated that 'Turkey's state of readiness to host the premier motorsports event was questionable. The decision to bring such a global event to Turkey required great vision (and risk)' (Ozerdim, 2012).

However, because of Istanbul's willingness to invest so much in the event, the risk was determined to be a worthwhile one, considering the potential economic benefits and international prominence the event could bring. Emery (2011) has pointed out that understanding the current market environment is crucial for investments of all kinds. However, prior to actually bidding for the event, there was no indication that the organizations responsible did as much as perform a SWOT analysis (strengths, weaknesses, opportunities, and threats) to determine the macro and micro-environmental conditions for marketing a Formula One Grand Prix race in Istanbul.

The most overlooked factor in Istanbul's bid for the Formula One event was the lack of an established 'racing' market in Istanbul. The country simply had no motorsports culture. While curiosity was expected to help attract consumers in the early years, the marketing team at race sponsor Mercedes-Benz expected an established motor sports fan base to develop into a 'core audience' with some international participation in the subsequent years (Bekdikhan, 2014). Even with this expectation, there was simply no 'core audience' in Turkey, and establishing one proved problematic. The marketing manager at Mercedes-Benz noted that there was no motorsports connection within Turkey (Bekdikhan, 2014) because Turkey did not have a team participating in any Formula One events, in contrast to India and Russia, which regularly sent racing teams to Formula One events. In the first years of the Istanbul race, Mercedes-Benz gave away thousands of tickets to promote the event, but after only a few years people refused free tickets, citing a lack of interest in the Formula One events (Bekdikhan, 2014). The lack of interest by Turkish consumers resulted in an unprofitable Formula One Grand Prix and essentially sealed the fate of the race.

All those involved in the development and implementation of the Istanbul Formula One Grand Prix, including Formula One Management, the Turkish government, and sponsors, knew of the risks associated with building a track and bringing Formula One to Istanbul, but the Turkish government accepted these risks. Although poor market analysis was only one reason why the Formula One event in Istanbul was unsuccessful, it was the only one that could have been addressed prior to construction of the race track. The problems that faced the Istanbul Formula One race initially continued throughout the subsequent series of events.

Construction phase

The construction of the Istanbul track began in 2003. Although the track's proximity to one of Istanbul's major airports and highways made it the best possible location in Istanbul, the construction of the track itself was mismanaged. Significant budget discrepancies, problematic infrastructure, and a poorly designed track were the three major track-related issues that contributed to the failure of Formula One in Istanbul.

Masterman (2004) has claimed that there are two levels of objectives involved in the management of events. First, there are the organizational objectives that are desired by the event owners for the future direction of the organization. Secondly, there are business objectives that are set for events, that is the maximization of sales, the maximization of profits, improved return on investment through dividends to shareholders, and/or the reinvestment of profits into the business for growth, and so on. In this case the financial or business objectives had no significant importance or urgency. The Turkish government subsidized the event without requiring specific return on investment (ROI) estimates. In addition, the problem of goal incongruence increases with the size of the organization (Berry and Jarvis, 1999), and this lack of ROI measures became the foundation for the subsequent budgetary issues.

According to an independent economic analysis, race track construction costs were estimated at US$20 million, but the actual cost exceeded US$230 million (Uras, 2007). The vast discrepancy is evidence of inaccurate cost analyses, incompetence, and lack of financial oversight and/or fraud. The manager of Formula One in Istanbul contended that the estimated cost for track construction varied because some estimates contained costs for infrastructure (i.e. roads, water/gas piping) but other estimates did not. He put the total cost of the track at approximately US$150 million (Ozerdim, 2012). Another source indicated that the Turkish government financed the Istanbul Park Grand Prix circuit at a cost of 80 million euros (Altinordu, 2015). The government's willingness to invest this much money and to exceed established budgets demonstrates not only a misunderstanding of the long-term viability of Formula One in Istanbul, but also effective financial risk management.

There was also a logistical problem with the track. While it was located close to one of Istanbul's international airports, it was far from the city centre. Giles (2001) noted the traffic jams after the race, and customer satisfaction surveys noted the substandard mobility services (i.e. public transportation and parking). Nearly 65 per cent of survey respondents were unsatisfied or only partially satisfied with these services (Ozbay 2009). The marketing manager of Mercedes-Benz, even though he personally thought the location of the track was the right choice, noted that, after the first few years of the race, the strong demand diminished and his customers cited the distance of the track from the city centre as a major factor deterring them from attending Formula One events (Bekdikhan, 2014). While the surrounding neighbourhoods developed as a result of the track construction, the track's neighbours were not interested in supporting Formula One events, and as a result most of the event's potential fans remained far from the site.

The final negative factor related to the track construction was its design. There were simply too many seats, and even when ticket sales were high, the stadium appeared empty. The manager of Formula One in Istanbul noted that 'no other Formula One track had a main tribune capacity as large as the Istanbul facility (27000)' (Ozerdim, 2012). He added, 'in some races the main tribune becomes full with 5,000–6,000 spectators but ours was empty with 8,000–9,000 spectators' (personal communication, 2012). In solving this problem, the Formula One manager noted that there should have been more research into the 'level of request and build some additional tribunes if needed' (personal communication, 2012).

The curiosity on the part of the public that inspired the first year of ticket demand was not sustainable. The cost of the track was underestimated, the fan base was unsatisfied, and the Istanbul track itself contributed to the impression that there was little interest. As a result, Istanbul Park could not meet the needs of government investment, and when costs continued to increase and profits continued to fall, the government decided to cancel the Formula One event series.

Early races

The first race was held at Istanbul Park in 2005. The novelty of the Formula One event attracted a large number of spectators in the first years, but slowly the numbers of attendees dropped precipitously. For example, by 2009 only 36,000 spectators attended the event on race day. That same year 120,000 people attended the British Grand Prix (Giles, 2011). Low interest combined with high ticket prices discouraged attendance. In 2005, the first year of the event, tickets in the first category cost US$490 and the open area tickets cost US$53. In 2008 the prices were then increased to US$570 and US$82 respectively, but by 2010 the prices had dropped dramatically. At US$350 and US$44 respectively, the prices were still not low enough to attract fans.

The lack of interest of fans contributed to lack of interest of the media and sponsors, from which a large percentage of revenues would normally be generated. In addition, the number of television viewers was low. A normal Formula One race in Europe might be viewed by approximately 6 to 7 million people. In Turkey, that number was unofficially between 300,000 and 400,000 (Ozerdim, 2012). In fact, the manager of Formula One in Istanbul claimed that organizers actually paid the media to broadcast the race (Ozerdim, 2012).

Sponsors therefore lost their initial interest in the race. Petrol Ofisi, Turkey's leading fuel products and lubricants distribution company, signed a three-year contract with Formula One in 2006, but then terminated the contract in 2008 (Ozerdim, 2012). Mercedes-Benz developed an extensive marketing strategy, but the low spectator interest could not sustain their efforts. The Mercedes-Benz marketing manager reported that they 'did not launch any advertisement campaign but [they] directly targeted [their] customers, employees and business partners and tried to create awareness' (Bekdikhan, 2014).

While there is a lack of motorsport culture in Turkey, race organizers did little to develop any interest. The manager of Formula One in Istanbul noted that grass-roots activities such as cart racing could have helped introduce the sport to potential fans on a smaller scale. Education or training sessions could also have fostered interest in the sport (Ozerdim, 2012). Rather than finding ways to bring motorsports to the Turkish people, the track was left on the edge of the city, with few people interested in making the trip and buying tickets for the events.

The end of Formula One in Istanbul

In 2011 Ecclestone doubled Istanbul's race licensing fee from 8 million GBP to 16 million GBP. Increased competition from other markets such as Russia and India required a fee increase. The Turkish government, however, was unwilling to pay such a high fee, and failed negotiations led to Formula One dropping the Istanbul Grand Prix from the calendar. In general, however, Formula One was not satisfied with the market in Turkey. They were not making money either from ticket sales or broadcast rights. The empty stadium did not convey the idea of an elite sport, and the management of the Istanbul Formula One Grand Prix did little to convey a sense of professional competence to sponsors and fans.

QUESTIONS

1. What potential did Formula One Management see in the Istanbul market?
2. What reasons do you think explain the lack of market analysis undertaken before Istanbul was chosen as a Formula One host city?
3. The construction of the track was problematic on a number of levels. How significant a factor was this in the overall failure of Formula One in Istanbul?
4. How did the focus (or lack of focus) on short-term and long-term goals affect the success of Formula One in Istanbul?
5. How do you think Formula One could avoid similar results in other new markets?

CONCLUSIONS

In 2012 the Istanbul Park track was rented to private investors, and although the current owner of the track has claimed to be in contact with Ecclestone with a view to restarting Formula One races in Turkey, the future plans for the space are still unclear. Possible plans for the track include organizing local races, concerts, and various entertainment, staging an open air car market, and renting suitable areas to a car dealer (Otomobilsayfasi.com, 2012). Other potential activities include a driving academy, cycling and running activities, FIA Rally Cross RX championships, and Ferrari Racing Days (Intercity Park, 2014).

The case analysis of the Formula One Istanbul Grand Prix reveals several complex factors that contributed to the discontinuation of Formula One in Turkey. The most important factor was low spectator attendance, but high costs and increased competition were also key factors. Insufficient growth and lack of financial accountability of organizers, sponsors, media, and other stakeholders brought an end to the Istanbul Formula One race. Overall, government investors saw the potential benefits of increased prestige, positive destination image, and enhanced tourism income as outweighing the risks. The Turkish organizers and investors focused on short-term goals rather than long-term sustainability. When Formula One doubled its licensing fee seven years after the first race in Istanbul, the Turkish government was forced to confront its initial lack of due diligence.

Istanbul is not the only city that has failed to maintain Formula One events. Similar failures have occurred since Formula One first attempted to break into new markets. Although Formula One has earned a reputation as an elite European and North American organization, it is likely that it will need to make changes to its approach in order to appeal to new markets without an established motorsport culture. Only then will Formula One be able to be considered a truly global organization.

RECOMMENDED READING

A book such as *Event Marketing: How to Successfully Promote Events, Festivals, Conventions, and Expositions* by Leonard H. Hoyle (2002) might be helpful to students as an introduction to event planning and marketing. *Events Management* by Bowdin *et al.* (2002) provides useful information on event management. The most comprehensive report on Formula One business, Formula Money: Formula One's Financial Performance Guide, prepared by Sylt and Reid on its annual operations, provide all the facts on the business of Formula One. For specific cases, students should look at two articles: *The Formula One Australian Grand Prix: Exploring the Triple Bottom Line* by Fairley *et al.* (2011) and 'The impact of mega sporting events on live spectators' images of a host city: a case study of the Shanghai F1 Grand Prix' by Liu and Gratton (2010).

BIBLIOGRAPHY

Altinordu, A. (2015), Ruzgar gibi gecti, Socrates Dergi, accessed 21 July 2015 from www.socratesdergi.com/hic-unutmam/f1-turkiye-gp/.

Baldwin, A. (2011), F1 revenues set to double by 2016-report, Reuters, accessed 14 November 2012 from http://in.reuters.com/article/idINIndia-57453820110602.

BBC News (2011). Turkish Grand Prix poised to lose 2012 F1 calendar spot, accessed 1 July 2012 from www.bbc.co.uk/sport/0/formula1/14348303.

Beech, J. and Chadwick, S. (eds) (2004). *The Business of Sport Management*. Pearson Education, Harlow, UK.

Berry, A. and Jarvis, R. (1999). Chapter 14: Planning and Control and Chapter 19: Budgets. *Accounting in a Business Context*, 3rd edn, International Thomson Business Press, London.

Burns, J. P. A., Hatch, J. H. and Mules, T. J. (1986), *The Adelaide Grand Prix: The Impact of a Special Event*. Centre for South Australian Economic Studies, Adelaide.

Champion, M. and Parkinson, J. (2011). Turkey's Economy Surged 11% in Quarter, *The Wall Street Journal*, accessed 1 July 2012 from http://online.wsj.com/article/SB1000142405270 23045840045764170730767640318.html.

Cousens, L. (1997). From diamonds to dollars: The dynamics of change in AAA baseball franchises. *Journal of Sport Management*, 11, 316–34.

Davies, W. (2013). Formula One Drops Korean Grand Prix, *The Wall Street Journal*, accessed 24 April 2014 from http://blogs.wsj.com/scene/2013/12/05/formula-one-drops-korean-grand-prix/.

Derudder, B. and Witlox, F. (2008). What is a world class city? Comparing conceptual specifications of cities in the context of a global urban network, in M. Jenks, D. Kozak and P. Takkanon (eds), *World Cities and Urban Form: Fragmented, Polycentric, Sustainable?* Routledge, London, pp. 11–24.

Donahay, B. and Rosenberger III, P. J. (2007). Using brand personality to measure the effectiveness of image transfer in Formula One racing. *Marketing Bulletin*, 18(1), 1–15.

Emery, P. (2011). *The Sports Management Toolkit*, Routledge, Oxford.

Fairley, S., Tyler, B. D., Kellett, P. and D'Elia, K. (2011). The Formula One Australian Grand Prix: exploring the triple bottom line. *Sport Management Review*, 14, 141–52.

Formula1.com (2010). Formula One returns to the United States, accessed 15 January 2013 from www.formula1.com/news/headlines/2010/5/10824.html.

Giles, R. (2011). Turkey set to lose F1 grand prix from 2012 after dispute over race fee, *The Guardian*, accessed 17 June 2011 from https://www.theguardian.com/sport/2011/apr/22/turkey-f1-grand-prix.

Hoyle, L. H. (2002). *Event Marketing: How to Successfully Promote Events, Festivals, Conventions, and Expositions*, John Wiley & Sons, Inc., New York.

Intercitypark.com (2014). Intercity Park Etkinlikler, accessed 10 January 2014, from http://intercitypark.com/.

Liu, D. and Gratton, C. (2010). The impact of mega sporting events on live spectators' images of a host city: a case study of the Shanghai F1 Grand Prix. *Tourism Economics*, 16(3), 629–45.

Marcuse, P. (2008). Globalization and the forms of cities, in M. Jenks, D. Kozak and P. Takkanon (eds), *World Cities and Urban Form: Fragmented, Polycentric, Sustainable?*, Routledge, London, pp. 25–40.

Masterman, G. (2004). *Strategic Sports Event Management: An International Approach*, Elsevier Butterworth-Heinemann, Oxford.

Mehrotra, K. and MacAskill, A. (2011). F-1 brings $650 million race to Delhi after struggles in Asia, Bloomberg, accessed 20 September 2012 from www.bloomberg.com/news/2011-10-28/formula-one-brings-650-million-race-to-new-delhi-after-struggles-in-asia.html.

Ntvmsnbc.com (2003). Formula 1 macerasi basladi, accessed 10 November 2013 from http://arsiv.ntvmsnbc.com/news/233203.asp.

Olson, S. (2010). Speedway, F1 discussing race's return to Indianapolis. *Indianapolis Business Journal*, accessed 26 August 2016 from www.ibj.com/articles/18684-speedway-f1-discussing-race-s-return-to-indianapolis.

Otomobilsayfasi.com (2012). Formula 1 ihalesi Intercity'e kaldi, accessed 15 January 2013 from www.otomobilsayfasi.com/haber/formula-1-ihalesi-intercity_e-kaldi/203575.

Ozbay, E. (2009). Formula 1'in Türkiye'de Düzenlenme Süreci, Ekonomik Etkileri, Bu Etkilerin Algilanmasi ve Istanbul Park Izleyici Memnuniyeti [The Organization of Formula 1 Turkish Grand Prix, Measuring its economical effects and spectator's satisfaction level], Unpublished Master's Thesis, Marmara University, Istanbul.

Peters, T. (1992). *Liberation Management: Necessary Disorganization for the Nanosecond Nineties*. Macmillan, London.

Rao, C. R. (2013). India says shift in F1 dates a scheduling issue, Auto Racing, accessed 8 February 2014 from http://racing.ap.org/article/india-says-shift-f1-dates-scheduling-issue.

Slack, T. (1997). *Understanding Sport Organizations*. Human Kinetics. Champaign, IL.

Smith, A. C. T. (2004). Complexity theory and change management in sport organizations. *E:CO*, 6(1–2), 70–9.

Sylt, C. and Reid, C. (2012). *Formula Money*, Sport Media, London.

Tourism Highlights (2013). United Nations World Tourism Organization, accessed 26 August 2016 from www.e-unwto.org/doi/book/10.18111/9789284415427.

Turkiyef1.com (2002), Ecclestone Türkiye'de, accessed 10 November 2013 from www.turkiyef1.com/haberler/998/ecclestone-turkiye-de.html.

Uras, G. (2007). Formula 1'i getirenler ortadan kayboldu, Milliyet, accessed 1 July 2012 from www.milliyet.com.tr/2007/04/16/yazar/uras.html.

Weaver, P. (2012). Bernie Ecclestone resists calls to cancel Bahrain Grand Prix, *The Guardian*, accessed 18 May 2013 from www.guardian.co.uk/sport/2012/feb/14/bernie-ecclestone-bahrain-grand-prix.

Westerbeek, H., Shilbury, D. and Deane, J. (1995). The Australian sport system, its history and an organizational overview. *European Journal of Sport Management*, 2(1), 42–58.

RECOMMENDED WEBSITES

BBC (2014). Bernie Ecclestone: I don't know how to fix F1 finances, accessed 2 February 2015 from www.bbc.com/sport/0/formula1/29868355

BBC (2014). F1 Marussia: Folded team's assets auctioned, accessed 15 December 2014 from www.bbc.com/news/uk-england-30394940

BBC (2015). Silverstone boss questions Formula 1 entertainment value, accessed 28 April 2015 from www.bbc.com/sport/0/formula1/32506582

Crash.net (2013). Istanbul GP return 'ruled out' by Turkish PM, accessed 18 December 2014 from www.crash.net/f1/news/187193/1/istanbul-gp-return-ruled-out-by-turkish-pm.html

The Guardian (2014). US sounds warning to Formula One, a sport teetering on the brink of crisis, accessed 10 January 2015 from www.theguardian.com/sport/blog/2014/oct/27/us-grand-prix-formula-one-mario-andretti-f1

C. Tinaz, D. M. Turco, J. Santomier

CASE 9

HOW DID A SMALL-TOWN ICE HOCKEY CLUB BECOME A EUROPEAN TROPHY WINNER? THE CASE OF JYVÄSKYLÄ ICE HOCKEY CLUB, FINLAND

AILA AHONEN

LEARNING OUTCOMES

Upon completion of this case study, the reader should be able to:

- evaluate the importance of entrepreneurship in team sport organization;
- identify individual entrepreneurial characteristics;
- distinguish the different actions that can affect growth entrepreneurship in sport organization.

OVERVIEW OF THE CASE

Jyväskylä Ice Hockey Club (JYP) is an entrepreneurially-oriented ice hockey club in the small town (130,000 residents) of Jyväskylä, Finland. The club used to be an indebted non-profit sport club, but since 1999 when the current owner took over and changed it into a limited company, it has grown both financially and operationally. Today it is one of the most successful ice hockey clubs in Finland and it also won the European Trophy League in 2013. Behind this success is its owner's entrepreneurial growth orientation.

CASE STUDY

Introduction

Top-level sport in Finland has become an area of business only in the late 1990s. This development started with some reluctance since the message from the community was that professional sports organizations could no longer identify themselves as non-profit organizations. Ice hockey players' contracts were listed as contracts of employment, and professional leagues were identified as profit-seeking businesses. Not-for-profit sport associations became businesses, as their national league teams were required to become business enterprises.

Ice hockey has been the most popular sport in Finland for the past three decades. In Jyväskylä the first ice hockey team was established in 1947 by Jyväskylä Ice Hockey Club (JYP). It played mostly in the second-level national league with varying success until the 1980s and qualified for the top national league in 1985. At the beginning of the 1990s an economic depression hit Finland very hard, and sport sponsorship money decreased. JYP's financial situation became worse, and the player budget was far too small for a national league team. Finally, in 1999 JYP was corporatized and JYP Jyväskylä Ltd was established. JYP Juniors had been separated from the league team in 1995. The new company bought the first league team and its place in the national league, together with the A-juniors. At that time, an entrepreneur joined the board and became one of the owners and the managing director.

The beginning of the entrepreneurial path

In 2000 the national league became a closed series with 13 teams, all limited companies. JYP played in the league with limited success, and the owners concentrated on coping with a relatively small budget. In 2004 JYP published a strategy called 'Mission 2007', the aim of which was to raise JYP to be among the best teams in the league. In 2005 the managing director invested more money in JYP and with an associate bought the majority of shares together, in order to be able to make decisions on his own and increase risk-taking. In addition, a professional marketing manager, who became the managing director later on, was hired, together with a new head coach. In 2006 JYP saw its first profitable year as a result of an innovative marketing strategy, risk-taking and successful recruitments. JYP's financial position stabilized during the decade; it made major partnership deals and reduced its debts, even though its performance in the league was no better than in the 1990s. Mission 2007 succeeded in terms of marketing and finances, but still failed in terms of sporting success.

Growth enterprise

In the 2007–2008 season JYP made its first international sale and sold its number one goalkeeper to the Russian Kontinental Hockey League (KHL) for a half-year, even though there was a risk of also selling the team's success as a result. In 2008 JYP used external funding for the first time and built a new ice hockey arena together with the City of Jyväskylä, and finally in 2009 JYP won the national championship. The success story had begun. In 2010 JYP won the bronze medal, in 2011 the team was fourth and in 2012 they won the championship again. In 2013 JYP was the first Finnish ice hockey team to win the European Trophy.

JYP has maintained its position amongst top ice hockey clubs in Finland, and in terms of finances it was very successful in the period 2008–2012, even though its arena capacity is the smallest in the national league. JYP Jyväskylä's turnover grew by 40.7 per cent from 2008 to 2012 and the number of sponsorships and partners grew steadily in relation to turnover growth. Overall income can be divided equally into ticket sales, sponsorship and restaurant services with 25 per cent comprising TV rights and international player sales. Personnel numbers have not increased over the years since some of the services are bought from partner organizations. However, personnel expenses have grown due to bigger player budgets and higher salaries. JYP's turnover showed a major increase in 2010 due to player sales to the Russian KHL league. The biggest trade was one player sale that was worth 1.1 million euros. KHL sales have since played a remarkable role in JYP's returns. JYP's profits have been growing through the whole five-year period, but the profits have been fairly small, on average 3.8 per cent. However small the return, it has allowed the JYP organization to achieve a range of other objectives.

QUESTIONS

1. What are the actions that have led to entrepreneurial growth in this case?
2. What are the entrepreneurial characteristics that have been important in maintaining this success?
3. In order to develop its businesses further, JYP needs to recognize new business opportunities. What possibilities do you think they have to advance their business?

CONCLUSIONS

Entrepreneurial opportunities exist in sport business, and entrepreneurial activities are widely needed in order to develop sport-related organizations. JYP's recent entrepreneurial success has been based on its entrepreneurially-oriented owner and managing director. As sport business is regarded as a rapidly changing industry, entrepreneurs are expected to be innovative, willing to take risks and capable of identifying business opportunities. The emphasis in JYP's case has been, on the one hand, in a value-creation process for shareholders and, on the other hand, in social entrepreneurship. The owners and managers of JYP are not only motivated by profit, but also by the possibility of making a social contribution by developing the JYP juniors and by offering business knowledge and professionalism to the club's development and growth.

Proactivity is often identified as an important characteristic in sport entrepreneurship together with risk-taking. Sport business owners bear financial risk by employing expensive athletes based on their reputation and future development possibilities. In JYP's case the biggest risk was in season 2007–2008 when the player budget was increased by 1 million euros and, fortunately, the return was outstanding: victory in the Finnish championship in 2009 and sales to the KHL. In addition, the investment in the new arena and its services was a risk, since the outcome was partially dependent on the team's sporting success, and the capacity was not as large as originally desired. However, it paid off in terms of service improvements and season ticket sales.

RECOMMENDED READING

A basic text of entrepreneurship, such as *A General Theory of Entrepreneurship: The Individual-Opportunity Nexus* by Shane (2003) or *Small Business and Entrepreneurship* by Storey and Greene (2010) are good starting points for students to develop an understanding of entrepreneurship theories. Students should also look at texts concerning sport entrepreneurship. Cilletti and Chadwick's *Sport Entrepreneurship* (2012) is one of the few books introducing sport entrepreneurship from various perspectives. Ratten's 2011 paper introduces a theory of sport-based entrepreneurship and provides interesting insights into this phenomenon.

BIBLIOGRAPHY

Cilletti, D. and Chadwick, S. (eds) (2012). *Sport Entrepreneurship, Theory and Practice*. West Virginia University, Morgantown.
Covin, J. and Slevin, P. (1991). A conceptual model of entrepreneurship as firm behavior. *Entrepreneurship Theory and Practice*, 16(1), 7–25.
Gallagher D., Gilmore, A. and Stolz, A. (2012). The strategic marketing of small sports clubs: from fundraising to social entrepreneurship. *Journal of Strategic Marketing*, 20(3), 231–47.
Hardy, S. (1986). Entrepreneurs, organizations, and the sport marketplace: Subjects in search of historians. *Journal of Sport History*, 13(1), 14–33.
Kreiser, P. and Davis, J. (2010). Entrepreneurial orientation and firm performance: The unique impact of innovativeness, proactiveness, and risk-taking. *Journal of Small Business and Entrepreneurship*, 23(1), 39–51.
Ratten, V. (2011). Sport-based entrepreneurship: towards a new theory of entrepreneurship and sport management. *International Entrepreneurship and Management Journal*, 7, 57–69.

Ratten, V. (2011). Social entrepreneurship and innovation in sports. *International Journal of Social Entrepreneurship and Innovation*, 1(1), 42–54.

Santomier, J. (2002). Sport business entrepreneurship. *New England Journal of Entrepreneurship*, 5(1), 5–7.

Shane, S. (2003). *A General Theory of Entrepreneurship: The Individual-Opportunity Nexus*, Edward Elgar, Cheltenham–Northampton.

Shane, S. and Venkataraman, S. (2000). The promise of entrepreneurship as a field of research. *Academy of Management Review*, 25(1), 217–26.

Storey, D. and Greene F. (2010). *Small Business and Entrepreneurship*, Pearson Education, Harlow, UK.

RECOMMENDED WEBSITES

European Trophy, Europe's Premium Club Competition, accessed 30 September 2016 from www.championshockeyleague.net

Finnish Ice Hockey Association, accessed 18 June 2015 from www.finhockey.fi/info/in_english

Jyväskylä Hockey Team (JYP), accessed 18 June 2015 from http://jypliiga.fi

Kontinental Hockey League (KHL), accessed 18 June 2015 from http://en.khl.ru

CASE 10

THE STRATEGIC REPOSITIONING OF OLYMPIQUE LYONNAIS: TOWARDS A NEW BUSINESS MODEL

AURÉLIEN FRANÇOIS AND EMMANUEL BAYLE

LEARNING OUTCOMES

Upon completion of this case study, the reader should be able to:

- define the concept of a business model for professional sports clubs;
- identify the factors that lead to decision to change a business model over time;
- consider the importance of these strategies to professional sport;
- critically assess the opportunistic transition of a model with an economic base to one that is more socially based.

OVERVIEW OF THE CASE

This case study focuses on the French soccer club Olympique Lyonnais (OL), which has a number of features that are different from other French clubs. In France, OL is the only club listed on the stock exchange market and is the only one to privately own a stadium, which is due for completion in 2016.

The OL case is particularly interesting as several recent economic and sporting failures pushed the club's managers to rethink their traditional business model. The cornerstone of this new strategy is that the stadium must support the model by following a pattern that manifests a more social dimension.

CASE STUDY

Originally formed in 1896, OL was officially established in 1950. Until the end of the 1980s it existed in the shadow of neighbouring club AS Saint-Étienne, and suffered in comparison with its neighbour's success. In 1987 OL was taken over by Jean-Michel Aulas, a young owner of a local company with a passion for sport. In that year, OL had a projected deficit of 1.5 million euros. This deficit represented 60 per cent of its 2.5 million euro turnover, even though the club operated, technical staff excepted, with only four employees.

Aulas instigated a complete restructuring of the club using his entrepreneurial skills. During his first year as president, he applied a plan entitled 'OL Europe', with several stages of commercialization through which the club had to proceed rapidly. In 1992 the French Football Association required all clubs to become companies, hence Lyon changed its status. Aulas then recruited communication and marketing personnel. But it was the changes that were made at the end of the 1990s that undoubtedly brought OL into the 'sportainment' era. In 1999 Aulas opened up part of the club's equity for investment. Jerome Seydoux, CEO of the cinema corporation Pathé, invested 15 million euros in the club, becoming its second-largest stockholder and also its vice president.

Those two men then extensively restructured the club by creating OL Groupe, a holding company owning various capital stakes in several subsidiary companies such as OL Voyages, OL Images and OL Merchandising. The activity of these subsidiaries embodied a double strategy. First, they allowed the internalization of costs previously paid to external service providers. Secondly, they participated in enhancing OL's brand value. Several licences and by-products were thus created, enlarging the club's marketing products offer. Even though the number of subsidiary companies has now decreased, the organization is almost the same today (see Figure 10.1). In 2002 the club's commercial company became an SASP (Société Anonyme Sportive Professionnelle), and then in 2012 it became an SAS (Société par Actions Simplifiée).

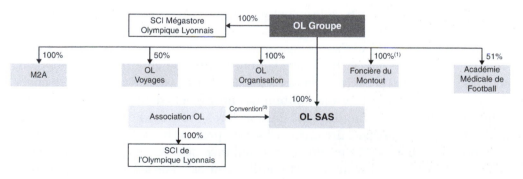

Figure 10.1 Simplified OL Groupe organization chart as of 30 June 2014

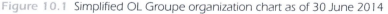

Thus the club's status is now even closer to the common status reserved for mainstream businesses, which allows the redistribution of profits to shareholders and also the remuneration of managers.

This strong drive towards commercialization allowed OL to reach higher sporting and economic levels. On the sporting side, OL started to dominate French soccer by winning seven championships in a row between 2002 and 2008 and, at a European level, it participated regularly in the very competitive Champions League. On the economic side, the club became the first (and so far the only) French club to enter the financial market. In 2007 the OL Groupe stock was introduced at a nominal price of 24 euros per share and this allowed the leveraging of almost 90 million euros in the days following its introduction. In 2008 the club's turnover was 211.6 million euros with a profit of 15.6 million euros, and it employed 256 people.

In the mid 2000s the emerging models of construction and private exploitation of stadiums in Europe reinforced Aulas' conviction to build a new stadium to generate some extra revenue streams, and to maintain OL's successful position. Even with the remodelling works that were carried out for the 1998 World Cup, the Gerland Stadium, built in 1926, was considered too old and too small. In particular, the stadium wasn't able to respond to the increased demand for tickets, which for some of the Champions League matches can go up to 200 per cent of capacity. Moreover, OL is obliged to pay a fixed rental charge to the city of Lyon, which owns the Gerland Stadium, and cannot currently enjoy financial benefits from the stadium other than ticket income. In 2004 a project to build a private stadium called OL Land was unveiled. It was first intended to build a 70,000-seat stadium, deliverable within 5 years for a cost of 140 million euros. In 2005 Aulas then proposed a less-ambitious remodelling project for the Gerland Stadium to Gérard Collomb, mayor of Lyon. However, this project was quickly abandoned. The new stadium project resurfaced after the announcement that the UEFA Euro 2016 tournament had been awarded to France, and for which Lyon is a host city. The search for a site for the location of such a complex was then focused on the east part of Lyon. In July 2013 work officially started on the construction of the Stade des Lumières.

The Stade des Lumières was designed with multifunctional arenas to ensure the ability to exploit it throughout the year. Inside the new OL Park, which included many non-sporting facilities (hotels, restaurants, meeting rooms, etc.) that were commercialized from the outset, the new stadium should be able to welcome 58,000 spectators, with 6,000 seats reserved for VIPs. Far above what was originally envisaged, the projected budget for the stadium has now reached 405 million euros. It is divided between internal funding (135 million euros) from the Foncière du Montout, a civil estate company specially created for this project, bank loans (136.5 million euros), issuing of bonds (112 million euros) and income from the commercialization of the park during its construction (21.5 million euros). The search for a sponsor to give its name to the stadium is still ongoing. The board of directors claims that the naming strategy will lead to annual income of 10 million euros for a term of at least 10 years.

However, the building project suffered criticism, especially among some of the residents of the 11 urban areas impacted by it. Politicians and ecologists also protested. Although the stadium was privately funded, the surrounding infrastructure, such as access roads, was funded by the public sector, and ultimately the taxpayer, with a cost estimated at 160 million euros. Because of all these issues, the construction of the stadium fell behind schedule between the late 2000s and early 2010s.

Besides the postponed stadium project, the new model the OL managers wanted responds to the economical and sporting difficulties which accelerated the decline of the former project. For this reason, since 2010 OL has been developing its OL Academy, which is aimed at boosting OL's sporting strategy by giving high priority to resourcing its training centre. This project was undertaken after many mistakes were made in player trading at the end of the 2000s and because of significant financial difficulties. The club then focused its recruitment efforts on a training policy, allowing it to alleviate payroll pressures by selling valuable players (Bastos, Lloris, Lopez, etc.). The nomination as head coach in 2011 of Rémi Garde, former player and in charge of the training centre, and the arrival of young players from the training centre each symbolized this new sporting strategy. This strategy was also adopted as a result of the increasing financial gap between OL and the richer French clubs (Paris Saint-Germain and Monaco) and other European clubs. From an economic perspective, the OL Groupe share price has continued its drop since its entry into the market in 2007, reaching as low as 2 euros in 2013. Finally, the relative failure of the OL brand in terms of marketing rates confirmed the difficulties the club was going through. In 2014, according to the last available report, OL Groupe reported gross profits of 120.5 million euros and a net loss of more than 26 million euros (partly due to the huge stadium investment) (see Table 10.1).

Table 10.1 Comparison of OL Groupe gross income and net profit/loss between 2007 and 2014

	2007–2008	2013–2014	Change
Financial gain	**211.6**	**120.5**	**− 43%**
Ticketing	21.8	13	− 40%
Sponsoring and advertising	20.4	19	+ 7%
Media and marketing rights	75	56.2	− 25%
Brand-related revenues	38.5	16.2	− 58%
Player trading	55.9	16.1	− 71%
Net result	**+ 15.6**	**− 26.4**	**− 269%**

All these factors led OL to promote the social dimension of the Grand Stade project. The replacement in 2011 of the OL Land project by Stade des Lumières symbolized this strategic reorientation. In 2012, in the club's financial statement, Aulas declared that the construction of the new stadium offered wonderful development perspectives, but also imposed a certain number of responsibilities.

In fact, OL adopted a corporate social responsibility (CSR) strategy at the beginning of the 2010s. Following the example of the great European clubs, OL wanted to emphasize its citizen role. By reaffirming the community dimension of its action, the CSR strategy planned by OL allows the justification of its legitimacy as a major social and economic actor in the city. This new orientation took its roots at first in the decision to rationalize the club's philanthropic initiatives with a private foundation, created in 2007. OL Foundation thus led to the maintenance of historic relationships created between OL and a pool of local non-profit organizations. But being more than a simple philanthropic strategy, the creation of the foundation was also the symbol of the start of OL's CSR strategy. In 2012 the board nominated one of the only two female administrators to head a CSR committee More recently, a CSR department was created to develop the social policy of OL, a first for a French sports club. OL managers gave significant amounts of money to its women's soccer section, to which the club allocated both important material and human resources as compared to what is generally seen in French and European soccer.

OL's current transitional model should be complete by the delivery of the new stadium. Initially forecast for 2013, the stadium's inauguration will now not be celebrated before 2016. Annual stadium revenues, which have been estimated at between 70 and 100 million euros by 2020, will make a strong contribution to the club's future financial performance. It remains to be seen whether these strategic orientations anchored in a strong social dimension are merely transitional, or if they will be at the core of this new business model.

QUESTIONS

1. What is a business model? What does it mean for a professional sports club?
2. The reasons for changing the OL traditional business model to a social one are numerous. List them and discuss them.
3. What is CSR? How does it take shape in this case?
4. Could CSR perspectives be fully integrated into the core strategy of a professional sports club?
5. Is the new OL business model sustainable? Expand your analysis to other professional soccer clubs, and more generally to the business of sport.

A. François, E. Bayle

CONCLUSIONS

The business models of professional football clubs have long been thought of as an answer to the needs of both sporting and economic performance. However, the introduction of new logics distilled by the sustainable development trend, such as the necessity for an organization to take into account the interests of its stakeholders, questions this traditional model.

Increasingly, club managers are asked to think according to global performance principles, aiming at the creation of new sustainable business models. The emergence of the model of private ownership of European stadiums, illustrated in this case, supports this view. Private ownership will enable the club to engage in more profitable and value-adding relationships. Therefore, analysing the change of business model is valuable for club managers wishing to have new managing strategies at their disposal, and also for those responsible for implementing these changes.

RECOMMENDED READING

The literature on the concept of the business model is flourishing. We first suggest referring to Drucker's 1994 article, published in the *Harvard Business Review*. Although he does not use the term 'business model' explicitly, he defines the concept. In the same journal, Johnson, Christensen and Kagerman's 2008 article enables us to go beyond the definition of the concept by introducing the benefits of a change of model with the help of recent examples.

Focusing on football management, a book such as Chadwick and Hamil (2010) allows the case to be put into perspective through the problems every professional football club is confronted with. French-speaking students could also refer to the work of Desbordes and Chanavat (2015), and more especially to the chapter by Scelles and Andreff (2015), allowing a contextualization of this study in respect to French football.

BIBLIOGRAPHY

Breitbarth, T. and Harris, P. (2008). The role of corporate social responsibility in the soccer business: towards the development of a conceptual model. *European Sport Management Quarterly*, 8(2), 179–206.

Chadwick, S. and Hamil, S. (2010). *Managing Football: An International Perspective*. Butterworth Heinemann, Oxford.

Desbordes, M. and Chanavat, N. (2015). *Le marketing du football*. Economica, Paris.

Drucker, P. (1994). The theory of the business. *Harvard Business Review*, 72(5), 95–106.

François, A., Anagnostopoulos, C. and Bayle, E. (forthcoming). CSR practices in the French professional sport context. *Sport, Business and Management: An International Journal*.

Johnson, M. W., Christensen, C. M. and Kagerman, H. (2008). Reinventing your business model. *Harvard Business Review*, 86(12), 50–9.

Paramio-Salcines, J., Babiak, K. and Walters, G. (2013). *Routledge Handbook of Sport and Corporate Social Responsibility*. Routledge, Oxford.

Scelles, N. and Andreff, W. (2015). Le modèle économique d'un club professionnel de football en France, in M. Desbordes and N. Chanavat (eds), *Le marketing du football*. Economica, Paris.

RECOMMENDED WEBSITES

Financial Times (2013). Jean-Michel Aulas: Football man who scores in big business, accessed 11 July 2015 from www.ft.com/intl/cms/s/0/bf238a34-80d6-11e2-9fae-00144feabdc0.html

Harvard Business Review (2015). What is a business model?, accessed 11 July 2015 from https://hbr.org/2015/01/what-is-a-business-model

Le Nouvel Economiste (2011). Le business model de l'Olympique Lyonnais – du club de foot à l'entreprise de spectacle, accessed 11 July 2015 from www.lenouveleconomiste.fr/le-business-model-de-lolympique-lyonnais-du-club-de-foot-a-lentreprise-de-spectacle-11702/ (in French)

Olympique Lyonnais (n.d.). New stadium – Stade des Lumières. Accessed 11 July 2015 from www.olweb.fr/en/team/new-stadium-167.html

A. François, E. Bayle

CASE 11

SOCIAL MEDIA AND MEDIA MANAGEMENT

RAYMOND E. BOYLE

LEARNING OUTCOMES

Upon completion of this case study, the reader should be able to:

- understand the key role played by social media in football PR;
- appreciate the importance of media training among football managers;
- understand the importance of briefing for live media interviews;
- be clear how important reputation management is in the 24/7 media environment.

OVERVIEW OF THE CASE

This case study highlights the importance of speed in the digital sports news environment, and the key role that communications experts need to play in helping managers and players understand the implication of media actions on the reputation of the club, and by extension its brand.

CASE STUDY

In 2011 the English Football Association was embroiled in a high-profile case involving allegations of racial abuse by Liverpool FC's Luis Suárez directed at Manchester United's Patrice Evra. During a league match between the two clubs at Anfield, Liverpool in October 2011, the French Manchester United full back Evra claimed that he had been racially abused by Liverpool's Uruguayan international Luis Suárez. A subsequent independent FA enquiry found Suárez guilty, fined him £40,000 and banned him for eight games. However, both before and after the FA investigation, Liverpool and then manager Kenny Dalglish rigorously defended Suárez in the media, including both manager and players wearing T-shirts supporting the player at a league match in Wigan in December 2011. Throughout this period there was a lack of contrition from the club or admission that any wrongdoing had taken place, despite intense media interest around debates about racism in football.

Following his ban, Suárez's first game was in February 2012 against Manchester United at Old Trafford and was broadcast live on Sky Sports. In the pre-match ceremonies Suárez refused to shake the hand of Manchester United's Patrice Evra, an event captured live on television and replayed in detail as the international audience watched on. What should have symbolized the end of the matter between the players inflamed an already tense situation.

However, what happened next illustrates how digital media had changed the environment within which sporting events and their participants now operated. For Liverpool manager Kenny Dalglish, it was an example of how he had simply failed to adapt to a media culture that had evolved since his previous time at the club 20 years earlier.

As live television coverage of the incident was broadcast, so social networking sites reported and commented on this event. Yet when Dalglish was interviewed live following the match, he not only indicated that he was unaware that Suárez had refused to shake hands with Evra, but accused the media of inflaming the situation. The initial exchange went as follows:

Geoff Shreeves: Your reaction to Luis Suárez refusing to shake Patrice Evra's hand?
Kenny Dalglish: I never knew he never shook his hand.
GS: He refused to shake his hand.
KG: I'll take your word for it but I don't know, I wasn't there so I never saw it. I didn't look at the handshakes, but that's contrary to what I was told.
GS: Well now that I have told you that, that he did do it, Kenny, what's your reaction to that?
KD: We'll ask him and take it from there.

GS: Do you think you have to take a serious look at his refusal to shake his hand and the way it set the tone?

KD: I think you are very severe and I think you are bang out of order to blame Luis Suárez for anything that happened here today, right. I think predominantly that both sets of fans behaved really well. They had a bit of banter between each other, no problem, right. How many bookings were there? End of story.

(The Telegraph, 2012)

Rather than being the end of the story, the Dalglish interview became the story, drew strong criticism from journalists and further damaged the reputation of the club as the interview went viral. Both Dalglish and Liverpool through Ian Ayre, the Managing Director of the club, later apologized for the behaviour of Suárez that day, but by then the racism story that should have ended that day had been given fresh impetus.

Liverpool launched an internal enquiry, presumably asking how Dalglish could be allowed to carry out a live post-match interview seemingly unaware that the incident had been seen around the world, had gone viral on social networks and was being extensively commented on by fans online. Dalglish was allowed to go on live television without having been instructed by his communication team to watch the event he was going to be questioned on. He only apologized after seeing the incident later. Any PR professional with a smartphone would have been aware of the damage being done to the club's reputation even 10 minutes after the incident. The fact that Ian Cotton, the club's Director of Communication, left Liverpool (having been there for 16 years) just three months later also suggests that the club and its US owners recognized their poor handling of the event. It also highlights the fact that Dalglish was not someone who felt he needed a communications expert to tell him how to deal with the media, yet that is precisely what is needed in the digital sports age.

QUESTIONS

1. How has social media changed the role of a club's communications officer on a match day?
2. To what extent does social media have the potential to enhance as well as cause damage to the reputation of a sports organization?
3. Why should PR training and strategy be taken seriously by clubs and all their officials?
4. How is the ability to access content on smartphones changing how clubs view their communications strategy?
5. With modern communication channels and methods, is there such a thing as 'off the record'? Discuss.

CONCLUSIONS

When Luis Suárez bit Chelsea's Branislav Ivanovic on the arm during a league match in April 2013, condemnation from the Liverpool manager Brendan Rodgers and club Managing Director Ian Ayre was swift and robust (with Ayre cancelling a trip to Australia to deal with the media fallout). Suárez took to Twitter to apologize for his 'inexcusable behaviour'. The speed and clarity of the club reaction, using Twitter as a news feed, and its robust sanctioning of the player was in marked contrast to the protracted and damaging incidents of 2011/12, suggesting lessons had been learned, at least in the communication operations of the club.

BIBLIOGRAPHY

Boyle, R. and Haynes, R. (2013). Sports journalism and social media: A new conversation? in B. Hutchins and D. Rowe (eds), *Digital Media Sport*. New York: Routledge.

Boyle, R. and Haynes, R. (2014). Sport, public relations and social media, in A. C. Billings and M. Hardin (eds), *Routledge Handbook of Sport and New Media*. London and New York: Routledge.

Lewis, R. and Kitchin, P. (2011). New communications media for sport, in M. Hopwood, P. Kitchin and J. Skinner (eds), *Sport Public Relations and Communication*. London: Routledge.

Stoldt, G. C., Dittmore, S. and Branvold, S. (2012). *Sport Public Relations: Managing Stakeholder Communication,* 2nd edition. Leeds: Human Kinetics.

The Telegraph (2012). Liverpool manager Kenny Dalglish's fractious post-match interview with Sky Sports: the full transcript. Accessed 9 June 2016 from www.telegraph.co.uk/sport/football/teams/liverpool/9077354/Liverpool-manager-Kenny-Dalglishs-fractious-post-match-interview-with-Sky-Sports-the-full-transcript.html.

Toney, J. (2013). *Sports Journalism: The Inside Track*. Bloomsbury: London.

CASE 12

THE DEATH OF COLONEL REB

CHARLES M. CARSON AND DARIN W. WHITE

LEARNING OUTCOMES

Upon completion of this case study, the reader should be able to:

- evaluate and critique the University of Mississippi's administration related to their decision-making regarding the naming of a new athletics mascot;
- explain how the University of Mississippi administration failed in its change management efforts related to the naming of a new athletics mascot;
- explain how the concept of escalation of commitments applies to the actions of the University of Mississippi administration;
- compare and contrast the 2003 mascot decision with the 2010 mascot decision at the University of Mississippi as it relates to administrative decision-making and involvement.

OVERVIEW OF THE CASE

Colonel Reb, the mascot for the University of Mississippi's athletic teams for decades, was removed during the summer of 2003. A subsequent vote for a new mascot during the fall of 2003 was met with controversy and voter apathy. This case examines the management implications around the decision to replace Colonel Reb and the failed efforts to find a replacement mascot. The case also offers insight into the University's new mascot, which was installed after a student-led vote in 2010.

CASE STUDY

How much trouble can a mascot cause? Mascots are traditionally used at sports events in a variety of ways to elicit positive emotional responses that elevate the audience's mood (Fetchko et al., 2013). Mascots, as generally conceived, are typically a loveable attraction for fans of all ages and in most cases a way for athletics teams to connect to younger fans – a gateway into fandom for children … that is unless your mascot, for some, is a symbol of the Confederacy, the Civil War, and slavery. Colonel Reb, the on-the-field mascot for the athletics teams of the University of Mississippi (Ole Miss) until 2003, has been described as "a white-haired old man who carries a cane and resembles a plantation owner" (ESPN, 2003).

For some citizens of the United States, Colonel Reb represents a part of American history they would like to forget. The Civil War was fought from 1861 to 1865 between the northern and southern states and it revolved around:

> whether the United States was to be a dissolvable confederation of sovereign states or an indivisible nation with a sovereign national government; and whether this nation, born of a declaration that all men were created with an equal right to liberty, would continue to exist as the largest slaveholding country in the world.
>
> (Civil War Trust, 2014)

Northern victory preserved the United States as one nation and ended the institution of slavery.

Over the course of the 150 years following the Civil War many southern states and institutions have sought to honor the hundreds of thousands of men and women who died in the conflict by including symbols of the Confederacy in everything from state flags to names of towns to school mascots.

Recently, symbols of the Confederacy have become a source of huge public debate. Many people (primarily southerners) believe that these symbols represent a sort of regional pride – a southern heritage. For those individuals, complaints about Confederate symbols "are an offense against their Confederate ancestors who fought and died in the Civil War" (Riley, 2002). Other people (primarily people who live outside the south) believe that Confederate symbols represent slavery and the continuing racism against African Americans. For those individuals, Confederate symbols are "an attack on racial identity and a symbol of the power of white America" (Riley, 2002).

Despite the fact that the vast majority of University of Mississippi students and alums wanted to keep Colonel Reb as their official mascot, the University administration attempted to change the mascot in the fall of 2003. They presented two options to the University community (students, graduates, employees, donors) on which to vote: "Rebel Bruiser" and "Rowdy Rebel." The results and participation levels were underwhelming and the administration was faced with a difficult

84

decision: should they accept the votes and name the leading vote getter, Rebel Bruiser, as the new mascot or pursue other options, including attempting to come up with new mascot options and have a new vote, extend the voting window and have more of a promotional campaign for each mascot, or have no mascot at all.

The administration chose the latter option, with Chancellor Robert Khayat stating at the time: "It is clear from the response received and from general public discussion that there is no community support for either of the proposed mascots. Therefore, the matter is closed" (ESPN, 2003).

QUESTIONS

1. What is a change agent and what role could a change agent have played in the University of Mississippi's attempted mascot change of 2003?
2. What is escalation of commitments and how does that concept apply to the decision-making of the University administration in 2003?
3. Compare and contrast the 2003 and 2010 mascot decisions from the perspectives of the multiple stakeholders (administration, alumni/students, fans).

CONCLUSIONS

Seven mascot-less years later the University had banned the sale of any Colonel Reb-imaged items and was ready to hold a new election for a mascot – this time under the banner of student leadership rather than an administration-led effort. The five new options again led to discord among the University's constituents. Eventually, the students voted to name a Black Bear the official mascot of the University's athletics teams. Even this decision was met with confusion and dissatisfaction: was the University team now the "Black Bears" and not the "Rebels?" To add to the confusion and frustration for most Ole Miss fans and alumni, the Black Bear mascot was named "Rebel." Like the Colonel Reb mascot, the term "Rebels" is also a symbol of the Confederacy as it is what the soldiers of the southern army were named – because the south had rebelled against the north and broken away from it.

The University had a new mascot but not without tremendous brand confusion, alumni and fan disenchantment, and administrative headache. The question was whether or not the University community would embrace Rebel the Black Bear in the same way they had embraced the dearly loved Colonel Reb.

RECOMMENDED READING

Most organizational behavior textbooks will have a chapter, or at least a section, dedicated to change management (change agents) and decision-making (escalation of commitments). We recommend Robbins and Judge, *Organizational Behavior*, due in part to the way in which the authors support conceptual material with citations and references to the theoretical and empirical works that undergird their textbook materials. The key work on escalation of commitments is B. M. Staw, "The Escalation of Commitment to a Course of Action."

REFERENCES

Civil War Trust (2014). A brief overview of the American Civil War. Available from: www.civilwar.org/education/history/civil-war-overview/overview.html (12 May).

ESPN (2003). "Ole Miss abandons search _ school won't have on-field mascot, officials say" Available from: http://sports.espn.go.com/espn/wire?id=1634547 (12 May).

Fetchko, M. J., Roy, D. P. and Clow, K. E. (2013). *Sports Marketing*. Pearson, Boston, MA.

Riley, K. (2002). "The long shadow of the Confederacy in America's schools: state-sponsored use of Confederate symbols in the wake of Brown v. Board". Available from: http://scholarship.law.wm.edu/wmborj/vol10/iss2/7.

Robbins, S. P. and Judge, T. A. (2017). *Organizational Behavior*, 17th edition. Pearson, United States.

Staw, B. M. (1981). "The Escalation of Commitment to a Course of Action," *Academy of Management Review*, 6(4), 577–87.

RECOMMENDED WEBSITES

Colonel Reb Foundation website: www.saveolemiss.com
ESPN: http://sports.espn.go.com/espn/wire?id=1634547
New York Times: www.nytimes.com/2010/09/20/us/20mascot.html?_r=1&

C. M. Carson, D. W. White

CASE 13

ANY PUBLICITY IS GOOD PUBLICITY? NIKE'S CONTROVERSIAL CAMPAIGNS AND MANAGEMENT OF CELEBRITIES

STEPHEN CASTLE AND GAYE BEBEK

LEARNING OUTCOMES

Upon completion of this case study, the reader should be able to:

- outline how and why celebrities are used by companies like Nike;
- assess the benefits celebrities bring to a brand;
- evaluate corporate values as exemplified by Nike and its celebrities;
- critically evaluate the relationship between celebrity brand and corporate brand.

OVERVIEW OF THE CASE

Nike has a portfolio of celebrities that it uses to endorse its products. In fact the company grew through celebrities using and endorsing its products. Tiger Woods is thought to have made Nike Golf the market player it is now rather than an 'also ran'. Celebrities do not always behave; Nike does not always behave. However, Nike has done well out of managing the situations it finds itself in with its celebrities and its marketing communications. This case study examines Nike's success in managing its celebrities and growing brand value.

CASE STUDY

The author and playwright Oscar Wilde once said: 'There is only one thing worse than being talked about and that is not being talked about' (Frater, 2007). Nike's controversial marketing strategy is an example of this. The company has been associated with a number of controversial campaigns and scandals, and has been talked about – a lot.

Nike chose not to pay the US$50 million fee to be an official sponsor of the 1996 Atlanta Olympics. Instead it used the money to cover the city in billboards and build an enormous Nike Centre that overlooked the Olympic stadium (Sauer, 2002). Nike's strategy of 'ambush marketing' was not the only issue, though. It also used a harsh slogan: 'You don't win silver, you lose gold'.

The slogan was heavily criticised by former Olympic silver and bronze medallists. Amy White, Olympic swimmer and silver medallist of the 1984 Los Angeles Olympics called the advert 'a slap in the face for whoever did not win a gold medal' (Payne, 2006). Another silver medallist, Townsend Saunders, told USA Today: 'it's just terrible for all the silver medallists' (USA Today, 2012). Olympic sponsors and spectators were equally unhappy with the message the advert gave, and it was argued that it negatively affected the athletes. NBC pulled the advert, and the *Financial Times* accused Nike of trashing the Olympic ideal. The response from the public, athletes and other sponsors of the games took the International Olympic Committee to the verge of banning Nike equipment from the games. Nike then backed down and toned down the advertising (Sauer, 2002).

The message was harsh and destructive, but Nike got a lot of coverage from the advert. Founder Phil Knight said it 'bombed' TV, and added it was 'one of the most downloaded ads of the year, so there were a few people who liked it' (USA Today, 2003). In fact, many thought Nike had been an official sponsor of the games.

Nike also has a history of having a very controversial portfolio of celebrity endorsement deals. Nike's endorsement obligations grew from $1.9billion in 2006 to $4.7billion in 2013 (Shropshire *et al.*, 2016).

One of the most famous scandals among Nike's endorsers was the sexual assault charges against Kobe Bryant in 2003. Bryant reportedly signed a five-year, US$40 million contract with Nike just days before the allegations were made. When charges were first filed, Nike was cautious about being publicly associated with the athlete. It even stripped Bryant's name from a shoe, but soon it saw the opportunity, and cleverly tested the waters of public opinion through back channels and underground methods. However, Nike's stock price did not suffer at all after the allegations were made, staying above US$53, and revenues continued to increase steadily in 2003 (Yahoo Finance, 2003).

Two years after charges were filed, Nike decided to fully and publicly stand behind Bryant by launching a new shoe bearing his name (Kang, 2005). Nike's decision definitely paid off when Bryant's image recovered and the Lakers won the NBA championship in 2009–2010. Nike even started to market Kobe shoes by underlining the image Bryant had created. After seven rounds of Kobe-themed Nike products, the company and the star have no reservations about packaging him as a 'predator': 'The Nike Kobe VII also tells a predator story that's inspired by Kobe's predator-like instinct' (Nike, 2011).

Memorably on 25 January 1995, it was a 'be-swooshed' boot that Manchester United's Eric Cantona wore when he kicked a football fan in the chest (Maysh, 2011). Not just any kick, but a full-on kung-fu kick – followed by a punch to the head. Nike was a sponsor of Eric Cantona, and on that fateful day he had demonstrated its slogan 'Just Do It' in the worst possible way. Instead of ditching him, Nike continued to sponsor Cantona – and played on his 'bad boy' image. Nike hired Cantona to play himself in an epic television commercial. As the captain of a team of Nike's top endorsees, Cantona did battle with evil gargoyles on a pitch set in Dante's Inferno. Life was imitating sport imitating art, and there was only one role for Cantona (Maysh 2011).

Another scandal that turned into success for Nike was Tiger Woods' infidelity. Nike has been a long-time sponsor of Tiger Woods (for instance, in 2000 signing a 5-year extension worth US$105 million). All of Woods' sponsors, including Accenture, Gillette, Electronic Arts, Tag Heuer and Gatorade, dropped him when the news of his infidelity came out, but Nike decided to stick by the golfer. It believed that when the time came for Woods to play again, he would compensate Nike for this. Nike even stated publicly: 'When he wins again, people will forget about everything.' The stock price repercussions of the decision to stand by Woods were minimal. Nike stock dropped a point or two following some events in the Woods story. The lowest price during this period was US$64.89 on 30 November 2009, down from US$65.70 on 25 November when the news of the scandal first broke (Yahoo Finance, 2009). The stock soon started recovering from its fall. On 1 May 2010 the stock was selling for US$75.91, compared to a 2009 low of US$48.76 (Adage, 2010). Overall, the Tiger Woods scandal is estimated to have cost Nike US$1.7 million in sales and 105,000 customers. However, the US$200 million endorsement was still worth it, as it is thought that Nike's loss would have been bigger if it had let Woods go (CBS Moneywatch, 2010). Nike even possibly regrets its cautious actions over the Kobe Bryant scandal (Powell, 2010).

After the Woods issue, the company's revenues had risen every year until 2012, when accusations that Lance Armstrong was using performance-enhancing drugs (PEDs) were made. Armstrong had been on Nike's Livestrong committee from 1997 and over the years Nike is estimated to have paid him US$40 million (Rovell, 2012). At the time Armstrong was still winning and Nike was still gaining profits from the deal, so it stood by him until the official announcement came in October 2012 that Armstrong was guilty. Nike dropped him immediately. Marketers interpreted the decision to drop Armstrong to be a manifestation of Nike as an elite sports performance brand, and a way to emphasise the difference between Armstrong's situation and that of Woods (Kay, 2012). Nike generated US$24.13 billion in revenues for the year 2012, increasing from US$20.86 billion in 2011 (Wikinvest, 2011).

Nike seems to be able to convert scandals into successes, but regardless of this controversial marketing strategy, it stands well clear from those scandals that could in any way associate the brand with an 'unfair game'. Nike has showed no reservations in cutting ties to athletes accused of using PEDs. Along with Armstrong, such athletes include baseball player Jason Giambi and Olympic track star Marion Jones (Business Insider, 2012). Equally, when Michael Vick was accused of involvement with unlawful dog fighting, Nike did not wait long to let him go. Nike suspended the release of the Vick V shoe, which cost the company US$1.5 million (CNBC, 2007). Nike's first action has always been to test the public reaction. With scandals like that surrounding Tiger Woods, there was always the chance that the celebrities would compensate for the negative publicity with even greater success in their sports (although this was difficult for Woods given his world ranking), and the public would 'forget' the misdemeanour, which they did. Yet with Vick, Nike could not risk being associated with a person who was accused of murdering dogs. Vick spent 21 months in prison, by which time the waters had calmed and Nike re-signed him in 2011 (ESPN, 2011).

A recent study by Elberse and Verleun (2012) showed that celebrity endorsements generate a 4 per cent increase in turnover and 0.25 per cent increase in stock returns, which are positively correlated to the athletic successes of the celebrity in question. Nike is cleverly choosing the scandals and the celebrities to use. PEDs are a no-no (Armstrong, Giambi); 'medium' scandals are positive if the athlete is popular (Cantona, Woods); and the strategy for the unthinkably horrendous scandals are to dismiss the athlete if they are not successful in their field, or if they are a successful athlete, dismiss them and then when the public forgets what they have done, re-sign them (Vick ... and Pistorius?).

Nike's strategy shows that any publicity can be good publicity if managed carefully.

QUESTIONS

1. Analyse Nike's management decisions and risk management in respect of its celebrity endorsement policy. Can you see any logic in Nike's support of some athletes and not others?
2. Is Nike right to think that PED charges damage the public's perception of the athlete in question more than other issues do? Will issues like this damage the Nike brand?
3. What evidence is there to support the concept that use of celebrities enhances the value of brands?
4. Consider the use of celebrities in corporate communications. How do celebrities communicate brand values?

5. What are the main considerations for an organisation when considering celebrity endorsement?

CONCLUSIONS

Nike has a long history of celebrity endorsement; indeed, the company was founded on such endorsement. In the early days of the company Steve Prefontaine (a well-known Oregon runner) sent pairs of Nike shoes to prospective runners along with personal notes of encouragement (Nike, 2014). The company courts controversy with its marketing and celebrity endorsement, as exemplified in its campaign at the Atlanta Olympics and its use of Eric Cantona to support the brand – and even taking the endorsement one step further after Cantona's kung-fu kick and punch to a football fan, when Cantona and his team of celebrity endorsers took on the devil in a TV advert. Nike lives its rhetoric and will 'Just Do It', though even for Nike there are some no-nos – drugs and murder. However, for Nike it is certainly a truism that 'there is only one thing worse than being talked about and that is not being talked about'. Good Oscar, Bad Oscar. You decide.

RECOMMENDED READING

To begin with, students might find it helpful to read an introductory text on marketing – specifically chapters on marketing communication and sponsorship. A book such as *Marketing: Real People, Real Decisions: Real People, Real Choices* by Solomon *et al.* (2009) is one example; Lagae (2005) is also a suitable resource. Thereafter, students should consider looking at texts on marketing communications (e.g. Fill (2013) or Cornelissen (2014)), and reputation management (e.g. Roper and Fill, 2012).

BIBLIOGRAPHY AND RECOMMENDED WEBSITES

Adage (2010). Standing by Tiger Woods helped Nike's Bottom Line, accessed 28 April 2014 from http://adage.com/article/news/study-standing-tiger-woods-helped-nike-s-bottom-line/147431/.

Business Insider (2012). The real reason why Nike canned Lance Armstrong has nothing to do with doping, accessed 28 April 2014 from www.businessinsider.com/reason-why-nike-fired-lance-armstrong-2012-10#ixzz2wQdwxV4S.

CBS Moneywatch (2010). Did Nike really gain from Tiger Woods' scandal as the numbers suggest, accessed 28 April 2014 from www.cbsnews.com/news/did-nike-really-gain-from-tiger-woods-scandal-as-the-numbers-suggest.

Cornelissen, J. (2014). *Corporate Communication A Guide to Theory and Practice.* Sage, London.

CNBC (2007). Nike: Drop Michael Vick right now, accessed 28 April 2014 from www.cnbc.com/id/19976022.

Elberse, A. and Verleun, J. (2012). The economic value of celebrity endorsements. *Journal of Advertising Research*, 52(2), 149–65.

ESPN (2011). Nike re-signs Michael Vick as endorser, accessed 28 April 2014 from http://sports.espn.go.com/nfl/news/story?id=6730833.

Fill, C. (2013). *Marketing Communications: Brands, Experiences and Participation, 6th edn*. Pearson, Harlow.

Frater, J. (2007). 40 quotes of Oscar Wilde, accessed 28 April 2014 from http://listverse.com/2007/10/08/40-quotes-of-oscar-wilde/.

Isidore, C. (2013). Nike suspends contract with Pistorius, accessed 28 April 2014 from http://money.cnn.com/2013/02/21/news/companies/nike-pistorius/.

Kang, S. (2005). Nike relaunches Kobe Bryant after two years of prep work. *Wall Street Journal*, 11 November.

Kay, E. (2012). Why Nike stands by Tiger Woods but dumps Lance Armstrong, accessed 28 April 2014 from www.sbnation.com/golf/2012/10/19/3526602/tiger-woods-nike-lance-armstrong.

Lagae, W. (2005). *Sports Sponsorship and Marketing Communications: A European Perspective*. Pearson, Harlow.

Maysh, J. (2011). Cantona as anti-hero, accessed 28 April 2014 from www.runofplay.com/2011/02/24/cantona-as-anti-hero/.

Nike (2011). Introducing the Nike Kobe VII System Supreme, accessed 28 April 2014 from http://nikeinc.com/news/nike-launches-the-nike-zoom-kobe-vii-supreme.

Nike (2014). History & Heritage, accessed 28 April 2014 from http://nikeinc.com/pages/history-heritage.

Payne, M. (2006). *Olympic Turnaround: How the Olympic Games Stepped Back from the Brink of Extinction to Become the World's Best Known Brand*. Greenwood Publishing Group, Santa Barbara, CA.

Powell, J. (2010). Tiger Woods needs to thank Kobe Bryant for keeping his Nike endorsement, accessed 28 April 2014 from http://bleacherreport.com/articles/356244-tiger-needs-to-thank-kobe-bryant-for-keeping-his-nike-endorsement.

Roper, S. and Fill, C. (2012). *Managing Corporate Reputation*. Pearson, Harlow.

Rovell, D. (2012). Nike drops Lance Armstrong, accessed 28 April 2014 from http://espn.go.com/olympics/cycling/story/_/id/8514766/nike-terminates-contract-lance-armstrong.

Sauer, A. (2002). Ambush Marketing Steals the Show, accessed 26 August 2016 from http://chatt.hdsb.ca/~harrisr/FOV1-000DECA0/U3_ambush%20marketing_online.doc.

Shropshire, K, Davis, T. and N. Duru (2016). *The Business of Sports Agents*. University of Pennsylvania Press, Pennsylvania.

Solomon, M. R., Marshall, G. W., Stuart, E. W., Barnes, B. and Mitchell, V. W. (2009). *Marketing: Real People, Real Decisions: Real People, Real Choices*. Pearson, Harlow.

USA Today (2003). Wake up consumers? Nike's brash CEO dares to just do it, accessed 28 April 2014 from http://usatoday30.usatoday.com/money/advertising/2003-06-15-nike_x.htm.

USA Today (2012). Silver medal a reminder how close he was to gold, accessed 28 April 2014 from http://usatoday30.usatoday.com/USCP/PNI/Front%20Page/2012-07-20-PNI0720met-townsend-silverPNIBrd_ST_U.htm.

Wikinvest (2011). Nike Revenue 2011, accessed 28 April 2014 from www.wikinvest.com/stock/Nike_(NKE)/Data/Revenue/2011.

Wikinvest, (2013). Nike Revenue 2013, accessed 28 April 2014 from www.wikinvest.com/stock/Nike_(NKE)/Data/Revenue/2013.

Yahoo Finance (2003). Nike, Inc. (NKE), Historical Prices (May 2003–September 2003, accessed 28 April 2014 from http://finance.yahoo.com/q/hp?s=NKE&a=04&b=30&c=2003&d=08&e=16&f=2003&g=d.

Yahoo Finance (2009). Nike, Inc. NKE, Historical Prices (November 2009–December 2009, accessed 28 April 2014 from http://finance.yahoo.com/q/hp?s=NKE&a=10&b=20&c=2009 &d=11&e=15&f=2009&g=d.

Yahoo Finance (2013). Nike Inc. NKE, Historical Prices (7 February 2013-20 February 2013, accessed 28 April 2014 from http://finance.yahoo.com/q/hp?s=NKE&a=01&b=7&c=2013& d=01&e=20&f=2013&g=d.

APPENDIX: QUESTIONS AND ANSWERS

1. ANALYSE NIKE'S MANAGEMENT DECISIONS AND RISK MANAGEMENT IN RESPECT OF ITS CELEBRITY ENDORSEMENT POLICY. CAN YOU SEE ANY LOGIC IN NIKE'S SUPPORT OF SOME ATHLETES AND NOT OTHERS?

Discussion can centre on management of brand and corporate reputation, as well as risk management.

It could be argued that everyone has a continuum of what is acceptable and what is not. But perhaps that continuum is not set in stone. Nike demonstrates this continuum in its endorsement (or not) of celebrities. It is acceptable to Nike for celebrities to be an *'enfant terrible'*, as with Eric Cantona, as it suits Nike's image of freedom of spirit/'just do it'. It appears to be acceptable to cheat on your partner, as in the case of Tiger Woods, but not acceptable to cheat at your sport, as in the case of Lance Armstrong, Jason Giambi and Marion Jones. It appears not to be acceptable to Nike to kill animals or people (Michael Vick and Oscar Pistorius, respectively), though as the case of Vick demonstrates, you can be rehabilitated after serving your time.

As with all reputation management, there is a balance between risk and benefit – risk to the brand/benefit to the brand. Nike management appears to be well attuned to customer and public opinion. Nike is willing to push the boundaries, as seen with its advertising at the Atlanta Olympics, and its continued (heightened?) endorsement of Eric Cantona and Kobe Bryant; yet it is keen to protect the brand from any association with cheating in sport.

2. IS NIKE RIGHT TO THINK THAT PED CHARGES DAMAGE THE PUBLIC'S PERCEPTION OF THE ATHLETE IN QUESTION MORE THAN OTHER ISSUES DO? WILL ISSUES LIKE THIS DAMAGE THE NIKE BRAND?

As with question one, Nike management seems to understand public sentiment in sport. The focus of this question is brand and reputation management. Just as organisations have reputations that need to be managed, so do individuals. A reputation needs to be managed, nurtured and developed. And that reputation can be destroyed

93

overnight if not managed successfully. Within sport use of performance enhancing drugs (PEDs) is certainly an issue. All sporting authorities have strict measures to deal with drug cheats including lifetime bans. Being caught, charged and found guilty of taking PEDs does damage the reputation of the athlete, and makes it difficult for them to regain the trust of the sporting authorities and the sports fans. However, Nike appears to be reasonably untouched by such controversies; the company is able to distance itself from the athlete and their actions.

3. WHAT EVIDENCE IS THERE TO SUPPORT THE CONCEPT THAT USE OF CELEBRITIES ENHANCES THE VALUE OF BRANDS?

The focus here is brand and values. What is a brand? What makes a brand?

'Value' can take on different meanings in this context. For instance, corporate values are an integral part of organisational culture and part of the core ideology – the philosophies, strategies and goals of the organisation. Shared values strengthen a corporate brand.

Brand equity consists of brand value, brand strength and brand description, and has both a financial and marketing perspective. The financial view is based on the brand's value as a definable, measurable value, whereas the marketing perspective is based on the beliefs, images and core associations consumers have about a particular brand. Hence, brand values are the meanings that consumers give brands, and the meaning brands give consumers. Conversely, brand value is the financial value given to the brand – the value added beyond just being a product.

The use of celebrity puts a face to a brand, a personality.

As such it can be seen that the celebrity has brand values and brand value, as does the actual consumer/service brand. The closer the alignment of these, the greater the value created for both brand and celebrity.

As shown in this case study, celebrity endorsements generate a 4 per cent increase in turnover and 0.25 per cent increase in stock returns, which are positively correlated to the athletic successes of the celebrity in question.

4. CONSIDER THE USE OF CELEBRITIES IN CORPORATE COMMUNICATIONS. HOW DO CELEBRITIES COMMUNICATE BRAND VALUES?

The use of celebrity puts a face to a brand, a personality. As seen above, brand values are the images, messages and associations that are communicated by the brand to the consumer, and from the consumer to the brand.

A consideration of the brand identity prism of Kapferer (2008) might be useful here:

* Physical facet	* Personality
* Relationship	* Culture (values)
* Reflected	* Consumer mentalisation

How well does the celebrity reflect the brand under the above elements, and vice versa? Consideration of this leads to consideration of the match between celebrity and brand value communication. Take, for instance, the personality of Tiger Woods, or Eric Cantona – what is the personality like? How does it appear? What is that personality communicating? Does the celebrity personality communicate the brand personality? Is this seriousness, perseverance, will to win, single-mindedness, focus? Or is it relaxed, partying, fun, frivolous? The idea is that the celebrity reflects the brand, which reflects on the consumer.

5. WHAT ARE THE MAIN CONSIDERATIONS FOR AN ORGANISATION WHEN CONSIDERING CELEBRITY ENDORSEMENT?

This question is designed to enable students to think about organisations, brands and celebrities as a whole and in a wider context. Celebrities can be used to build brands, and to establish strong brand identity and personality. According to Roll (2014), three considerations are:

Attractiveness of the celebrity: An 'attractive' endorser will have a positive impact on the brand. This is not just about physical appearance. The endorser should be attractive to the target audience in certain aspects such as personality, physical appearance, intellectual capabilities, athletic competence and lifestyle.

Credibility of the celebrity: For any brand–celebrity collaboration to be successful, the personal credibility of the celebrity is crucial. An organisation must appear credible; likewise, a celebrity must appear credible, where credibility is perceived expertise and trustworthiness. A celebrity acts as an external cue, the personality of the brand, that helps consumers understand the brand meaning, enhancing acceptance by consumers.

Meaning transfer between the celebrity and the brand: This principle states that the success of the brand–celebrity collaboration heavily depends on the compatibility between the brand and the celebrity in terms of identity, personality, positioning in the market vis-à-vis competitors, and lifestyle. The celebrity is the brand personified.

Considerations around the use of celebrity can include (Roper and Fill (2012); Roll (2014)):

Product life cycle and portfolio management: Bear in mind the long-term strategic and enduring nature of the brand–celebrity relationship. It takes time to build brand/celebrity identity. Equally as with products, a celebrity will have a life cycle. It is important to know who and when to sign up (rising stars) and when to let them go at the end of their time (decline).

Compatibility: Are the values, ethics, culture – personality – of the brand and celebrity alike? Will the celebrity create a positive image of the brand in the eyes and minds of consumers?

Monitoring and management: As we have seen in this case study, the organisation needs to monitor the behaviour, conduct and public image of the celebrity to maximise their positive contribution to brand identity, and minimise any potential negative publicity.

Care with legal aspects: Celebrities should be signed up on proper legal terms so that they cannot endorse products of direct competitors, and the organisation can veto other endorsements, to avoid mixed messages of what the celebrity stands for (consider Scarlett Johansson and the Oxfam–SodaStream incompatibility). Also there should be adequate break-clauses to manage any negative behaviour.

Marketing management: Use of celebrity is one part of the communication mix, but the focus should be on the brand, not the celebrity. Again, care needs to be taken in the use and management of celebrity.

ROI: Organisations should have a system combining quantitative and qualitative mechanisms to measure the overall effect of celebrity endorsements on their brands. There should be effective return on investment (e.g. Tiger Wood's building (creating?) Nike Golf).

REFERENCES

Kapferer, J. (2008). *The New Strategic Brand Management*. Kogan Page, London.

Roll, M. (2014). Branding and celebrity endorsements, accessed 28 April 2014 from www.venturerepublic.com/resources/branding_celebrities_brand_endorsements_brand_leadership.asp.

Roper, S. and Fill, C. (2012). *Managing Corporate Reputation*. Pearson: Harlow.

STRATEGIC REPOSITIONING OF CONCACAF: REBUILDING TRUST IN THE 'BEAUTIFUL GAME'

AARON BURKS, MICHAEL M. GOLDMAN AND NOLA AGHA

LEARNING OUTCOMES

Upon completion of this case study, the reader should be able to:

- identify the role of leadership in creating a shared vision;
- examine the core ideology and intended future components of an organisational vision;
- evaluate an organisation's strategy development process;
- develop an appreciation of the complexities involved in the strategic repositioning of an organisation.

OVERVIEW OF THE CASE

This case study presents the strategic repositioning challenge faced by the Confederation of North, Central American and Caribbean Association Football (CONCACAF) after a period of leadership and strategy instability. It reports the allegations and findings of misconduct, and discusses the steps taken by the new leadership to define a new mission and strategy.

Acknowledgements

The authors thank Jurgen Mainka for his support and assistance with the research for this case study, including approving the comments attributed to him in the case study. The authors also acknowledge the initial research contributions of Giovanni Vaglietti and Trenton Lively in preparing this case study.

CASE STUDY

Jurgen Mainka stepped out of the main conference room at the Ritz-Carlton, Grand Cayman in October 2013 to take another call from a journalist interested in the discussions underway at the CONCACAF Sports Summit. As a spokesperson for CONCACAF, Mainka was delighted to share the positive developments of the previous year, which had seen a marked shift in the way football fans and other stakeholders were viewing the organisation. He spoke of the increasing number of social media followers who were now regularly engaging with content about the confederation's tournaments and development programmes, and the greater awareness and optimistic associations now linked to CONCACAF. Mainka recalled how even his business travel experiences had been impacted – with customs officials, who previously stared blankly when he provided his reason for visiting their country, now recognising CONCACAF and excitedly sharing their views on recent games.

As Mainka slipped back into the room, he also knew that the job was not yet done. Questions remained about whether CONCACAF had made a clean enough break from its difficult past. Observers also wondered whether the strong words and new vision could be carried through to tangible actions on the fields of play and administration boardrooms across the region. Mainka took his chair just as FIFA President Sepp Blatter began speaking about the power of football:

> There are three powers in our game. The first one is the social power – football is education, entertainment, based in discipline, respect and fair play. But more than that, football gives emotions and hope ... The second power, a big power, it is the economic power. Football has become, and specifically in the past 25 years, a very significant economic power ... Naturally football has a political dimension. It is important for the development of the game all around the world but especially in smaller countries.
>
> (CONCACAF, 2013)

CONCACAF

The Confederation of North, Central American and Caribbean Association Football (CONCACAF) is one of six continental confederations of FIFA (Fédération

Internationale de Football Association). It serves as the governing body of football for the national associations from Canada in the north to Guyana, Surinam and French Guyana in the south. It includes 3 North American countries, 7 Central American countries and 31 Caribbean countries. As the administrative body for the region, CONCACAF manages competitions, offers technical and administrative training courses, and actively promotes and develops the game of football. This mandate is located within the objectives of FIFA to improve the game of football constantly and to promote integrity, ethics and fair play. A General Secretariat, Executive Committee, Congress and several committees lead CONCACAF. The Executive Committee is composed of seven elected members, including a president, three regional vice-presidents and three other members, and serves as the Board of Directors of this non-profit company.

Prior to 2012, three presidents had led CONCACAF during its 50-year history: Ramón Coll Jaumet from Costa Rica from 1961 to 1968, Joachín Soria Terrazas from Mexico from 1968 to 1990, and Austin Jack Warner from Trinidad and Tobago from 1990 to 2011. When Warner assumed his leadership position, CONCACAF was a 'languishing confederation with few resources, little or no sponsorships or broadcast revenues, and events and competitions that, at best, had achieved limited success' (Simmons *et al.*, 2013: 5). Supported by his General Secretary, Charles 'Chuck' Blazer, Warner oversaw an extended period of development and prosperity for the organisation. By 2010 CONCACAF reported annual revenues of over US$25 million, with assets of more than US$45 million.

Allegations of misconduct surfaced in 2006 when Warner was implicated in the reselling of large blocks of tickets for the 2006 FIFA World Cup at inflated prices (Longman and Carvajal, 2011). Other reports in 2011 alleged that Warner sought funds from the English Football Association to cover some of the US$1.6 million cost of broadcasting rights for the 2010 FIFA World Cup at Haitian public viewing venues after the devastating 2010 earthquake. FIFA confirmed that no public viewing licence had been granted for Haiti (Bond, 2011). In June 2011 FIFA's ethics committee found 'comprehensive, convincing and overwhelming' evidence that Warner and Mohamed bin Hammam, the president of the Asian Confederation and candidate for the FIFA presidency, were involved in attempted bribery (Phillips, 2011). The investigation was conducted at Blazer's request as a member of FIFA's Executive Committee, and followed an affidavit from the vice-president of the Bahamas soccer federation stating that he had been offered US$40,000 as a gift from bin Hammam. Warner resigned as FIFA vice-president and president of CONCACAF on 20 June, essentially ending the FIFA investigation with 'a presumption of innocence' (Phillips, 2011). Later that month, Warner accused Blazer of misusing and misappropriating CONCACAF funds. Blazer resigned from CONCACAF at the end of 2011.

After a period of instability during which CONCACAF Vice-President Alfredo Hawit acted as president, Jeffrey Webb was elected president in May 2012, becoming 'one of the most important men in the sport of football worldwide' (Cayman Islands Government, 2012). Webb had served as president of the Cayman Islands Football Association since 1991 and was deputy chairman of the FIFA Internal Audit Committee and a member of the FIFA Transparency and Compliance Committee (Simmons *et al.*, 2013). Within a month, Webb announced the establishment of an Integrity Committee to oversee investigations of alleged misconduct as part of his pledge to promote transparency, accountability and reform within CONCACAF. By April 2013 the Integrity Committee had determined that Warner had committed fraud against CONCACAF and FIFA in the development, financing and ownership of the Centre of Excellence, a multipurpose sports complex in Trinidad and Tobago (Simmons *et al.*, 2013). The Committee's report concluded that Blazer misappropriated more than US$15 million of CONCACAF funds and violated US Federal tax laws by failing to file tax returns from 2006 to 2010. The Committee also found that Warner and Blazer repeatedly issued financial statements that they knew contained misrepresentations and material omissions, while employing a non-independent accountant as an auditor (Simmons *et al.*, 2013).

A new mission

As Webb accepted the presidency at the CONCACAF Congress in Hungary on 23 May 2012, he declared: 'What has our focus been? Politics and economics; let us focus on our game … We must move the clouds and allow the sunshine in' (Liburd, 2012). He went on to say:

> Over the last year, our mission and our vision have been blurred, from lawyers, to audit reports to compensation. We have deviated from our mission. I am here; we are here, because of our love for football. The passion for the game drives and motivates our every action. Our core focus must be football: its development, its growth and its ability to transform nations. We must … restructure our confederation. The events over the past year will not define and determine our destiny. We have a responsibility to ensure that history isn't repeated. Let us use the events over the past year as a catalyst to promote positive change. Let's see it as an opportunity to return to the core values of the beautiful game – the values which enchanted and sparked our love affair with this game.
>
> (Cayman Net News, 2012)

Webb appointed Columbian-born Enrique Sanz as the new general secretary in July 2012, replacing Deputy General Secretary Ted Howard, who had held the position in an acting capacity since Blazer had resigned. Sanz had been vice-president of

South American soccer marketing agency Traffic Sports USA. Additional personnel changes followed in November with the appointments of Horace Donovan Reid as director of competitions and Jurgen Mainka as director of communications and marketing. Reid had previously served as general secretary of the Jamaica Football Federation and as the chairman of CONCACAF's Administration Committee. Mainka was born in Mexico and grew up idolising Argentinian goalkeeper Ubaldo Fillol. Mainka had previously worked as vice-president of community relations for the New York Red Bulls Major League Soccer (MLS) franchise, and was also responsible for MasterCard's Latin American sponsorship activations during his time at Octagon.

Crafting a new strategic agenda

As Mainka walked into his new office in Miami, the leadership of CONCACAF was defining a new strategic agenda. Webb stated, 'I want to focus on the field of play and on the players and on grassroots programs and player development. The game is about players, coaches and referees and that should be the foundation of the game' (Evans, 2012). Reflecting on the role of the Confederation as the hub for member countries, Webb questioned whether it had adequately serviced that responsibility: 'I think we should be sharing the wealth with those countries, helping them participate in competitions' (Evans, 2012).

For Mainka, the new strategic agenda was captured in two core messages: 'The development of the game was 100% of our focus, regardless of how big or small our member associations were', and 'CONCACAF works for its members, not the other way around'. In repositioning the public perception of CONCACAF, Mainka's goal was to regain the business trust of the market and stakeholders, including commercial partners, through 'very clear transparency in everything we did'. Specifically, Mainka's first objective was to develop a stronger platform for the organisation's external messaging, in order to raise communication levels with all stakeholders. Secondly, Mainka set an objective to change the stakeholder's negative perceptions of CONCACAF. These goals were echoed in Webb's public comments that, 'in rebuilding the vision and the image of the confederation, actions speak louder than words. We have to rebuild that trust and integrity and reestablish that credibility that we've lost' (Wahl, 2013).

Mainka's team employed a SWOT (strengths, weaknesses, opportunities and threats) analysis to reassess the internal and external context facing the organisation. As he arrived, Mainka recognised strength in the passion for the game felt by many of the management team based in Miami. One of the important weaknesses the analysis found was the passive way in which CONCACAF had performed marketing activities, which Mainka felt was 'very different to the way in which I would do it'. Looking externally, the SWOT analysis suggested that the increasing use of social media by fans presented an opportunity to communicate more consistently and frequently where 'nothing was done in the past'. Mainka was conscious that the window of opportunity to effect change was small and needed to be capitalised on to avoid the dominant themes of corruption and fraud setting in for good. Given FIFA's espoused commitment to the spirit of fair play, Mainka recalled the example of a worrying Facebook post in March 2013, exclaiming 'Fair play does not exist in Concacaf!!!' (Jimenez, 2013). With this primary context, and reinforced by weekly strategic conversations with Sanz, the new general secretary, Mainka focused his team on execution.

> We began by revamping our webpage to be able to have a direct touch point with not only the fans but every single stakeholder, whether it was a member of the association or a sponsor, a partner, or whether it was any official within the football world ... to make sure that our information was accurate, current, and really reflected that transparency we spoke about.

These actions followed a set of new business practices that Sanz led to professionalise the administration of the organisation, which incorporated a strict budget for every division, including marketing, public relations and competitions.

Capitalising on the Gold Cup and Champions League

One of the implications of the new strategic agenda was the intent to involve all 41 member countries in all CONCACAF activities. Reassessment of the confederation's competitions such as the Gold Cup and Champions League were seen as immediate remedies in achieving a new strategy.

The Gold Cup is a biennial international tournament involving 12 qualified national teams within the CONCACAF region. Tournament games are held on US soil and televised by Fox in English and Univision Deportes in Spanish. The Gold Cup is the premier tournament competition within CONCACAF, with the 2011 edition contributing nearly US$20 million in revenue (Wahl, 2013). In fact, the 2011 Gold Cup match between the United States and Mexico drew a 93,000 sell-out crowd at the Rose Bowl in Pasadena in addition to its record-setting 1.43 Nielsen viewership rating in the US. In 2013 the United States and Panama Gold Cup match achieved the second-highest television rating for any soccer match in the US. The Gold Cup results determine which CONCACAF national teams will earn a place in the FIFA World Cup every four years.

The CONCACAF Champions League is an annual tournament of 24 qualified club teams from within the CONCACAF region. Spots are allocated based on each country's strength of inter-league quality. For example, the United States and Mexico are given four spots each. Costa Rica, Panama and Honduras are provided with two spots each. Canada and the remaining countries within the region are left with one spot each. The current CONCACAF Champions League group stage is a six-week process with several scheduled matches per week. In many cases the competition receives no coverage by traditional sports media broadcasters, raising questions about the value of the tournament for teams across the region (Hickey, 2013).

Mainka recognised that 'people didn't quite understand what it meant to win the league ... You are the reigning champions of CONCACAF? And?' From his time with the New York Red Bulls, Mainka knew that teams would rather focus on their more lucrative national tournaments, with the Mexican Liga MX recognised as the league attracting the fourth-highest average attendance in the world. Eighty per cent of CONCACAF countries, however, were without a professional league (Nicholson, 2013). Because the CONCACAF Champions League winner qualifies automatically for the annual FIFA Club World Cup, Mainka's team therefore focused their communication with clubs on the prestige and financial rewards of this global tournament. The Club World Cup involves seven teams competing for the title at venues within the host nation over a period of about two weeks. The seven participating clubs include the winners from the AFC Champions League (Asia), CAF Champions League (Africa), CONCACAF Champions League (North America), Copa Libertadores (South America), OFC Champions League (Oceania) and UEFA Champions League (Europe), along with the host nation's national champions. In December 2012 Club de Fútbol Monterrey, the Mexican representative of CONCACAF at the tournament in Japan, beat Al Ahly Sporting Club from Egypt to take third place, which included prize money of US$2.5 million.

Beyond the brand positioning and appeal of the CONCACAF Champions League, Mainka focused on 'reassessing the structure of the entire tournament, from dates we are playing, to formats, to really exploring in language with the new approach to everything'. Mexican clubs had won the previous 5 years of the tournament, with 9 of the 10 finalists and 14 of the 20 semi-finalists being from the Liga MX. Critics of the tournament also pointed to the poor broadcast and online streaming product, when it was covered at all (Hickey, 2013).

QUESTIONS

1. Identify and discuss the ways in which Webb created a shared vision.
2. Discuss the extent to which CONCACAF's core ideology and intended future are related.
3. Critique CONCACAF's strategy development process.
4. What risks does CONCACAF face in executing its strategic agenda?
5. How should CONCACAF mitigate these risks to enhance the likelihood of successful execution?

CONCLUSIONS: ONGOING TRANSFORMATION

Jeffrey Webb kicked off the CONCACAF Sports Summit in the Cayman Islands on 22 October 2013 by highlighting the 43 million athletes playing football at various levels across the region. With the theme of 'Transformation through partnership', the two-day event aimed to 'build bridges; create dialogue; examine and highlight some of the best practices throughout the region; analyze strengths and to set goals and objectives to improve shortcomings' (Wilson, 2013). For the first time in the region's football history, sports ministers from each of the 41 countries were invited to join CONCACAF's regional and country leadership teams. In addition, business, media and non-profit stakeholders were invited to 'create synergies and dialogue ... to foster the development of the game for the future' (Wilson, 2013).

Nic Coward, the general secretary of the English Premier League, argued during the summit that their transformation from a 'league that brought in a few million pounds a year to one that brings in over two billion [was] directly attributable to the partnerships we have built with the media, fans, businesses and above all with the local communities where our teams play' (Riccio, 2013). Webb suggested that the Caribbean nations should cooperate to create a professional, region-wide Caribbean League. This league could bolster the chances of a Caribbean nation qualifying for the World Cup. In addition, it could change the balance of football revenues in the region where currently 80 per cent of revenues are generated by less than 20 per cent of the countries (Nicholson, 2013). The CONCACAF president also suggested that the region should have the opportunity to host the FIFA World Cup in 2026.

Mainka wondered whether his team's efforts over the previous year had reestablished a strong-enough foundation for CONCACAF's ambitious growth intent. As the numbers of Twitter followers and Facebook likes for CONCACAF continued to grow, Mainka questioned whether a strong-enough strategy was in place to achieve the developmental goals of the organisation. Reflecting on his role in executing the new strategic agenda, Mainka wondered whether the Gold Cup and Champions League products were aligned strongly enough to the new mission, and pondered what else he needed to do to accelerate the transformation of CONCACAF.

RECOMMENDED READING

In order to deepen analysis of this case study, students are encouraged to read the following strategy development resources. First, students are directed to review Collins and Porras' (1996) and Kouzes and Posner's (2009) *Harvard Business Review* articles on developing a corporate vision. An additional view on this step in the strategy process is offered by Colakoglu's (2012) *Thunderbird International Business Review* article. In order to fully critique CONCACAF's strategy development process in question three above, students should refer to Kaplan, Norton and Barrows' (2008)

Harvard Business Publishing Newsletters contribution. Finally, students are directed to review Neilson, Martin and Powers' (2008) *Harvard Business Review* article when reflecting on strategic risks and execution.

BIBLIOGRAPHY

Bond, D. (2011). E-mail adds pressure on Fifa's Jack Warner, BBC, 26 May, viewed 14 April 2014, www.bbc.com/sport/0/football/13559384.

Cayman Islands Government (2012). Congrats to Cayman's CONCACAF President, viewed 14 April 2014, www.gov.ky/portal/page/portal/cighome/pressroom/archive/201205/ congratstocaymansconcacafpresident.

Colakoglu, S. (2012). Shard vision in MNE subsidiaries: The role of formal, personal, and social control in its development and its impact on subsidiary learning. *Thunderbird International Business Review*, 54(5), 639–52.

Collins, J. C. and Porras, J. I. (1996). Building your company's vision. *Harvard Business Review*, 74(5), 65–77.

CONCACAF (2013). President Sepp Blatter focuses on the Power of Football, 22 October, viewed 26 August 2016, www.concacaf.com/article/president-sepp-latter-focuses-on-the-power-of-football.

Evans, S. (2012). Webb keen to usher in new era for CONCACAF, Reuters, 12 July, viewed 14 April 2014, www.reuters.com/article/2012/07/12/us-soccer-concacaf-webb-idUSBRE86B1 G820120712.

Goal.com (2012). Webb was officially named president and eyes 2026 World Cup, while officials from Central America and the Carribbean vote for Blazer's removal from FIFA, viewed 27 October 2016, www.goal.com/en-us/news/1616/concacaf/2012/05/23/3122991/concaca f-elects-jeffrey-webb-as-president-looks-to-oust.

Hickey, K. (2013). The CONCACAF Champions League may currently not be up to standard, but a few changes could make it a competition worth watching all the way through, Sporting News, 26 September, viewed 26 August 2016, www.goal.com/en-us/news/594/concacaf-champi-ons-league/2013/09/26/4289900/keith-hickey-how-to-fix-the-concacaf-champions-league.

Jimenez, A.S. (2013). Fair play does not exist in Concacaf!!!, Facebook, Facebook post, March, viewed 14 April 2014, www.facebook.com/concacafcom/posts#.

Kaplan, R. S., Norton, D. P. and Barrows, E. A. (2008). Developing the strategy: vision, value gaps, and analysis. Harvard Business Publishing Newsletters (B0801A-PDF-ENG), Harvard Business School Publishing, Boston, MA.

Kouzes, J. M. and Posner, B. Z. (2009). To lead, create a shared vision. *Harvard Business Review*, 87(1), 20–1.

Liburd, L. (2012). No business as usual yet at CONCACAF, Play the Game, 4 June, viewed 14 April 2014, www.playthegame.org/news/detailed/no-business-as-usual-yet-at-concacaf-5401.html.

Longman, J. and Carvajal, D. (2011). FIFA power broker is out after years of whispers, *New York Times*, 20 June, viewed 14 April 2014, www.nytimes.com/2011/06/21/sports/ soccer/jack-warner-fifa-and-concacaf-power-broker-resigns.html?pagewanted=4&_ r=0&pagewanted=all.

Neilson, G. L., Martin, K. L. and Powers, E. (2008). The secrets to successful strategy execution. *Harvard Business Review*, 86(6), 60–70.

Nicholson, P. (2013). Webb calls for CONCACAF federations to grasp their future, Inside World Football, 23 October, viewed 14 April 2014, www.insideworldfootball.com/ world-football/football-americas/concacaf-news/13484-webb-calls-for-concacaf-federations-to-grasp-their-future.

Phillips, M. (2011). FIFA found "overwhelming" evidence of bribery, Reuters, 22 June, viewed 14 April 2014, www.reuters.com/article/2011/06/22/us-soccer-fifa-idUSTRE75L4PY20110622.

Riccio, R. J. (2013). CONCACAF 2013 Sports Summit in the Cayman Islands concludes, Examiner.com, 22 October, viewed 14 April 2014, www.examiner.com/article/concacaf-2013-sport-summit-the-cayman-islands-concludes.

Simmons, D. A. C., Urbina, R. M. and Hempe, E. (2013). CONCACAF Integrity Committee Report of Investigation, Report presented to the Executive Committee of CONCACAF, 18 April, Business of Soccer, viewed 14 April 2014, www.businessofsoccer.com/wp-content/uploads/2013/04/CONCACAF-IntegrityCommittee-ReportofInvestigation-20120418.pdf.

Wahl, G. (2013). Jeffrey Webb hopes his presidency will transform CONCACAF, Sports Illustrated, 10 July, viewed 26 August 2016, www.si.com/soccer/2013/07/10/jeffrey-webb-concacaf-gold-cup.

Wilson, F. (2013). Historic CONCACAF Sports Summit opens today in Cayman Islands, Kaieteir News Online, 22 October, viewed 14 April 2014 www.kaieteurnewsonline.com/2013/10/22/historic-concacaf-sports-summit-opens-today-in-cayman-islands/.

RECOMMENDED WEBSITES

CONCACAF: www.concacaf.com
Official CONCACAF: www.facebook.com/officialconcacaf
@CONCACAF: www.twitter.com/concacaf
FIFA: www.fifa.com
Harvard Business Review, Strategy Execution: http://hbr.org/balanced-scorecard

A. Burks, M. M. Goldman, N. Agha

CASE 15

THE CANADIAN SPORT DELIVERY SYSTEM: CHALLENGES FACING RECREATIONAL SPORT

JONATHON EDWARDS, CHARLENE SHANNON-MCCALLUM, AND TERRI BYERS

LEARNING OUTCOMES

Upon completion of this case study, the reader should be able to:

- gain an understanding of how the complexity and importance of a sport system affects the delivery of recreational sport;
- assess the challenges that exist within a complex sport system with regards to recreational sport where the focus is on elite sports;
- gain an understanding of the interrelationships that exist within a complex elite sport/recreational system;
- assess the importance for sport and recreation management to understand the need for collaborative governance within a sport system.

OVERVIEW OF THE CASE

Recreational sport has always been an important part of Canadian culture. It is viewed as a way to build social capital and strengthen communities, improve the health and well-being of citizens, foster positive youth development, and contribute to economic development and renewal. Sport exists in nearly every community across Canada with significant numbers of Canadians participating directly. In 2010, 7.2 million (26 percent) of Canadians over the age of 15 were active in sport (Canadian Heritage, 2013). Five years earlier, data collected on youth 15 years of age or younger found 55 percent of boys and 44 percent of girls were active in sport (Ifedi, 2008). The value of sport in Canada is also reflected in the 5.3 million Canadians who volunteer with sport and recreation organizations and the

> sport volunteers who each contribute an average of 143 hours per year to sport (Doherty, 2005).
>
> Recreational sport (both in organized and unorganized forms) is delivered mainly within communities by schools, sport clubs, and municipal recreation departments. Although competition may be an element of the experience, having fun and accessing health and social benefits is considered the main objective. Despite the shared objective, the Canadian sport system faces challenges in delivering recreational sport, which lacks the well-integrated delivery system that exists for elite sport.

CASE STUDY

In Canada, sport, including recreational sport, is delivered and managed across three sectors – the public or government sector, the voluntary or non-profit sector, and the private or commercial sector. Within the public sector, three levels of government (federal, provincial, municipal), each with their own mandate, are involved in sport delivery. The federal government is involved with sport through shaping policy, collaborating with provinces and territories to set priorities, and contributing financially to sport through Sport Canada (a branch of the Department of Canadian Heritage). The provincial government role is primarily to assist and enable municipalities and community groups in providing services (e.g., financial support, consulting, and resources). Broadly, provinces provide leadership in policy development; consultation services to governing bodies such as Provincial Sport Organizations (PSOs) and Community Sport Organizations (CSOs); assistance with building partnerships or strategic alliances; financial investment in municipalities and sport organizations; and they also champion the benefits of sport and physical activity. However, the provincial departments in which sport is housed vary (e.g., Parks, Culture, and Sport in Saskatchewan; Department of Tourism, Heritage and Culture in New Brunswick), as do the specific mandates of each department. Municipal governments are responsible for direct provision of recreational sport opportunities to residents by providing basic, affordable programs (e.g., swimming, tennis, and skating lessons) and indoor and outdoor facilities that both facilitate residents' sport participation and also support local voluntary sport organizations in the services they provide. Public sector recreational sport delivery is further complicated by an affiliated public delivery system – education – which engages youth in sport education and facilitates competitive sport opportunities.

Non-profit sport organizations exist at the national, provincial, and local/regional level and include single sport (e.g., Swim Canada) and multi-sport (e.g., SportNB) groups. Local CSOs comprise the membership of PSOs and help to make up National Sport Organizations (NSOs). NSOs, the majority with financial support from Sport Canada, provide support for athletes and competitions, prepare national teams, and develop

J. Edwards, C. Shannon-McCallum, T. Byers

coaches and officials. CSOs deliver both recreational and competitive sport opportunities directly to participants. Furthermore, CSOs have a limited paid staff (e.g., coaches) and operations are managed by volunteers.

While not well linked with other delivery systems, commercial recreation organizations do provide opportunities for sport participation at a cost (e.g., bowling alleys, golf courses, ski hills). However, while these organizations may offer instructional opportunities that contribute to sport literacy and recreational participation, the main goal of these organizations is to make a profit.

The challenging facet to consider when examining Canada's sport delivery system in the context of recreational sport is the variation in policy, procedures, communication, and management that exists at the three different levels – federal, provincial, and municipal – and between commercial and not-for-profit sport organizations. This type of system can be described as a decentralized system that is highly complex. As a result of this complexity, non-profit sport organizations are challenged with delivery of recreational sport. For the purposes of this discussion, we will focus on non-profit sport organizations such as NSOs, PSOs, and CSOs. As an example, Figure 15.1 shows the structure of the sport system in the province of New Brunswick regarding the span of control.

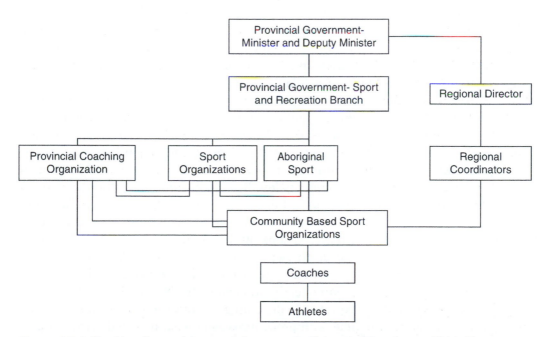

Figure 15.1 The New Brunswick sport delivery system (Edwards & Leadbetter, 2016: 7)

We now outline three challenges organizations face regarding the complexity of this system within the context of recreational sport.

Resources

The first challenge that recreational sport faces within the Canadian sport system is access to resources. Resources can be understood in one of two ways: financial and human. Financial resource challenges exist where the board members of PSOs and CSOs debate whether resources should be allocated to recreational or high-performance sport. The centralized premise of the debate exists with training, facilities, and coaching, as these have a higher cost at the high-performance level and recreational sport needs fewer resources to operate effectively. Recreational sport has less importance for management and board members of an organization because it has less visibility. When recreational sport is forced to compete with high-performance sport in a decentralized system for the necessary financial support, managers and board members lean more towards providing financial assistance to high-performance athletes, largely because of the visibility that high-performance sport garners.

The complexity of the Canadian sport system increases as the span of control increases, where there are multiple organizations operating at multiple levels (i.e., tall structure) within the delivery of recreational sport. This complexity also increases between provinces and between levels of government through the funding that is provided by each of these organizational actors. Managers of non-profit sport organizations must attempt to understand this complex structure in order to identify from where financial assistance is available at the various levels – national, provincial, and municipal. Since sponsorship opportunities are limited, non-profit sport organizations depend upon government assistance for their survival. Furthermore, depending on the size and resources of the NSO, PSO, and CSO, it is not uncommon that these organizations are volunteer-based and do not have paid staff members, while paid staff members are more commonly seen at the national and provincial levels. For example, in the province of New Brunswick approximately 20 percent of the PSOs have paid staff members, while the remaining 80 percent of PSO management are volunteers with various skills and experience, including stay-at-home parents, business executives, tradespersons, and/or education professionals. This becomes a human resource issue, as there is a concern regarding whether the executive board members and management have the time and expertise to understand the system to deliver recreational sport effectively. Leaders in CSOs and some PSOs who do not have the time and/or expertise to develop grant proposals, seek sponsorship, and construct formalized policies and procedures can constrain the delivery of programs within recreational sport, as their focus is on areas where they have knowledge and/or experience. Seemingly this will often dictate the goals and managerial decision-making processes of the organization.

Communication

Effective communication is a challenge in any type of organization, but increasingly so in a complex, decentralized system. In linking the human resource issue and the complexity and decentralization of the Canadian sport system, management can be challenged with effectively determining the communication chain and communicating with the necessary actors to gain access to resources. In the case of recreational sport, the perception often exists that the organization is not deemed legitimate, resulting in less communication and guidance from the governing body. The delivery of these programs therefore exists primarily at the municipal level, where there is arguably less funding. Hence, less funding and options for guidance signifies the perceived importance of recreational sport within the context of the Canadian sport system.

The lack of communication that exists could be attributed to geography and the design of the overall system. Ultimately the argument could be made that the system design is focused on elite athletes as opposed to mass participation. In terms of communication, Green's (2005) basic model of athlete development (see Figure 15.2) shows that recreational sport is the foundation from which management and coaches are able to identify talented athletes and transition these individuals to higher competition levels. At key transition points it becomes imperative that there is a communication link between and/or within organizations to move athletes upward.

For example, in the Edmonton region of Alberta, Canada, youth male hockey players transition at 12 years old from recreational-based hockey (mass participation) to club hockey (competitive level). Communication becomes key at this transition point for two reasons: first, club hockey is the "stepping stone" to competing in the Canadian Hockey League (CHL, a semi-professional, for-profit hockey league for players between the ages of 16 and 21), which is a pathway for players to reach the National Hockey League (NHL). Second, if the player chooses to continue playing

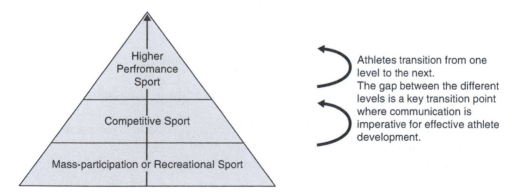

Figure 15.2 Pyramid model for sport development (Green, 2005: 235)

recreational hockey, the likelihood that the player will be able to make a high-performance team in the future decreases.

"Missed opportunities for growth"

The fundamental challenge with the design of this type of system is that its focus is on high-performance sport, which ultimately limits the growth potential for recreational sports (unless the intention of the participant is to progress to the elite level). In some of the more popular sports in Canada (e.g., ice hockey, golf, and softball) the recreational component is fairly strong. However, in some of the less popular sports (e.g., wrestling, volleyball, badminton, and cricket), there becomes a "missed opportunity" for providing recreational sport services to the 20+ age group. Recreational sports for the 20+ age group are commonly organized by "ad hoc committees" (e.g., community softball leagues), where there is a less formalized delivery of the sport. Conversely, organized recreational sport is often delivered by CSOs, PSOs, universities or colleges (e.g., campus recreation), or provided through commercial recreation organizations (e.g., private ski hills, and/or private golf courses) with higher price points for participation.

The value of recreational sport for the 20+ age group has a particular importance, as there is a common initiative at the various governmental levels that there is a need for physical activity as Canada's provinces are facing an obesity epidemic. For example, the Federal Government enacted the Physical Activities and Sport Act, which stipulates that "the Government of Canada wishes to encourage and assist Canadians in increasing their level of physical activity and their participation in sport" (Canadian Government, 2014: 1). However, the design of the current sport system does not facilitate the promotion and organization of recreational sport for participants in the 20+ age group, unless the individuals have higher levels of disposable income. As a result, entire segments of the population are missing opportunities for and access to recreational sport services.

QUESTIONS

1. Why would it be important to have a strong recreational sport system for the overall system?
2. What organizational strategies could be used to address the challenges faced within recreational sport?
3. What marketing strategies could be used to increase the visibility of recreational sport and the importance of being physically active?
4. What opportunities are NSOs, PSOs, and CSOs missing regarding recreational sport in Canada?

5. What are the challenges of managing a change in the formal system to put greater emphasis on recreational sport participation, given the size and complexity of the Canadian sport system and geography?
6. Discuss the process of developing a new strategy for the Canadian sport delivery system that balances recreational and elite sport.

CONCLUSIONS

The challenges that organizational actors face with regard to recreational sport are ones that are often contingent upon the overall design of the sport system, where the focus of most organizations is on the development of elite sports. Some of these challenges include lack of resources, communication, and "missed opportunities for growth." Furthermore, these challenges are often a result of lack of expertise and knowledge on the part of management and volunteer board members, high turnover rates, leadership, lack of governance structure, and an overall struggle to establish the legitimacy of recreational sport within a particular sport system. Governments, such as the Canadian government, have enacted policies to directly and indirectly motivate sport organizations based on Green's (2005) pyramid model, as it is arguable this is a foundation from which a healthy society, and ultimately an elite sport program, can be built.

RECOMMENDED READING

The challenging aspect to this case study is that there is a dearth of background literature in the area. Students should begin by reading the textbook *Leisure and Recreation in Canadian Society* by Karlis (2011). Next, students should consider readings that discuss sport systems (e.g. Green, 2005; Sotiriadou et al., 2008), governance (e.g., Byers et al., 2014; Shilbury and Ferkins, 2011, 2015), collaborative governance (e.g., Shilbury and Ferkins, 2015), and PSOs (e.g., Edwards et al., 2009). The above readings provide a foundation for students in understanding the delivery of recreational sport within the context of a broader complex sport system, such as the Canadian sport system.

BIBLIOGRAPHY

Byers, T., Anagnostopoulos, C. and Brooke-Holmes, G. (2014). Understanding control in non-profit organisations: Moving governance research forward? *Corporate Governance*, 15(1), 134–45.

Canadian Heritage. (2013). *Sport Participation, 2010*. Ottawa: Statistics Canada. Catalogue No. CH24-1/2012E-PDF.

Doherty, A. (2005). *Profile of Community Sport Volunteers*. Toronto: Parks and Recreation Ontario and Sport Alliance of Ontario.

Edwards, J.R., & Leadbetter, R. (2016). Collaborative governance in a sport system: A critique of a "one-size-fits-all" approach to administering a national standardized sport program. *Managing Sport and Leisure*. DOI:10.1080/23750472.2016.1220811.

Edwards, J. R., Mason, D. S and Washington, M. (2009). Institutional pressures, government funding and provincial sport organisations. *International Journal of Sport Management and Marketing*, 6(2), 128–49.

Green, C. B. (2005). Building sport programs to optimize athlete recruitment, retention, and transition: Toward a normative theory of sport development. *Journal of Sport Management*, 19, 233–53.

Ifedi, F. (2008). Sport Participation in Canada, 2005, accessed 10 July 2015 from www.statcan.ca/bsolc/english/bsolc?catno=81-595-MIE2008060.

Karlis, G. (2011). *Leisure and Recreation in Canadian Society*. Toronto: Thompson Educational Publishing, Inc.

Shilbury, D. and Ferkins, L. (2011). Professionalisation, sport governance, and strategic ability. *Managing Leisure*, 16, 108–27.

Shilbury, D. and Ferkins, L. (2015). Exploring the utility of collaborative governance in a national sport organizations. *Journal of Sport Management*, 29(4), 380–97.

Sotiriadou, K., Shilbury, D. and Quick, S. (2008). The attraction, retention/transition, and nurturing process of sport development: Some Australian evidence. *Journal of Sport Management*, 22, 247–72.

RECOMMENDED WEBSITES

Canadian Government. (2014). Physical activity and sport act, accessed 26 August 2016 from http://laws-lois.justice.gc.ca/eng/acts/p-13.4/FullText.html

Government of New Brunswick. (2008). New Brunswick Sport Plan, accessed 9 July 2015 from www2.gnb.ca/content/dam/gnb/Departments/thc-tpc/pdf/Sport/NBSportPlan.pdf

Government of New Brunswick. (2015). Tourism, Heritage and Culture, accessed 28 July 2015 from www2.gnb.ca/content/gnb/en/departments/thc/sport.html

CASE 16

SELLING THE RIGHTS TO BROADCAST FOOTBALL GAMES IN EUROPE: THE CONTROVERSY STILL CONTINUES

JON GUEST

LEARNING OUTCOMES

On completion of this case study, the reader should be able to:

- appreciate the significance of broadcasting revenue for the financial performance of teams in European football leagues;
- compare and contrast the individual with the collective selling model of broadcast rights;
- outline the different approaches taken by various competition authorities in Europe towards the selling of broadcast rights;
- critically assess the economic arguments both for and against the adoption of the collective selling model for broadcast rights;
- evaluate the extent to which the evidence supports the view that the adoption of the collective sales model helps to maintain competitive balance in a league.

OVERVIEW OF THE CASE

Media companies have to pay football clubs a fee in order to purchase the rights to broadcast their matches on television, the internet or radio. In recent years these companies have been willing to spend very large amounts of money to obtain the rights to show live games on television. For example, for the three seasons from 2016 until 2019, BSkyB are paying just under £1.4 billion each year for the rights to broadcast 126 English Premier League (EPL) games per season in the UK. For the same period BT Sport are paying £320 million per year for the rights to broadcast 42 EPL games per season. The BBC is also paying £68 million per season to be able to broadcast a highlights package on its *Match of the Day* programme. In addition to selling the rights to broadcast games in their own domestic market, football teams can also sell the rights to have their games broadcast in other countries. Cable Thai Holdings paid £205 million for a 3-year deal to show EPL matches in Thailand while NowTV paid £128 million for a similar deal in Hong Kong. The biggest five leagues in Europe combined (EPL in England, Serie A in Italy, La Liga in Spain, Bundesliga in Germany, Ligue 1 in France) are generating over £5 billion per season from the most recent sales of their domestic and international media rights.

The sale of these broadcasting rights raises two interesting, controversial and much-debated issues:

1. The organisation of the sale – individual club selling vs. collective selling by the league/association.
2. The distribution of the revenue between the teams in the league.

This case study will focus on the first of these two issues.

CASE STUDY

Different approaches to the sale of the broadcast rights

There are two distinct methods of organising the sale of TV rights. They can either be sold individually or collectively. In the Individual Sales Model (ISM) each club is responsible for selling the rights to broadcast its home games to the media providers in the market. The ISM was used in both La Liga in Spain and Primeira Liga in Portugal for the 2014–15 season. For example, Real Madrid and Barcelona sold the rights to their home games to TV production company Mediapro for approximately €150 million per year. The ISM was also used from 1999–2010 in Serie A. In the Collective Sales Model (CSM) the rights are sold jointly by the league, federation or national association on behalf of the teams involved. The CSM is currently used by the majority of the football leagues in Europe, including the EPL, Bundesliga, Ligue 1 and Serie A. As previously stated, the EPL will receive just over £1.7 billion per season from BSkyB and BT Sport as a result of the deal negotiated for the period 2016–2019. This money is then distributed to the clubs using an agreed formula. In May 2015 the Spanish government announced that it was introducing a new law so that the CSM could be used for the rights to La Liga matches from 2016 onwards. Although the legislation was supported by the National Professional Football League (LFP), it was opposed by the Spanish Football Federation (SFF) and the Spanish players' association (AFE) and nearly resulted in a strike.

116

The economic case against the CSM – the cartel argument

Originally all the leagues in the European Union used the CSM. However, concerns were expressed over the legality of this practice. Some economists and policy makers have argued that selling the rights in this way effectively creates a cartel. A cartel is an arrangement whereby a group of organisations agree to restrict the extent to which they compete against one another. In many instances these agreements relate to the quantity of the good or service supplied. Instead of choosing how much to sell purely on an individual basis, the organisations instead jointly agree to regulate or restrict the quantity of the good/service that each of them supply. This usually results in higher prices for the customer and higher profits for the members of the cartel. The cartel then has to agree how to split the extra profits made between its participants. These types of agreement are usually prohibited under competition law as they are thought to be against the best interests of society.

If clubs in a league are judged to be the equivalent of firms in a traditional industry, then the CSM does appear to be an example of a restrictive agreement. The argument that they are comparable to firms is based on a number of observations about their behaviour. They:

- are each separately owned and submit their own individual set of accounts;
- compete with each other to buy inputs (i.e. the players) to produce an output (i.e. a match);
- individually market and set the price for the output they produce (i.e. the tickets for the games and prices of merchandise such as football shirts).

Taking this view, the league or federation looks rather like a monopoly seller of the broadcast rights that restricts output and leads to prices that are above the level that would exist if there were free and open competition. As evidence to support this interpretation of the CSM, reference is often made to the details of the contract between the EPL and BSkyB and BT Sport. As part of this agreement the number of live games that can be broadcast per season is restricted to 168. This represents just over 44 per cent of the maximum total of 380 that could be shown. Teams are effectively prohibited from individually selling the rights to matches that are not selected for broadcast in the collective deal as they must seek permission from the EPL. Because of the exclusivity granted to the media companies in the collective deal, it is clearly indicated to the clubs that such permission will not be granted. A number of economists and policy makers have argued that this restriction on the number of games broadcast is clear evidence of anti-competitive/cartel behaviour and should be prohibited. In September 2014 Virgin Media made a formal complaint to Ofgem about the CSM. In particular, Virgin argued that the collective selling of rights in the UK led to a smaller proportion of EPL games being broadcast compared with other leading European leagues, and this contributed to consumers having to pay higher prices. Following the complaint, Ofgem announced in November 2014 that it would undertake an investigation into how the EPL sells its live media rights. The EPL has always defended its actions by arguing that any major increase in the number of televised games would significantly reduce attendance at its matches.

The judgments of different competition authorities in Europe

Against the use of CSM

During the 1990s a number of competition authorities took this anti-competitive view of the CSM and prohibited the practice. For example, in 1993 a ruling in the Spanish competition court made the collective selling of rights illegal and so made the move to individual selling by teams compulsory. A similar ruling was made by the Italian competition authorities in 1999, which resulted in the ISM being used for a 10-year period. In Germany, the competition authorities ruled that the collective selling of games was anti-competitive and should be prohibited. However, in this case politicians intervened and passed an act in May 1998 which exempted the CSM from the German Competition Act. This allowed the Deutsche Fussball Liga to continue to sell the broadcast rights on behalf of the teams in Bundesliga and Bundesliga 2.

In favour of CSM

The competition authorities in the UK and France came to a different conclusion. In France, the Sports Law of 1984 and amendments in 1992 stated that the legal ownership of the rights to a sporting event belonged to the organiser of that event. In the case of football, the organiser of the event was considered to be the league or sport federation/association, so the CSM was judged to be legal. In the UK, the CSM was challenged in 1999 when the Office of Fair Trading (OFT) referred the case to the Restrictive Practices Court (RPC). The Director General of the OFT stated that: 'The net effect of cartels is to inflate costs and prices. Any other business acting in this way would be subject to competition law and I see no reason why the selling of sport should be treated differently (*Irish Times*, 1996).

However, much to the surprise of many people at the time, the RPC ruled against the OFT. It concluded that the collective selling of games was in the public interest with the benefits outweighing any of the costs of the restrictive agreement. Therefore, the CSM was allowed to continue in the UK.

The European Union has also taken a more positive stance. In its 2007 White Paper on sport it stated that 'while joint selling of media rights raises competition concerns, the commission has accepted it under certain conditions'.

Article 101(1) of the Treaty on the Functioning of the European Union (TFEU) prohibits agreements or undertakings that restrict or distort competition in the internal market. However, exemptions to the prohibition can be made under article 101(3), which identifies that the restrictive effects of some agreements on competition might be outweighed by the potential benefits, in particular where the agreements that restrict competition 'contribute to improving the production or distribution of goods'.

The European Union has also concluded that that the potential benefits of the CSM model on the quality of the output (i.e. the matches) outweigh the costs caused by the restrictive nature of the agreements on competition.

How can collective selling improve the quality of matches? The unique characteristics of sport

It has previously been explained how teams in a league can be viewed as equivalent to firms in an industry as they each purchase inputs to produce a match. If this approach is accepted, then adoption of the CSM does appear to result in a cartel being created. However, some authors have argued that the relationship between the teams in a league is very different to that of firms competing in a traditional industry. Reference is often made to the peculiar or unique characteristics of sports leagues. Two key factors are usually identified:

- the extra levels of co-operation required between the teams, and
- the importance of competitive balance.

It is argued that these two features mean that sports leagues should be given exemptions from the normal application of competition policy.

Extra levels of co-operation

The central idea is that the level of co-operation required between teams and a league in order to produce matches is far greater than that required by firms to produce output in any other industry. A team cannot produce a match on its own – it needs a competitor. Therefore, teams need to co-ordinate their activities to produce a game. Amongst other things, the rules under which the game will be played need to be agreed, as well as the timing and venue of the fixture. However, this would only produce a 'friendly' game. The entertainment value of the games can be further increased if the teams co-ordinate within a league. Games that are part of a league can have increased meaning and significance, that is they determine which team will be the champions, which teams will qualify for the Champions League and which teams will be relegated. This is something that fans appear to value, given the much higher attendance levels at league games as opposed to friendly matches. Agreements have to be made between the teams and the league about the rules and the fixture list. However, unlike a traditional cartel arrangement these agreements do not simply restrict output. They also improve the entertainment value of the game and hence the quality of the product.

Some authors have argued that because of these unique characteristics of sport, the league, rather than the individual team, should be thought of as the equivalent to a firm in a more traditional industry. In this 'single entity theory' teams are viewed as divisions of a single organisation, that is the league. The league is treated as a natural monopoly that legally owns the broadcast rights of the clubs rather than a cartel of separate organisations (e.g. see the decision of the French Competition Authority previously outlined in this case study). Others have argued that it is more sensible to think of the league as a joint venture between the teams.

Competitive balance

The second unique characteristic of sport leagues is how the viability and profitability of the teams are affected by the performance of their rivals. Not only do teams need rivals in order to produce the matches, but the strength of these rivals could also have an unusual impact on their own financial performance. Imagine a situation where a firm in a traditional industry weakens the position of its competitors by investing in more productive inputs that enable it to run its business more effectively. Faced with weaker competitors, the firm would make more money. However, imagine if this happened in a sports league. Assume an owner improves the quality of his/her team by investing in more productive inputs, that is buying significantly more of the most talented players. By employing a larger share of the most talented players available, the owner would weaken the playing strength of its competitors, making matches more one-sided and predictable. If fans value matches where the outcome is uncertain, then this increased predictability may reduce their interest in the sport and their willingness to pay to watch a game either in the stadium or on television. A team in a league may generate less revenue if its rivals become significantly weaker.

It has been argued that unregulated leagues have an inherent tendency to become competitively unbalanced with the most talented players concentrated in a few of the bigger clubs. Therefore, regulations that implement a more equal distribution of the revenue from the sale of broadcast rights could help to maintain competitive balance and produce a successful league. Some competition authorities have accepted the argument that only through the use of the CSM can the appropriate distribution of broadcast revenue be achieved. For example, in its judgment in July 1999 the RPC concluded that if the CSM model were prohibited in the UK, then the ability of the EPL to maintain competitive balance by ensuring a more equal distribution of TV money would be lost or seriously diminished. The White Paper on sport published by the European Union in 2007 also stated that 'collective selling can be important for the redistribution of income and can thus be a tool for achieving greater solidarity within sports'.

QUESTIONS

1. Using relevant diagrams, explain why cartel agreements usually lead to lower output and higher prices.
2. Evaluate the arguments that have been used to justify the contention that league sports are different from other more traditional industries and so should not be subject to conventional competition policy.
3. Using economic theory, what other arguments could be used to justify the use of the CSM for the sale of broadcasting rights?
4. Critically assess the argument that unregulated leagues have an inherent tendency to become competitively unbalanced with the most talented players concentrated in a few of the bigger clubs.
5. To what extent does the evidence suggest that the use of the CSM, for the sale of broadcasting rights, leads to a more competitively balanced league?

CONCLUSIONS

Different competition authorities in Europe have come to conflicting judgments about the relative merits of using either the ISM or CSM for the sale of broadcasting rights. Those that have prohibited the use of the CSM, such as Spain, have emphasised the restrictive nature of the agreements on competition. Those competition authorities that have allowed the CSM to continue have tended to stress the unique characteristics of sports when compared to other industries and the relative importance of competitive balance to ensure the future success of the league. One of the key assumptions that tends to underpin these decisions is the belief that the CSM is required in order for there to be an effective and appropriate distribution of the broadcast revenues. Some authors have challenged this assumption and have suggested that it would be perfectly feasible to have the less restrictive system of the ISM combined with appropriate measures that ensure an adequate distribution of the revenues generated.

RECOMMENDED READING

To begin with, students might find it helpful to read an introductory text on economic theory – specifically chapters on market structure, competition and collusion. A book such as *Essentials of Economics* by Sloman and Garratt (2013) is a good example of such a text. Students could then move onto read relevant chapters in books that have focused specifically on the economics of sport. Examples include the chapter on the economics of competitive balance by Guest in *The Business of*

Sport Management, edited by Beech and Chadwick (2013). Chapters 3 and 5 in *Sports Economics* by Fort (2011) are also useful. The European Commission's website is a good source for explaining how competition policy operates. Thereafter students should focus on reading the literature that applies economic theory to the issue of broadcasting rights. A good example includes the chapter by Andreff and Bourg in *Economics of Sport and the Media*, edited by Jeanrenaud and Kesenne (2006). Peeters' paper 'Broadcasting Rights and Competitive Balance in European Soccer' (2011) presents some interesting empirical evidence on the impact of the method used to sell broadcasting rights on the level of competitive balance in football leagues in Europe.

REFERENCES

Andreff, W. and Bourg, J. (2006). 'Broadcasting rights and competition in European football', in C. Jeanrenaud and S. Kesenne (eds.), *Economics of Sport and the Media*, Cheltenham: Edward Elgar.

Buraimo, B. (2008). 'Stadium Attendance and Television Audience Demand in English League Football', *Managerial and Decision Economics*, 29, 513–23.

Cave, M. and Crandall, R. (2001). 'Sports Rights and the Broadcast Industry', *The Economic Journal*, 111, 4–26.

Cox, A. (2012). 'Live Broadcasting, Gate Revenue, and Football Performance: Some Evidence', *International Journal of the Economics of Business*, 19(1), 75–98.

Falconieri, S., Palomino, F. and Sakovics, J. (2004). 'Collective vs Individual Sale of Television Rights in League Sports', *Journal of the European Economic Association*, 2(5), 833–62.

Flynn, M. and Gilbert, R. (2001). 'The Analysis of Professional Sports Leagues as Joint Ventures', *The Economic Journal*, 111, 27–46.

Forrest, D., Simmons, R. and Szymanski, S. (2004). 'Broadcasting, Attendance and the Inefficiency of Cartels', *Review of Industrial Organisation*, 24, 243–65.

Fort, R. (2011). *Sports Economics*, 3rd edn, Boston, MA: Prentice Hall.

Guest, J. (2013). 'The economics of competitive balance in sport', in J. Beech and S. Chadwick (eds), *The Business of Sport Management,* 2nd edn, New York: Pearson Education.

Massey, P. (2007). 'Are Sports Cartels Different? An Analysis of EU Commission Decisions Concerning Collective Selling Agreements for Football Broadcasting Rights', *World Competition*, 30(1), 87–106.

Peeters, T. (2011). 'Broadcasting Rights and Competitive Balance in European Soccer', *The International Journal of Sport Finance*, 6(1), 23–39.

Sloman, J. and Garratt, D. (2013). *Essentials of Economics*, 6th edn, Harlow: Pearson Education.

Tonazzi, A. (2003). 'Competition Policy and the Commercialization of Sport Broadcasting Rights: The Decision of the Italian Competition Authority', *International Journal of the Economics of Business*, 10,1), 17–34.

RECOMMENDED WEBSITES

Bundesliga Fanatic (2013). The Bundesliga TV Rights and their Place in Europe, accessed 15 May 2014 from http://bundesligafanatic.com/the-bundesliga-tv-rights-and-their-place-in-europe/

European Commission (2012). Competition: Sports, accessed 3 June 2014 from http://ec.europa.eu/competition/sectors/sports/overview_en.html

Financial Fair Play Latest News (2012). TV revenue distribution – comparing Italian and English models, accessed 15 May 2014 from www.financialfairplay.co.uk/latest-news/tv-revenue-distribution-%E2%80%93-comparing-italian-and-english-models

Forbes Sports Money (2014). Dividing the TV Money Pie or How Some Soccer Leagues Are More Equal than Others, accessed 15 May 2014 from www.forbes.com/sites/bobbymcmahon/2014/05/10/dividing-the-tv-money-pie-or-how-some-soccer-leagues-are-more-equal-than-others/

Irish Times (1996). Premier League television deal taken to court of fair trading, 7 February, accessed 30 September 2016 from www.irishtimes.com/news/premier-league-television-deal-taken-to-court-of-fair-trading-1.28804

Ofcom (2015). Competition Act investigation into the sale of live UK audio-visual media rights to Premier League matches, accessed 24 June 2015 from http://stakeholders.ofcom.org.uk/enforcement/competition-bulletins/open-cases/all-open-cases/cw_01138/

Soccernomics – The Blog (2014). accessed 17 May 2014 from www.soccernomics-agency.com/?page_id=9

The Swiss Ramble (2015). The Premier League TV Deal – Master And Servant, accessed 24 June 2015 from http://swissramble.blogspot.co.uk/2015/02/the-premier-league-tv-deal-master-and.html

CASE 17

LEVERAGING THE BENEFITS OF SPORT SPONSORSHIP: A GLOBAL BRAND'S LOCAL ENGAGEMENT THROUGH SPORT SPONSORSHIP

ADAM JONES AND JOHN NAURIGHT[1]

LEARNING OUTCOMES

Upon completion of this case study, the reader should be able to:

- describe the benefits of sport sponsorship;
- identify the opportunities for extending the benefits of sport sponsorship beyond communication objectives;
- evaluate the mechanisms by which sports clubs can integrate sport sponsorship into their operation;
- construct an integrated sport sponsorship opportunity that goes beyond communication objectives.

OVERVIEW OF THE CASE

This case study evaluates the additional benefits of sport sponsorship over and above the usual marketing communication objectives. It explores the sponsorship by an international financial services company, American Express®, of a local professional football club, Brighton & Hove Albion. In addition to the traditional sponsorship of the club's stadium and team shirts, the agreement also includes a partnership between the sponsor and the charity arm of the club, Albion in the Community. This case study reviews the methods by which these benefits are realised, evaluates the outcomes for the sponsoring organisation and poses questions about the ways in which additional value can be gained from sport sponsorship, particularly in this case at local and regional levels, which can also influence enhancement of a brand's image when it is engaged with the communities in which it operates.

CASE STUDY

In a globally competitive world, companies are aware of the significance of attracting customers and sustaining their loyalty. As an integrated key component of the marketing mix, the promotion mix is used as a method of communicating to gain attention, provide information and raise awareness. The promotional mix is composed of advertising, public relations, sales promotion, personal selling and sponsorship. Sponsorship has developed as a valuable tool in the promotion mix as a method of escaping the clutter of traditional channels of promotion. There is recognition that it provides a solution to the challenge of how to gain attention and support loyalty at a time when many consumers are apathetic or even hostile to traditional methods of marketing communications. Considered originally as a tactical tool and regarded as a component of public relations, with the benefits of its use for (re)positioning brands and creating customer loyalty, sponsorship has developed into a strategic instrument for marketers.

In addition to the purely marketing benefits to be gained as identified above, companies may also sponsor local organisations, financially or through donation of products and services, in order to act as a good citizen or give something back to the local community (Bovaird *et al.*, 2002). Sport, which is regarded as a valuable vehicle for sponsorship, as its products, services, events and venues are associated with positive feelings and strong brand images, is therefore a good vehicle for organisations wanting to make a contribution to their local communities (Smith and Westerbeek, 2007).

Sponsorship is the investment, in cash or in kind, in an activity in return for access to commercial potential associated with that activity (Meenaghan, 1991: 36). The importance of sponsorship can be seen from the amount invested by companies. IEG, in its annual survey of sponsorship, reported a projected global spend of US\$53.3 billion in 2013, up by US\$9 billion from 2009. They report that, in North America, sports, with 69 per cent of all reported spending, take the lion's share of all sponsorship arrangements (IEG, 2013). Sport sponsorship can take many forms, such as individuals, teams and kit, and more recently there has been an increase in sponsorship of iconic buildings and sports stadia. The sponsor provides funds for the 'space' that is sponsored, as this is regarded as a revenue generation opportunity by the sports organisation. For the sponsor, by attaching the brand name to the sports team, sports event or sports team building, there is the prospect of raising awareness and providing occasions to support either public relations exercises or traditional promotion activities.

There are, however, risks associated with sponsorship, especially when involved with sport. If the team is knocked out of a competition early, there is limited publicity; relegation to a lower division can mean a sharp decline in visibility; and inappropriate behaviour by a team or an individual being sponsored can create considerable bad publicity and associated brand damage. During the America's Cup in Valencia, Spain, the BMW Oracle-sponsored team sailboat was eliminated before the competition had even started, while Nike was forced to drop its sponsorship of cyclist Lance Armstrong as it did not want to be associated with the ensuing scandal connected with his admission of taking performance-enhancing drugs.

American Express and sponsorship of Brighton & Hove Albion Football Club

Companies enter sponsorship agreements to support key business objectives. Sponsorship of teams or sporting events, which impact on or are supported by a local community, provides the opportunity to attain associated local benefits. This case study concerns itself with the way in which American Express is supporting its corporate social responsibility objectives from its sponsorship of Brighton & Hove Albion Football Club. International financial services firm American Express is the headline sponsor for Brighton & Hove Albion Football Club. In 2010 they acquired the official naming rights to the (then) first division football team's newly built stadium in the city's suburb of Falmer. Henceforth, the award-winning venue would be referred to as the 'American Express Community Stadium'. This successful partnership developed further, in 2011, with the company also becoming the headline sponsor of the club's charitable arm, Albion in the Community.

American Express has been operating within the city of Brighton & Hove for almost 50 years; in that time it has become the largest private employer in the city. The success of the organisation is therefore important to the city, and the city to American Express. The American Express organisation, as part of its stated values, considers serving the needs of the local community as integral to running a successful business. It regards these values as part of its responsibilities as world citizens. By supporting communities in ways that enhance the company's reputation with employees, customers, business partners and other stakeholders, it brings to life the American Express value of good corporate citizenship. This they achieve by supporting not-for-profit organisations that preserve and sustain unique historic places for the future, by developing new leaders for tomorrow and by encouraging community service where its employees and customers live and work.

Albion in the Community (AITC) has delivered community programmes since 1990 and became a registered charity in 2005. It uses the power of football and the reach of Brighton & Hove Albion FC to engage and inspire local people of all ages, abilities and backgrounds. Through their programmes, they help people to improve their health and well-being, overcome challenges and build their confidence and skills. They raise people's aspirations and help them to use their potential to the full.

When the partnership was established, AITC and American Express worked jointly to create the 'Realise the Potential of the Community' programme. Delivered by AITC and supported by American Express – both financially and through engagement of hundreds of their employee volunteers – in 2016 it is in its fourth year. The programme harnesses the talents and enthusiasm of American Express staff to support the charity in positively influencing the lives of local people. This community-oriented partnership between American Express and the club's charitable arm builds on the 'community' component of the stadium's name, and addresses both organisations' aspirations. The central piece of the partnership is an Employee Volunteering Programme (EVP) that engages local American Express employees in AITC-coordinated projects taking place within the community.

Since its inception in October 2012 the programme has engaged over 2,000 American Express employee volunteers. In recognition of the importance of the partnership, American Express created a dedicated full-time stadium relationship team to ensure effective management of and employees' engagement in activities. Employee engagement is achieved through a mix of internal communications, including office roadshows and senior leader support, and is reinforced internally through word of mouth. As part of the engagement programme, time is taken to promote the relationship and activities internally and to provide advice on the most beneficial opportunities and training. Every employee is trained before being allowed to participate, enabling volunteers to play a full and active supporting role. In addition, this training is intended to challenge the American Express employee, develop their transferable skills and provide job satisfaction. Volunteers come from all areas of the business, from operational staff through to members of the senior leadership team. The level of support provided by American Express is evidence of the importance they place on the programme and their commitment to community engagement.

'Realise the Potential of the Community' projects currently focus on the following three areas.

Social inclusion

The social inclusion projects include two activities. The first of these is 'Get Ready to Work' – an employability programme for jobseekers in Sussex. Albion in the Community uses its local links to recruit participants onto these free two-day sessions. During the sessions, volunteers from American Express mentor learners and apply their professional experience to help learners produce CVs, write job applications and prepare for job interviews.

The second project is the Kicks Football Tournament for 11–19 year olds from areas of social deprivation within Sussex. Up to 200 players from across Sussex attend this annual tournament at Preston Park in Brighton. It is free to attend and to avoid financial barriers, coaches and minibuses are provided to shuttle participants from known areas of deprivation to the tournament. Led by the charity's coaches, American Express provides volunteers on the day to assist with refereeing.

Disability

The largest disability activity is 'Gully's Days Out'. These consist of visits to local attractions for people with disabilities, accompanied by a staff member from Albion in the Community and volunteers from American Express. The scheme not only takes away the financial pressure from people with disabilities, thus enabling them to enjoy days out, but also helps parents and carers in giving extra support: often families attending these days have more than one child and this project ensures that all children in these families can enjoy social experiences to the full.

In 2015 the organisations launched two sporting activities for people with disabilities. A football tournament tailored to the needs of people with Down's Syndrome was organised by the charity's disability sports staff and supported by American Express volunteer referees. Following its success, Powerchair football coaching sessions were hosted by AITC with American Express volunteers assisting their coaches.

Education

Using the American Express Community Stadium as an inspirational venue to examine sport as a business, the Schools' Masterclasses programme provides commercial insight into the sport to groups of schoolchildren. AITC's tutor and American Express mentors support students in developing business knowledge and understanding that football is big business and extends past the 11 players on the pitch.

QUESTIONS

1. Why is the link between American Express and Brighton & Hove Albion a positive relationship between the two organisations?
2. What are the benefits for the football club of linking such sponsorship opportunities?
3. What benefits, if any, accrue to the wider community through corporate sponsorship of community-focused groups such as Albion in the Community?
4. Are such benefits available in other examples of sport sponsorship?

CONCLUSIONS

The generally recognised value of sponsorship is in raising brand awareness and the promotion of products and services. However, in this instance it is the commitment to support the local community, where its employees live and work, that is the key indefinable benefit for American Express. The community appears to be at the heart of the sponsorship agreement, with the name of the stadium specifically including the word 'community'. This combination of 'community' and 'American Express' is a reflection of the importance the sponsoring organisation places not only on linking their brand name with the sports team and the venue – typical sponsorship activity – but also using it to promote their commitment to the local community.

The 'Realise the Potential of the Community' programme has engaged over 2,000 of American Express's locally based employees, representing a significant proportion of the organisation's local work force. Their volunteering has provided increased job satisfaction by enabling them to be involved in something meaningful within the community. To achieve American Express's objective of good corporate citizenship, the sponsorship provides awareness of the company within the community, and through its engagement with AITC has placed American Express at the heart of the community. This sponsorship helps enhance the company's reputation with employees, customers, business partners and other stakeholders; it therefore helps to bring to life the organisation's commitment to serve the needs of the local community as an integral component of running a successful business.

RECOMMENDED READING

To place sponsorship within the context of sport marketing, a text such as *The Marketing of Sport* by Beech and Chadwick (2007) would provide a good starting point, whilst Lagae's *Sports Sponsorship and Marketing Communications: A European Perspective* (2005) provides a more comprehensive analysis of the specific role of sponsorship. For a more detailed understanding of the role of corporate social responsibility and sport, Levermore's paper 'CSR for development through sport: examining its potential and limitations' (2010) is good starting point, whilst Plewa and Quester's review in 'Sponsorship and CSR: Is there a link? A conceptual framework' (2011) provides a theoretical basis for sport, sponsorship and CSR.

NOTE

1 Thanks to Mel Dunn, Albion in the Community, and Melanie Green, American Express for assistance in developing this case study.

BIBLIOGRAPHY

Beech, J. and Chadwick, S. (eds) (2007). *The Marketing of Sport*. Harlow: Pearson Education Limited.

Bovaird, T. E, Loffler, E. and Parrado-Diez, S. (2002). Finding a bowling partner. The role of stakeholders in activating civil society in Germany, Spain and the UK. *Public Management Review*, 4(3), 411–31.

IEG (2013). 2013 Sponsorship Outlook: Spending Increase Is Double-Edged Sword. Available at www.sponsorship.com/iegsr/2013/01/07/2013-Sponsorship-Outlook--Spending-Increase-Is-Dou.aspx (accessed 18 August 2015).

Lagae, W. (2005). *Sports Sponsorship and Marketing Communications: A European Perspective*. Harlow: Financial Times, Prentice Hall.

Levermore, R. (2010). CSR for development through sport: Examining its potential and limitations. *Third World Quarterly*, 31(2), 223–41.

Meenaghan, T. (1991). The role of sponsorship in the marketing communication mix. *International Journal of Advertising*, 10(1), 35–47.

Plewa, C. and Quester, P. G. (2011). Sponsorship and CSR: Is there a link? A conceptual framework. *International Journal of Sports Marketing and Sponsorship*, 12(4), 301–17.

Smith, A. C. and Westerbeek, H. M. (2007). Sport as a vehicle for deploying corporate social responsibility. *Journal of Corporate Citizenship*, (25), 43–54.

RECOMMENDED WEBSITES

Albion in the Community (2016). Accessed 15 November 2016 from www.albioninthecommunity.org.uk/about-us/

American Express (2015). Accessed 15 June 2016 from http://about.americanexpress.com/csr/

BBC (2010). Brighton reveal sponsorship deal for new stadium, accessed 18 August from http://news.bbc.co.uk/sport1/hi/football/teams/b/brighton/8753418.stm

IEG (2014). 2014 recap: sponsorship spending by property type, accessed 18 August from www.sponsorship.com/iegsr/2014/12/22/2014-Recap--Sponsorship-Spending-By-Property-Type.aspx

CASE 18

IMPACTS OF AN INTERNATIONAL MOTORSPORT EVENT ON A SMALL CARIBBEAN ISLAND

CRISTINA JÖNSSON

LEARNING OUTCOMES

Upon completion of this case study, the reader should be able to:

- ■ analyse a motorsport event from a social and environmental impacts perspective;
- ■ evaluate social and environmental impacts of a motorsport event on residents living adjacent to motorsport racetracks;
- ■ formulate criteria for a socially valuable event.

OVERVIEW OF THE CASE

The year 2014 marked 25 years for the Barbados Rally Club's (BRC) blue riband all-stage event 'Rally Barbados'. This premier event has grown into the Caribbean's largest annual international motorsport event, held across two days on either the last weekend in May or the first weekend in June. Since the first overseas competitors took part in the International All-Stage Rally in the early 1990s, nearly thirty countries have been represented, including six from the wider Caribbean, with Jamaica and Trinidad and Tobago providing the best support. The biggest competitor base is from the UK, but the event has also attracted competitors from Australia, Canada, Japan, Kenya, South Africa and the United States, as well as mainland Europe.

This case study focuses on social and environmental impacts of the annual Sol Rally Barbados motorsport event on the local community. There is a growing concern about the impact of the rally on the residential areas located in the vicinity or directly situated within the event's stages. In order to gain a full picture of the perceived environmental impacts of the rally, the perceptions of local residents, spectators and the event organiser have been included in this case study.

CASE STUDY

There are environmentally conscious practices and policies in place for the Sol Rally Barbados, but there is a commonly held view among residents that much of it is done simply to meet the standard basic levels or as a civic duty. In the case of noise pollution, the Barbados Rally Club (BRC) has adopted a noise limit based on the rules set by the Fédération Internationale de l'Automobile (FIA). Although the FIA has rules in regard to carbon emissions for competition vehicles, there are no standards in place for carbon emission control in motorsport events in Barbados. This is due to the fact that there is a general lack of environmental policies on air pollution from vehicles in Barbados. As a result, carbon emission control standards are not applied to motorsport events in Barbados. Under competition rules, as they relate to noise pollution, an adopted noise limit of 108 decibels for competitive vehicles is in place, which is the standard set by the FIA. Also in place are rules governing the service areas where there is a zero-garbage policy and the protection of service areas by the mandate of appropriate ground cover.

There are no environmental guidelines in the BRC internal regulations; however, the BRC accepts its responsibility for impacts of the event and has rules and practices in place to ensure that some inherent externalities from hosting the event are controlled, especially in the areas of noise pollution and waste disposal, and to a lesser extent crowd control. The BRC does 'not believe that the residents should suffer from the spectator littering that occurs, furthermore we do not want the event to be seen as a burden on society … but we don't have full crowd control'.[1] The BRC and its governing committees are working to ensure the most prevalent externalities of the sport that affect the environment are policed. However, for those physical areas where the BRC believe they have no direct jurisdiction (some spectator vantage points along the stages), the responsibility is thrown on the spectators to be environmentally conscious. In cases where this is ignored, the BRC removes itself as the responsible party with the statement that it does not have full control over spectators and can only focus on areas that it has control over, such as service parks, special stages, scrutinising locations and other premises used for promotional activities.

Motorsport arouses human senses with the need for thrills, dangerous action and excitement. Some spectators at the Sol Rally Barbados (BRC, 2013) expressed the importance of the event's focus on the action: 'who cares about the environment? I came to see backfire and exhaust at the best vantage point so I don't care if the BRC had to cut down plants for us to get a good view of the rally.' Another participant said, 'Rally is noise, expect noise pollution'. But some spectators said that they have consideration for the environment surrounding the Rally area: 'I think about the environment when it comes to the duck pond and the ducks, and how people harm them and the fields nearby where produce are being grown.' Another spectator thought of his actions only as a means of securing the event's future by not irritating the residents and persons whom the rally directly affects: 'I try to respect people's

C. Jönsson

property to keep the area clean and safe to avoid future problems for the Rally.' 'I never thought of rally in that way [considering the environment]. I think it is about not littering and the drivers and rally club would have to focus on that [good environmental practices].' Even in the area of waste disposal practices, many participants believe that not enough provisions have been made by the organisers regarding infrastructure like waste bins and portable toilets.

Residents living in close proximity to the racetrack have little tolerance for the event and find that there is no respect for the environment. 'The tolerance for the event has deteriorated over the years ... in the beginning we were enthusiastic about the Rally being held in our area, but now it feels like it has been forced on us.' Noise pollution is the most prevalent negative impact on residential communities. Residents complain that the noise levels from both the cars and spectators are intolerable. In the case of one resident whose location is at the start of one of the rally's stages, he alluded to the noise generated by the cars as killing a vast number of his young chickens; as he is a farmer, this is cutting into his livelihood. Another participant with a newborn baby said the noise from the event was very disturbing and 'the baby was unable to sleep and I am not in a position to move location out of this residence to avoid the noise'. Some residents said, 'the unfortunate nature of motorsport is its noise level, but it has decreased throughout the years, so we are more tolerant'.

With regard to damage to the physical environs, residents are concerned about 'spectators trampling through our gardens and property, the cutting down of vegetation and the blatant disregard for the natural landscape'. One resident said, 'the organisers [BRC] cut down vegetation to set up tent areas ... on the event days marshals and officials use agriculturally ploughed land as a footpath to access certain areas ... they destroy our crops'. Another participant referred to a spectator who 'reversed his car into my hedge and just left without acknowledging the damage he did'. The general view of the residents is that both groups within the motorsport community (organisers and spectators) have negative impacts on the physical environment.

Air pollution is another impact of motorsports. While one participant was adamant that moving the rally away from residential locations was the way to alleviate such a problem, others were more practical in offering the view that the onus is also on those who will be affected to put measures in place to ensure that they protect their environment and themselves. Some residents admitted that, having lived in the rally event venue throughout the event's lifetime, the reduction in noise from the competition cars and in gas emissions was evident, something they believe has to do with the improvement in technology and the organisers' understanding of some environmental issues.

The main environmental concern of residents is that of waste disposal, especially with regard to garbage disposal. Garbage is left all over event areas. One participant in a rural area said, 'an adjacent sugar cane field was left like if it was the dump, people left cups and food containers all over the field and for those who showed a little more consciousness bagged the garbage but still left it in the cane field'. The common view held by the residents is the lack of proper provision for receptacles for garbage disposal and one participant was proactive in providing garbage bags for spectators to use during the event, which minimised the impact of garbage being left on their property. Another resident mentioned the spin-off from improper garbage disposal as causing a rodent problem. Some residents believe that the spectators are responsible for the negative impacts on the communities around the rally fields. Other residents 'blame the Rally Club as they promote the sport in the country areas, they need something in place to clean up after the event and to educate people of not trespassing and tolerance of noise and respect for a person's space'.

QUESTIONS

1. How can there be more collaboration among Rally Barbados stakeholders?
2. In what ways can the BRC reduce environmental impacts from Rally Barbados?
3. How can Rally Barbados become a more socially valuable event?

CONCLUSIONS

The BRC, rally spectators and residents discussed with the case writer whether or not the environmental impacts of Rally Barbados are the responsibility of the event organiser or the spectator. This situation could be used to implement policies that would benefit all parties. A spectator said, 'I try to respect people's property to keep the area clean and safe to avoid future problems for the Rally'. The organiser believes that it is the spectators' responsibility to play their part in minimising negative environmental impacts. A resident believes that the BRC needs to educate spectators about respecting residents' private spaces. What is your conclusion?

RECOMMENDED READING

Ritchie, B. W. and Adair, D. (eds) (2004). *Sport Tourism: Interrelationships, Impacts and Issues*, Channel View Publications, Buffalo.

This book examines the economic, social and environmental impacts and issues associated with the development of sport tourism globally, including the lack of research and coordination between industry and government. The book suggests the need for a more balanced analysis of the impacts and issues associated with future sport tourism development.

NOTE

1 Anonymous interview with Cristina Jönsson at The Barbados Rally Club, 9 March 2015.

BIBLIOGRAPHY

The Barbados Rally Club (2013). Welcome to Sol Rally Barbados! 2013. Accessed 4 April 2014 from www.rallybarbados.bb/.

Faulkner, B. and Tideswell, C. (1997). 'A framework for monitoring community impacts of Tourism. *Journal of Sustainable Tourism,* 5(1), 3–28.

Fredline, L. (2004). 'Host Community Reactions to Motorsport Events: The Perception of Impact on Quality of Life' in B. W. Ritchie and D. Adair (eds), *Sport Tourism: Interrelationships, Impacts and Issues,* Channel View Publications, Buffalo.

Gibson, H. (2005). Sport tourism: concepts and theories – an introduction. *Sport in Society,* 8(2), 133–41.

Totally Barbados/Brecal (2008). Motor sport in Barbados. Accessed 26 March 2014 from www.totallybarbados.com/barbados/Entertainment/Sports/Car_Racing_and_Motor_Sports/.

Tourism South East Research Unit (2004). Motorsport tourism cluster study. Accessed 10 March 2014 from www.sws.ci.austin.tx.us/sites/default/files/files/AustinGrandPrix/Motorsport-Tourism-FINAL-REPORT.pdf.

RECOMMENDED WEBSITES

Barbados Rally Club: http://barbadosrallyclub.com
Fédération Internationale de l'Automobile (FIA): www.fia.com/home
Sol Rally Barbados: www.rallybarbados.bb/

GUIDELINE ANSWERS

1. How can there be more collaboration among Rally Barbados stakeholders?
    Motorsport is a relationship-oriented industry because it provides a product-service in coordination with other stakeholders (e.g. tuning companies, sponsors, fans). These relationships are inherently human-focused, which is a plus for resource advantage because the stakeholders are able to provide more resources. Usually a resource-based view of the team allows for starting, developing and improving year by year its sustainability activities and operations. Stakeholders have their own social and environmental impacts and sustainability strategies. Including these groups in strategic social and environmental planning and tactics would offer not only a competitive advantage, but would also work to strengthen the already existing coordination between fans and sports organisations.

2. In what ways can the BRC reduce environmental impacts from Rally Barbados?
    Environmental impacts can be reduced by implementing strategies to minimise air and noise pollution. Greening motorsports might have a negative effect on the event itself and on the passionate following of fans. However, green racing uses motorsport competition to help to rapidly develop cleaner, more fuel-efficient vehicle propulsion systems that will eventually be used in consumer vehicles. Technologies initially developed for green racing cars can foster faster general

introduction of automotive technologies that reduce greenhouse gases and exhaust pollutants, and increase fuel economy. The high level of interest in motorsports could bring this technology to the attention of the public and accelerate its acceptance in the new market. The Green Racing Protocols can be adapted for any racing series. The protocols promote the development of energy-efficient technologies, and the reduction of greenhouse gases and auto emissions. They also encourage the use of renewable fuels and regenerative energy powertrains (hybrids). EPA, DOE and SAE International will also provide national awards and recognition to the auto companies that build the racing cars that go the fastest while using the least amount of energy and creating the fewest greenhouse gas emissions.

Elements of Racing Protocols are based on five principles:

1. the use of renewable fuels;
2. the use of many different engines, fuels and propulsion systems in one race;
3. the use of regenerative energy powertrain technologies that recover and reuse braking energy;
4. the use of energy allocations instead of detailed sporting regulations; and
5. the use of exhaust pollution control strategies and systems.

3. How can Rally Barbados become a more socially valuable event?

    The BRC can provide knowledge and subsequently empower people in the community to make informed decisions regarding the environment. Furthermore, lessons learned from Rally Barbados can result in an overall change in behaviour which could reduce the government's expenditure on resources, waste removal and skills training, resulting in an overall saving to Barbados in the long term. This reiterates the importance of seeing these events as investments and not expecting an immediate or even measurable return. As quantifying social impacts is extremely subjective and can be interpreted in a number of ways, the following are criteria that outline the overall social impacts:

    ■ Community involvement: opportunities for the community to participate in the event, either during the event or in the planning/preparation phases.
    ■ Interaction with other community members: create opportunities for people to interact with other community members to form and improve social ties and to promote a feeling of connectedness.
    ■ Sense of pride in community: give people the opportunity to feel pride in their community or surroundings from a cultural, historic or social perspective.
    ■ Recreational opportunities: provide recreational opportunities for local residents at all participation and skill levels.
    ■ Employment opportunities: provide employment opportunities for the local community, especially young people who may be looking for a part-time job. Providing this group with supplementary income will help to give them opportunities and increase their mobility.

- Opportunities to garner new skills: provide people with the opportunity to garner new skills either through working at the event or through participating in the event.
- Heritage preservation/interest in local heritage: through the event, increase knowledge and interest surrounding heritage in the area.
- Give community members the opportunity to volunteer their time to help organise and/or facilitate the event and subsequently learn new skills and improve social connections.

CASE 19

MK DONS FC AND AFC WIMBLEDON: MOVING THE GOALPOSTS AND RISING FROM THE ASHES

DAVID COOK AND CHRISTOS ANAGNOSTOPOULOS

LEARNING OUTCOMES

Upon completion of this case study, the reader should be able to:

■ define and highlight the features of franchising;
■ consider the cross-cultural perspectives on franchising and the resulting implications for management;
■ compare and contrast different ownership and governance models within professional sports teams and their impact upon stakeholders;
■ critically evaluate the value of the relationship between professional sports teams and their local communities.

OVERVIEW OF THE CASE

This case study provides an insight into a unique and unprecedented event in English professional football: the relocation of a major club to a completely different geographical area.

The ruling, in 2002, was hugely controversial, and effectively spawned two entirely new entities: MK Dons FC, who took the place of Wimbledon FC in the Football League and based themselves in Milton Keynes, 60 miles away from the original club; and AFC Wimbledon, a fan-owned 'phoenix' club which started again at the bottom of the football pyramid and is located near to Wimbledon FC's original home.

Despite their creation resulting from the same event, the two newly created clubs are notable for their contrasting ownership models and the reaction they have received from both the media and the wider football community in Great Britain.

CASE STUDY

Wimbledon FC (1889–2004)

Wimbledon FC had enjoyed an illustrious history as a team that had climbed from non-league level to the top division of English football, where they remained for 14 years. The highlight came in 1988 when they defeated Liverpool to win the FA Cup. This was followed by the quote from BBC commentator John Motson that 'the Crazy Gang have defeated the Culture Club', which helped to define Wimbledon's brand. Known as the 'Dons', they were the underdogs, and their brand associations were direct, uncompromising football with a 'loveable rogue' element that helped to endear them to fans and boost their brand profile as a prominent English football club.

Unfortunately, Wimbledon FC lacked a permanent 'home' venue following the closure of their Plough Lane ground in 1991. The ground was considered to be beyond redevelopment to meet the FA criteria for all-seater stadia following the Taylor Report. They subsequently rented Crystal Palace's Selhurst Park, which denied them crucial revenue streams and arguably limited the size of their fan base. Crucially, Wimbledon's then owner, Lebanese businessman Sam Hammam, decided to sell off Plough Lane and the club as separate assets. The ground was sold to a supermarket chain for £8 million, whilst the club fell into the hands of a Norwegian consortium who knew little about English football, attracted by an ultimately unsuccessful proposal of relocating it to Dublin. The Norwegian owners later came to regret their £28 million purchase, lamenting Wimbledon's lack of tangible assets and income-maximising opportunities, summarised by the new chairman Charles Koppel thus:

> We can't maximise the potential of hospitality, of advertising hoardings, of anything here. This club has to find a home of its own or it will die. Simple as that.
>
> (White, 2003)

In comparison, some other English football clubs during this period were enjoying an unprecedented branding boom, powered by Sky's coverage of the Premier League. Fellow London-based rivals such as Chelsea and Tottenham Hotspur were reaping the rewards of becoming far more market-orientated and employing brand extension tactics. These included Chelsea's building of a hotel and entertainment complex known as 'Chelsea Village'.

While the construction of a new stadium was deemed essential to secure the club's future, available land in Wimbledon and surrounding areas of London was scarce and its purchase regarded as financially unviable. Plans to relocate the club away from Wimbledon emerged, which seemed far-fetched, as relocation of a professional football club to a completely different town and borough had never previously happened in post-war English football.

However, with the club rapidly losing money and the owners desperate for a return on their investment, they were eager to take up an offer from music magnate and property developer Pete Winkleman to relocate to a new, purpose-built stadium in Milton Keynes, a rapidly growing and well-populated town without a professional football club but with a vast potential market of supporters.

In US sport, 'franchising' – moving the name and goodwill of a sports outfit to wherever it might be more profitably exploited – is commonplace, but has rarely proven successful in the UK. Recent US examples include:

- baseball (in 2005 the Montreal Expos moved to Washington DC to become the Washington Nationals);
- ice hockey (in 2011 the Atlanta Thrashers relocated to Winnipeg to form the Winnipeg Jets); and
- basketball (in 2012 the New Jersey Nets were transferred to Brooklyn, becoming the Brooklyn Nets).

In America, these franchises are viewed as being a form of entertainment, but their primary objective, as for any successful business, is to make money. Indeed, within American Major League Soccer (MLS) there has been a long history of franchising, with clubs historically disappearing from one location and then being reintroduced in another. Two more teams created an 'expansion' in 2015 – including New York City, which is part-owned by English Premier League giants Manchester City. In the future, global sporting icon David Beckham is set to launch what will become the twenty-second team in the MLS, based in Miami, on a so far undisclosed date. Unlike the British model of competitive league team sports, major US sports operate closed leagues where new teams appear based on market growth and profit potential, as opposed to success on the field of play.

In Britain, where football clubs have largely grown out of the communities where they are situated, the term 'franchising' was practically unheard of until Wimbledon FC was, highly controversially, granted permission by the English Football Association to relocate to Milton Keynes in May 2002.

AFC Wimbledon (2002–)

With the vast majority of original Wimbledon FC fans unwilling to travel to Milton Keynes and left feeling outraged about the 'theft' of their club, the supporters decided to found a new 'phoenix' club, AFC (A Fans Club) Wimbledon, in June 2002. Traditionally in football the acronym AFC stands for Athletic Football Club, but in this case the different meaning of AFC was important in defining from the outset the ethos of the club: 'by the fans, for the fans'.

Erik Samuelson, Chief Executive of AFC Wimbledon, stated that the brand value of his club had been built entirely on a straightforward sense of knowing what is

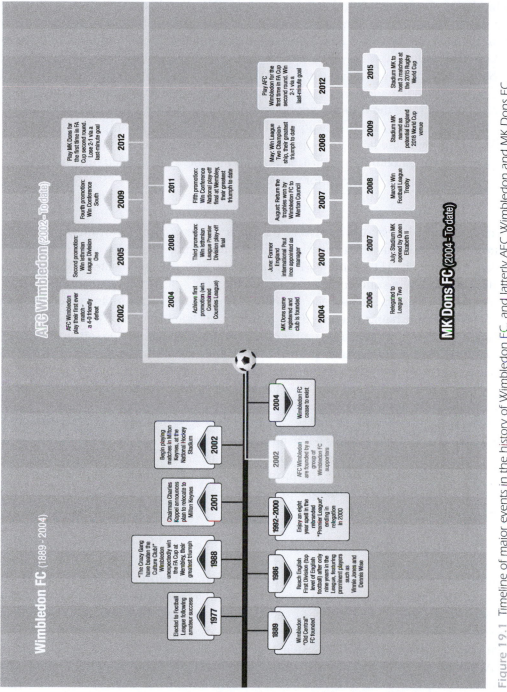

Figure 19.1 Timeline of major events in the history of Wimbledon FC, and latterly AFC Wimbledon and MK Dons FC

right and what is wrong: acknowledging the new club's historical links to the old Wimbledon FC (such as retaining the original 'Dons' nickname), but believing that the key to the success of the new venture has been the overall attempt to get away from the past and establish AFC Wimbledon as a new identity completely independent of Wimbledon FC.

Samuelson picks up the case of AFC Wimbledon's fortunes:

> We do not have the resources or finance to be able to afford specialist marketing staff and have up to this point relied completely on the help and support of volunteers. We have no tools to measure anything, but the fans genuinely are part of the club. We have 1,500–1,600 members who effectively own the club, paying £25 each year for one share.
>
> (Samuelson, 2009)

This fan ownership set-up, known as the Dons Trust, is a not-for-profit organisation committed to safeguarding the club's decision-making processes and community links. As a result, AFC Wimbledon is run democratically by elected officers, with each member having one vote.

The Dons Trust has also been beneficial from a marketing point of view, with AFC Wimbledon being perceived by many to be 'genuine' and 'straightforward', according to Samuelson. These brand characteristics have helped to attract financial backing right from the beginning of AFC Wimbledon's origins, such as a shirt sponsorship deal with computer games firm Sports Interactive. Miles Jacobson, managing director of Sports Interactive, appears to concur with Samuelson's comments regarding AFC Wimbledon's brand values:

> There are a lot of parallels between Sports Interactive and AFC Wimbledon, which is why we're so keen to support the team. AFC Wimbledon has shown that because of football the community will pull together at times like these – a sure sign this remains the people's game.
>
> (AFC Wimbledon, 2014)

The Dons Trust has been proactive in its efforts to re-establish the brand values and in many ways create a much stronger brand than the former Wimbledon FC possessed. For instance, the website is constantly updated with requests for volunteers to help out in many different ways, such as cleaning the stadium and taking minutes at general meetings. The club has even learned from its lack of residual income in the past, hosting revenue-generating events such as a regular comedy night at its currently owned home ground, Kingsmeadow.

Although in Britain supporter-governed football clubs are usually created as a result of a crisis situation, in German football this model is widespread. All but 2 of the 36 clubs in the Bundesliga and second tier are controlled by members, their

D. Cook, C. Anagnostopoulos

supporters, with at least 50 per cent plus one of votes required to take important decisions. This model has kept the clubs rooted within their communities and traditions, with average attendances in the Bundesliga being the highest of any league in Europe.

On the pitch, AFC Wimbledon has performed remarkably well, achieving five promotions during the first nine years of their existence. In May 2011 they beat Luton Town on penalties in the Conference Premier Play-Off final to reclaim the football league place they believe was 'stolen' from them amidst euphoric scenes at the City of Manchester Stadium. In the process they became the first club formed in the twenty-first century to qualify for the Football League, thus becoming the league's youngest club by a considerable margin.

A few months later, AFC Wimbledon found themselves playing their now bitter enemies, the newly evolved MK Dons, in the FA Cup second round. Widespread media coverage and national interest followed the event, with the focus on the attempts of both sets of supporters to lay claim to the historical achievements of Wimbledon FC and the 'Dons' nickname. MK Dons defender Dean Lewington was in the unique position of having started his career with the original Wimbledon FC, and staying with the club throughout its transition to MK Dons, where he still remains today. According to Lewington, neither of the two new clubs can rightfully lay claim to the origins and history of the original Wimbledon FC (Mail Online, 2013).

AFC Wimbledon eventually lost the tie 2–1 to an agonising late goal, with manager Neil Ardley commenting:

> This moment that our fans have dreaded has come and gone and it's turned into a celebration of how far this club has come. From the fans' point of view I don't think they will ever forget about the relocation, but it's a milestone for them that they've got this out of the way.
>
> (James, 2012)

In closing, Erik Samuelson offered his opinions as to the major reason why AFC Wimbledon has been so successful in establishing a thriving reputation based on a brand famous for its ethical and community-based values:

> Koppel [the former owner of Wimbledon FC] turned up unaware of the unique relationship between a club and its customers. These are not customers in the traditional sense, who will shop by price or convenience. Their affiliation with the organisation is much closer to a religious connection. It is a faith.
>
> (Samuelson, 2009)

MK Dons FC (2004–)

Whilst AFC Wimbledon re-formed, MK Dons were able to effectively start where the previous Wimbledon FC left off in terms of their position in the English football league in 2004. This angered supporters of many clubs across the country, some of whom even chose to visit AFC Wimbledon's ground rather than the MK Dons when their team were due to be playing an away match at MK Dons' ground, Stadium MK. The club were dubbed 'Franchise FC' by certain sections of the British media, portraying the concept of franchising in a negative light. The club is 100 per cent owned by the holding company InterMK Group Ltd, which in turn is wholly owned by Winkleman.

The team initially played in a temporary venue, the National Hockey Stadium, and was relegated from League One to League Two in an early period of instability. However, since moving into its new stadium in 2007, the club has not looked back, both on and off the pitch.

The club won its first trophies in the 2007–2008 season, lifting the League Two Championship and thus gaining immediate promotion back into League One, and also winning the Johnstone's Paint Trophy, a notable knockout competition for football league teams.

The MK Dons brand has certainly begun to grow and gather momentum. Stadium MK was officially opened by Queen Elizabeth II and this royal endorsement immediately put the club and its new stadium into the spotlight with a mass of free publicity. In stark contrast to the former Wimbledon FC, brand extension strategies and diversification are arguably the hallmarks of the MK Dons brand.

The MK Dons brand is developing at a fast pace, as demonstrated by the steady rise in matchday attendances. These have more than doubled from an average of below 5,000 supporters in 2004 to over 10,000 ten years later. The club has a sophisticated customer relationship management (CRM) and database system which allows extensive analysis and measurement of sales and loyalty trends. This affords MK Dons a competitive advantage over many rivals at this level of football. Like many other clubs, MK Dons believe targeting young supporters is essential, and a spokesperson from the club lays claim to another impressive statistic:

> We focus on capturing the attention of junior supporters, with research showing that football fans choose their teams by the age of 8. To encourage this, under 7s enter the stadium free. At present, 32 per cent of our season ticket holders are under the age of 16, which is, we believe, the highest in the country.
>
> (Gardner, 2009)

Combined with this impressive targeting and measurement of young supporters, there is another major factor which could contribute to the future success of the club. In Milton Keynes, MK Dons are the only football club occupying such a large catchment area without direct competition from another league club. Other large urban settlements without a league club, such as Dudley, Poole and Slough, may make for an interesting proposition.

MK Dons embrace a strategy designed to alleviate the 'distance' that appears to have been created between supporters and several clubs at the top of English football. Their philosophy is that supporting a Premier League team has almost become an armchair activity, with fans still following their clubs but without attending matches.

Rather than feel dwarfed by the clubs of the Premier League, MK Dons appear to view being able to provide an authentic matchday experience at a reasonable price as a key form of competitive advantage over clubs in the Premier League.

The future looks bright for the emerging franchise of MK Dons. Stadium MK was named on a prestigious list of 15 stadia put forward by the Football Association as potential hosts of England's ultimately unsuccessful 2018 World Cup Finals bid, but the venue will host three matches in the 2015 Rugby Union World Cup. The latest company accounts show an annual turnover of £34 million with a profit of almost £2 million.

With an improving playing squad, a state-of the-art stadium with vast income-generating potential and the combined factors of having one of the youngest supporter bases in the country and a growing catchment area, the club will surely only prosper further in years to come.

QUESTIONS

1. What is franchising and what are its characteristics?
2. What lessons about ownership structures does the case reveal to the following stakeholders: (a) regulatory bodies such as the FA and Football League; (b) official sponsors such as Sports Interactive; (c) supporters of AFC Wimbledon; and (d) supporters of MK Dons FC?
3. From the perspective of a fan of a Bundesliga club, how might they react to David Beckham creating a franchised club in Germany?
4. Wimbledon FC's relocation to Milton Keynes was neither legal nor ethical. Discuss.

CONCLUSIONS

AFC Wimbledon was formed by the Dons Trust as a supporter-owned club with a similar governance model to the majority of teams in the German Bundesliga. The Trust concerns itself with safeguarding the club's decision-making and community associations, and in turn this has helped the club's brand to become set at the heart of its local community.

MK Dons set a precedent by becoming the first English club to be set up based on the franchising model prevalent in America, and have enjoyed some early success in their brief existence to date. Could such a model establish itself in England and other major European leagues? History, tradition and cultural forces all suggest not. But enough money over a long enough time frame can often overcome most hurdles. Do the US owners who bought Manchester United, Arsenal and Liverpool have a long-term aim to replicate the US franchise model on a global scale?

RECOMMENDED READING

To begin with, students might find it helpful to read an introductory text on marketing in sport, particularly sections on community identity and fan loyalty, such as *The Marketing of Sport* by Chadwick and Beech (2007), *Team Sports Marketing* by Wakefield (2007) or *Sport Marketing* by Blakey (2011).

Shropshire's text on sports franchising (1995) offers students an insight into cities in pursuit of sports franchises in the USA, and Rupert Cornwell's 2011 article in *The Independent* on the US Franchise system also provides a useful insight into how the concept of franchising may work in England.

BIBLIOGRAPHY

Beech, J. and Chadwick, S. (2007). *The Marketing of Sport*. Prentice Hall, London.
Blakey, P. (2011). *Sport Marketing*, Learning Matters, Exeter.
Gardner, A. (2009). Personal communication with lead author, 15 July.
James, A. (2012). We are Wimbledon! Fans stake claim for 'real Dons' tag during FA Cup grudge match. *Daily Mail* (online) 2 December. Available from www.dailymail.co.uk/sport/football/article-2241784/AFC-Wimbledon-v-MK-Dons--fans-clash.html (accessed 16 March 2014).
Samuelson, E. (2009). Personal communication with lead author, 29 June.
Shropshire, K. L. (1995). *The Sports Franchise Game: Cities in Pursuit of Sports Franchises, Events, Stadiums, and Arenas*. University of Pennsylvania Press, Philadelphia.
Wakefield, K. L. (2007). *Team Sports Marketing*. Elsevier, Oxford.
White, J. (2003). Pitch battle. *The Guardian* (online) 11 January. Available from www.guardian.co.uk/football/2003/jan/11/clubsincrisis.sport (accessed 16 March 2014).

RECOMMENDED WEBSITES

AFC Wimbledon (2014). Official Website, last accessed 16 March 2014 at www.afcwimbledon.co.uk/
BBC (2007). The Queen visits Milton Keynes, last accessed 16 March 2014 at www.bbc.co.uk/threecounties/content/articles/2007/11/30/queen_mk_2007_feature.shtml
BBC (2009). From Crazy Gang to Culture Club, last accessed 16 March 2014 at http://news.bbc.co.uk/sport1/hi/football/eng_conf/8018155.stm

BBC (2014). David Beckham 'living a dream' with MLS franchise in Miami, last accessed 16 March 2014 at www.bbc.co.uk/sport/0/football/26054220

Dons Trust (2014). Official Website, last accessed 30 September 2016 at http://thedonstrust.org/

The Guardian (2012). German model bangs the drum for club, country and the people's game, last accessed 16 March 2014 at www.theguardian.com/football/david-conn-inside-sport-blog/2012/dec/01/german-fan-owned-clubs-bundesliga

The Independent (2011). The US Franchise System ... coming to a league near you? Last accessed 18 March 2014 at www.independent.co.uk/sport/football/news-and-comment/the-us-franchise-systemcoming-to-a-league-near-you-2374155.html

Mail Online (2012). We are Wimbledon! Fans stake claim for 'real Dons' tag during FA Cup grudge match, accessed 16 March 2014 at www.dailymail.co.uk/sport/football/article-2241784/AFC-Wimbledon-v-MK-Dons--fans-clash.html

Mail Online (2013). Dean Lewington: My dad can't wait to assist in Brazil ... but I'm worrying about his hair! And who should claim Wimbledon's 1988 FA Cup win? Nobody, last accessed 16 March 2014 at www.dailymail.co.uk/sport/football/article-2518909/The-Footballers-Football-Column--Dean-Lewington-Im-worrying-dad-Rays-hair-Brazil-Wimbeldon-claim-FA-Cup.html

CASE 20

HOW TO SPEND 20 YEARS FILLING UP THE STADIUM, AND THEN LOSE FANS IN 4 YEARS

ALEXEY KIRICHEK

LEARNING OUTCOMES

Upon completion of this case study, the reader should be able to:

- compare and evaluate different approaches to fan engagement strategies in a professional sports club;
- write and examine their own opinion on processes and relations in club management, and evaluate the club's management organization chart;
- contrast and criticize different approaches to fan relations and pricing strategies used by different management teams;
- identify the pros and cons of different management styles and relations between stakeholders.

OVERVIEW OF THE CASE

This case study tells the story of the development of a professional football club in a post-USSR landscape, covering the stage to sport success and increasing wealth based on own financial income streams, for 20 years, and the crucial fall in fan relations in just 5 years. This case study is about relations within the top management of one of the most prosperous clubs in Russia and their dependence on the government as a shareholder. The development of FC Lokomotiv during these 25 years reflects the breadth and depth of stakeholders within the football club.

The focus of the case study is also to present the complexity and long-term nature of the development of fan engagement. The case study also includes an account of different pricing strategies used by the football club during the ups and downs of its sport path.

When the deeds of high resolve began (1922–1991)[1]

The word Lokomotiv was a suffix used by railway clubs – Kazanka (Moscow–Kazan railway) established in 1922; the October Revolution Club (KOR) that was playing during the period 1923–1930; and then again Kazanka (Moscow–Kazan railway) playing during the period 1931–1935. In fact, the Lokomotiv fan community celebrates the team's birthday twice every year, since 12 August is close to the Day of the Railway Worker, which is celebrated on the first Sunday in August.

Football championships in the Soviet Union were founded on 22 May 1936, and the 'railway' team ranked fifth at the end of that season. In 1936 they won the first trophy – the first Soviet Cup within the USSR.

The second half of the 1950s saw Lokomotiv's strongest line-up during the whole Soviet period of its history. To a large extent, the team was promoted by Boris Beshchev, the Railway Minister, who had been appointed to this position in 1948. In 1953 he brought to the team Boris Arkadyev, the then famous Soviet coach, the six-times champion of the USSR with other Moscow teams Dinamo and CDCA.[2] He gradually began to build the team that went on to win the second Soviet Cup of the USSR in 1957. During the final match, the 'railway' team beat Spartak Moscow thanks to the goal scored by Valery Bubukin, the team captain. The same year, the 'railway' team was ranked fourth in the League of the Soviet Union, scoring the same number of goals and having the same goal difference as Spartak, the bronze medal winner. The long-awaited medal was finally won in 1959; it was the silver medal in the championship of the Soviet Union

During the 1970s and 1980s, the team was moving between the two leagues. At that time, the team had a lot of talented football players, who then became well-known coaches, such as Yuri Semin, Valeri Gazzayev, Givi Nodiya, Valeri Petrakov, Vitali Shevchenko, and so on.

A new era of the club began when Yuri Semin became head coach in 1986. Lokomotiv's results improved considerably: after seven years in the First League, in 1988 the Club returned to the Top League of the USSR, and in 1990 played in the finals of the Soviet Cup of the USSR, where it lost to Dinamo Kiev, a much stronger opponent in those days, with a catastrophic score of 1:6.

Nevertheless, throughout the Soviet period the club was always the 'fifth wheel' in the 'cart' of Moscow football. While matches of the other Moscow clubs CSKA, Spartak, Dinamo and Torpedo were attended by thousands of fans, just a few hundred came to FC Lokomotiv games during the championships of the USSR.

The new era begins in Russia (1991–2006)

As the system of the USSR contests collapsed, and the economy turned into a market forces model, Lokomotiv entered the new age, which became its most successful period and lasted until Yuri Semin left the club in 2005. The club was firmly established among the domestic football elite, and achieved excellent results in the domestic championship and in international games. An important contribution to this was its stable management: from 1992 to 2006 the president of the club was Valeri Nikolayevich Filatov, and there was a partnership of coaches – Yuri Semin (head coach) and Vladimir Eshtrekov, who worked there until they were summoned to the national team in 2005.

It was after the appearance of this coaching partnership and with the direct involvement of President Filatov that the new era of the club began. During that period the club was at its most successful: it became the champion of Russia twice, won the Russian Cup four times and the Russian Super Cup twice, and was a multiple prize-winner in the Football Championship of Russia.

The team played many times, and at a highly professional level, in European club matches. In particular, in 1998 and 1999 the team reached semi-final games of the Cup Winners' Cup twice in succession. Note that in 1999 Lokomotiv lost to Rome's Lazio only because of a missed goal in a domestic game. During 2001–2004, Lokomotiv participated in the main round of the Champions League and reached the group stage twice. During the 2003/2004 league season, with a confident victory – 3:0 – over FC Inter, as the group leader Lokomotiv was recognized by UEFA as the best team of the third round in the Champions League.

Thanks to the club's achievements and the efforts of the management, attendance at matches grew. The club's long-time supporters remember that in the mid-1990s there were 200–300 people at the stadium, and that the voice of every person could be heard. But with the club's success, its army of fans increased. So by 2002 Lokomotiv matches were attended by over 6,000 people who came regularly to the club's games in the Football Championship of Russia. The club was actually the first in Russia to carry out dedicated efforts to attract fans to its stadium, or to use the current phraseology, to launch fan engagement programmes. The emphasis was laid upon the work with senior pupils, and college and university students, who became the backbone of the club's fan sector (the 'curve'). Gradually, the middle-class Muscovites began coming to the stadium, in the same way that female fans had already become an indispensable attribute in the stadium. Many fans of other clubs joined the team, for example, fans of Dmitry Sychev, who followed him when he was transferred from Spartak to Lokomotiv.

In 2002 Lokomotiv was the first Moscow club to obtain its 'home' – a new ultra-modern stadium with a seating capacity of 28,800. And the number of fans started increasing at a much higher rate, including VIP fans thanks to the introduction of hospitality boxes and other VIP seats available at the stadium.

The changes begin (2006–2010)

Lokomotiv's head coach Yuri Semin, with whom the team had achieved its best results, became the head coach of the national team of Russia in April 2005. At the end of 2005 he quit that position and hoped to return to Lokomotiv. However, club president Valeri Filatov, for a variety of reasons, decided he no longer wanted Yuri Semin around, and began looking for a new coach.

At the same time, OJSC Russian Railways, as the main shareholder and the primary sponsor of the club, decided to increase the efficiency of funds they gave to Club, including audit and control of these funds. They also asked to increase the level of money the Club takes for sport facilities from rent. Vladimir Yakunin, president of OJSC Russian Railways, probably did not want to dismiss Valeri Filatov immediately, since he, together with Semin, had contributed to the tournament successes of the club; so he appointed Sergei Lipatov as the club's chairman. Lipatov was the energetic, determined and successful president of TransTeleCom, an affiliate of OJSC Russian Railways. Lipatov was granted carte blanche to make any changes he felt necessary. He said he needed some time to ensure success of the club, just as he had done with all his previous projects.

Lipatov backed the initiative of club president Valeri Filatov, and the club appointed a foreign coach, Slavoljub Muslin, instead of reinstating Yuri Semin. At the same time, Lipatov provided extra funding from TransTeleCom. This funding enabled the club to settle its debts and to arrange a transfer campaign in the winter of 2006, since it was clear that the winning team of 2002 and 2004 had reached its peak and now needed some fresh blood, some new players.

The club made a bad start in the 2006 Championship; however, after 25 rounds out of 30 the team was ranked second and stood a good chance of becoming Champions of Russia. However, President Filatov was concerned about the team's failure in the UEFA Cup, and about a potential drop in their placement at the end of the season, so he decided to change the coach. Lipatov did not object to this decision. At the end of the season, the team was ranked third in the Championship. Since President Filatov had not achieved the target of reaching the first or second rank in the Championship, he resigned and Lipatov received carte blanche to direct the club in the 2007 season. He proposed Anatoli Byshovets as head coach. In order to unite the fans after the resignation of Valeri Filatov, who was an icon for them, he suggested appointing Yuri Semin as the president of the club. Lipatov believed that the return of Semin would help him to strengthen the updated club and consolidate the fan base.

In order to introduce changes to the club and to build it along the lines of professional English clubs, Lipatov began appointing to key positions professionals from other businesses who were oriented to the development of the club's commercial strategy. However, he did not take into account that there were some people in the club who were personal friends of Yuri Semin. All that, naturally, rendered the club more and more unmanageable; everyone was struggling to survive, and as the new president, Semin turned out to be much more than a figurehead.

In May 2007 the team won its fifth Russian Cup and started gaining momentum in the Championship of Russia too. At the same time, President Yuri Semin, who was committed to the team winning, and who still remained as a coach in his heart, saw himself as the Head Coach of Lokomotiv, too. Semin still had a certain influence among the players of the 2004 team, who now formed the backbone of the current team, and it is likely, although never proven, that he began to compete against the head coach, whose nature was always to search maniacally for enemies around him. Naturally, this situation had a negative impact on the whole team and its performance.

After Lokomotiv lost five games in a row, in July 2007 Lipatov, who understood his personal responsibility towards Vladimir Yakunin, president of OJSC Russian Railways, began investigating the reasons for the team's failure. He became more and more involved in team intrigues, started sending the team for various medical tests and hired new people (doctors, PT coaches, scouts). At the same time, he began losing the information war in the mass media and among the fans, who had been supporting Yuri Semin on the basis of his previous successful work as head coach of Lokomotiv.

As a result, the players, who saw the things that were happening around the team, became less professional in their training, and divided into groups. The fans (the 'curve'), who had supported Yuri Semin ever since he had been head coach, in their turn introduced an additional element of extremism during matches. They openly opposed the current head coach, which behaviour naturally affected the psychological climate in the team.

At the end of 2007 the team was only seventh in the championship. Both Yuri Semin and Anatoli Byshovets were dismissed immediately. Then Vladimir Yakunin invited his old contact, Nikolai Naumov, to become the president of the club. Naumov's main task was supervising the economic operations of the club and helping Lipatov. However, in fact this appointment was a warning to Lipatov from the president of OJSC Russian Railways: Lipatov's activities were under Yakunin's control now.

FC Lokomotiv invited the young Rashid Rakhimov, who was seen as having potential, to become head coach. Rakhimov was Lipatov's creature, and Naumov silently supported this decision. The mass media also backed Rakhimov. The club signed a 3-year contract with Rakhimov and granted him carte blanche to buy players. The players acquired by Rakhimov were not of higher calibre than those procured by the club in the past. However, the coach trusted these players and selected them to play in the team. From the point of view of sporting achievements, there were no improvements in the team during the 2007 season; there were a number of losses after some victories, even though Rakhimov had got everything he asked for to improve the team.

In their turn, the club fans throughout the season blamed Lipatov for all the failures, hung various banners and chanted obscenities addressed to him, and also demanded the return of Yuri Semin to the club as head coach. For his part, President Naumov worked with the fans in order to neutralize the negative effect of their actions, which he realized would in any case affect the team.

As a result, at the end of the 2008 season Lokomotiv again finished seventh in the championship. The club believed the failure in 2008 was due to the young age of the coach and that he needed time to build the team. Vladimir Yakunin supported this idea; he also supported Lipatov and Naumov and agreed that they would keep their positions. Yakunin gave them one last chance to improve the club's performance. At the same time, the global financial crisis began; it affected OJSC Russian Railways, which made the club optimize its financial situation, although it confirmed that the club would still be funded. And President Naumov took that chance to get rid of the people appointed by Lipatov, explaining the lay-off by the need to reduce administrative costs. Lipatov silently agreed, and this was really a signal that the power in the club had passed to Naumov from Lipatov.

At the same time, starting in 2009, the club began efforts to attract different kinds of fans considered to be beneficial from a long-term perspective:

- families, who have a higher buying power and who can spend more money to meet the needs of their children. It is important for families to spend their leisure time together and to obtain the live and unique experiences that only a football game can give, rather than those obtained from theatre, cinema or any other entertainment.
- schoolchildren, who must gradually replenish the fan army of the club in the 'curve'; in the future, they will go to different stands in the stadium with new price levels of tickets.
- VIP fans, whose presence would allow the club to earn more money without having to attract a large number of ordinary fans. In addition, VIP fans value this status, and the atmosphere of communication and self-satisfaction from sitting in VIP seats, more than the results of a match. The cost of one season ticket for VIP fans was 80,000 roubles (about €2,000). This price was equal to 50 fan tickets, so was an efficient way to raise revenue.

The formation of this new fan base was the long-term strategy of President Naumov and his staff. They understood that if they created nothing new, and kept losing fans because they were unhappy with the team's performance, they might lose the audience for the games, which would result in the loss of some revenues from the commercial sponsors not related to Russian Railways and from TV broadcasting. The club launched its own customer relationship management (CRM) system for working with the fans. The fans were offered a programme of stadium tours, which included the chance to visit the team's locker rooms 1.5 hours before the match(!). The club also began developing its own system of merchandizing, opening outlets close to customers in the centre of Moscow.

Before the 2009 season Rakhimov got all he wanted from the training process, but he failed to build the team. After seven matches (the team was ranked 12 out of 16), President Naumov spoke with Vladimir Yakunin and then dismissed Rakhimov.

The position of acting head coach was taken by Vladimir Maminov, a former player for the club, whose whole sports career was connected with Lokomotiv. He and the team gained 13 points out of a potential 15, and the fans were very happy, both with the team and with the fact that the management had appointed one of their 'icons'. At the same time, Nikolai Naumov started secret discussions with Yuri Semin concerning his return as head coach of Lokomotiv.

Meanwhile, Vladimir Yakunin decided to strengthen the role of the board of directors in the management of Lokomotiv and proposed new candidates as members of the board, including some top executives from OJSC Russian Railways and a number of independent candidates whose opinion he respected. In June 2009 Yuri Semin was appointed as head coach and also promoted to the board of directors. Vadim Morozov, first vice president of OJSC Russian Railways, became chairman of the board of directors, while Sergei Lipatov became an ordinary member of the board of directors.

At the end of the 2009 season the team was ranked fourth in the Championship of Russia, although it had stood a good chance of becoming a prize-winner. What is more, the team was allowed to participate in the European club competitions, which improved its brand, attracted new sponsors, increased the value of the players and, naturally, aroused the interest of the fans.

The fans again believed this success had been brought about by their icon, Yuri Semin. Lokomotiv had new hopes entering the 2010 season!

The new era: 'die'[3] Lokomotiv, or the beginning of the fall (2010 – today)

After 11 matches in the 2010 season, the club was ranked 8 among 16 teams and 9 points behind the leaders of the championship. The fans still believed in Semin, who asked for new players.

Meanwhile, the atmosphere among the board of directors hampered the normal development of the club. The new board members were very serious people, and they had serious ambitions regarding the management of the club, particularly in relation to sports results and transfer issues. Semin had some influence with certain members of the board of directors, who, in turn, did not like the partial independence of the president, who had been granted carte blanche by Yakunin. Semin was playing his own game within and around the board of directors – in fact, playing against Naumov. There was a general feeling that some changes would be made in the club.

And on 29 July 2010 the club saw these changes. Olga Smorodskaya, who had once worked in the CSKA[4] Sport Club, became the new president of the club and took over from Nikolai Naumov. Three months after her arrival, all the top managers of Naumov's team left the club. From the very beginning Smorodskaya did not get along with head coach Yuri Semin, because she thought she was a real expert in the sports component of the game. Gradually, controversy grew with the fans, too; they openly supported Semin and began acting against the new president.

At the end of 2010 Smorodskaya convinced all the members of the board of directors and Yakunin that the club did not need Yuri Semin for its further development. At the time of his dismissal, Semin said what has since become a catchphrase: 'I have no conflict with Olga Yuryevna. She has a conflict with football.' In fact, the logic of this event had been predetermined as early as in the middle of 2009, when Yuri Semin returned to Lokomotiv.

After half a year at Lokomotiv, in February 2011, Olga Smorodskaya said that the club 'needs to dramatically increase attendance, and we [the management] set ourselves ambitious goals – to raise it by 2–3 times. We are studying foreign experience, and have tried to adjust the ticket program for a specific buyer.' (www.fclm.ru/ru/publications/smi/7749).

During four years as the head of the club, Olga Smorodskaya appointed six different coaches. Reasons for their dismissals were very varied, and sometimes illogical – as, for example, in the case of head coach Yuri Krasnozhan. He had breathed new life into the team (and the team was ranked high in the tournament table at the time of his dismissal), but he was fired 'for certain omissions in his work'.

During 2011–2014 the Club saw both serious failures, as, for example, ninth place in the Russian Championship at the end of the 2012/2013 season (the worst result in the history of the Club), as well as successes. For example, the club won the bronze medal in the 2013/2014 season due, among other things, to head coach Leonid Kuchuk, who had been appointed before the 2013/2014 season. But the most important issue was that the club kept losing its main asset – the fans – relations with whom were getting worse.

QUESTIONS

1. Analyse the club's work with the fans during 1992–2014. Use the case study data to substantiate your conclusions; if necessary, use additional sources, specifying the source.[5]
2. Evaluate the ticketing programme of the club and attendance indicators; analyse the trends and changes, and to what extent these changes have matched the events described in the case study.
3. Evaluate and estimate potential attendance at the club's games by 2020, keeping in mind the World Cup 2018 in Russia, in relation to this case study and the sensitivity of fans to the sporting results of Lokomotiv. What changes can you suggest for club management to implement?
4. Analyse from different marketing perspectives why the level of decrease in attendance was higher or lower than the level of increase. When did the decrease in attendance actually start?
5. Produce a stakeholder map of Lokomotiv for the beginning of the 2000s and for the 2014 situation.

CONCLUSIONS

All through her years in the club, the fans openly expressed their discontent with Olga Smorodskaya and the decisions she took; to a large extent, such discontent was caused by Smorodskaya herself. In particular, at the meeting with the fans before the beginning of the 2011 season, she used the club scarf to wipe drops of water from the table in plain view of all the fans, which they viewed as disrespect to the club brand. During the 2012/2013 season, in response to the continuing insinuations of the fans against her, she prohibited selling tickets to the 'curve' for two domestic games (only holders of season tickets could attend the match). This dubious measure was also applied before the game against the club's most important opponent, Moscow CSKA, a match that a lot of club fans always attend.

But the worst of it was that, while losing one base of fans by preventing them from coming to the stadium, she did not do anything to encourage new fans to attend the games of FC Lokomotiv – fans who would come to the game for different reasons, and who would not comment openly about the performance of the team and the actions of its management.

After the successful 2013/2014 season, the prices of regular and season tickets for the 2014/2015 season were increased considerably – which caused the demand for season tickets to drop. No explanation for this measure has been found so far.

Unfortunately, attendance at FC Lokomotiv games in the 2014/2015 season dropped to between 3,000 and 7,000 people.[6] The following factors were the reasons for such a drop after the team's success in the Championship of Russia during 2013/2014: the new ticket prices, which rose significantly at the beginning of the season; the ongoing conflict between the fans and the club management; the lack of interest shown by the management in attracting fans and increasing the revenue base; the lack or inefficiency of marketing tools for attraction of fans to the stadium; and communication with the club.

Attendance at club games – when it has taken so long to create, grow and attract new fans, and having built a home for them by opening a new stadium in 2002 (the first club of the Premier League to do so) – has actually been decreasing since 2010.

ADDENDUM 1

Game attendance

In order to illustrate the work with fans, a number of indicators should be considered. The first is sales of season tickets. This is the key indicator showing the loyalty of the fans to the club, since they are bought only by the fans who are devoted to the club. The higher the sales of season tickets, the higher is the level of confidence in the club, the team and the management. In 2006 the club sold 2,779 season tickets, and with growth every year it reached maximum of 5,885 season tickets in 2010.

A. Kirichek

Tickets for the 2011 season were sold by the team of President Olga Smorodskaya, and sales dropped by 10 per cent.

Second, attention should be paid to game attendance; note that this is the average game attendance, taking into consideration fans of the opposing team. This factor should be taken into consideration during any analysis, especially in view of the fact that at certain matches, such as those with CSKA and Spartak, there may be more fans from these teams than Lokomotiv fans. And the more games there are with these teams, as during the 2011/2012 season, the higher is the average attendance. It is also necessary to note that the attendance statistics include (a) all season ticket holders, (b) owners of sky-boxes and (c) different types of invitations issued through the ticketing system, even if all of these people do not actually attend the match.

Figure 20.1 shows the official statistics of average attendance at club games in the Russian Premier Football League (RFPL).

What is the reason for decreasing attendance? Could it be the fact that the 'honeymoon effect' after the commissioning of FC Locomotiv's new stadium is over, and in the near future the number of fans will simply return to the figures seen in 2002–2003?

Both the fans of FC Lokomotiv and experts may note that, during 2002–2014, most fans have been members of the fan community based in the 'Southern Stands'

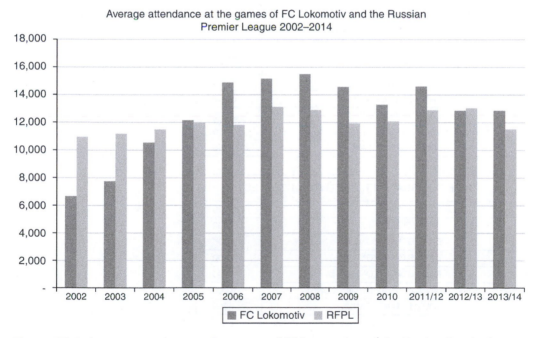

Figure 20.1 Average attendance at the games of FC Locomotiv and the Russian Premier League 2002–2014

(total capacity 6,000 people) of the Lokomotiv Stadium, which was full at almost every game during 2004–2010, especially at top-level matches. The average age of these fans ranges from 15 to 22 years, and it has not changed since FC Lokomotiv started playing at the new stadium. As a result, one may presume that if over the last 10 years even 50 per cent of the fans attending the 'curve' of the stadium during 2004–2006 had moved to any other stands due to changes in their age and social status, the occupation ratio of the stadium would have been as high as 70–75 per cent of its capacity.

ADDENDUM 2

Table 20.1 Price for season tickets to FC Lokomotiv matches, roubles

PRICE FOR SEASON TICKETS 2005, ROUBLES	
VIP	110,000
VIP ZONE 1	30,000
EAST STAND, ZONE 8	6,000
EAST STAND, ZONE 7	4,000
EAST STAND, ZONE 6	2,500
WEST STAND, ZONE 22 (FAMILY ZONE)	3,500
SOUTH STAND (FANS)	1,000

PRICE FOR SEASON TICKETS 2006, ROUBLES	
VIP	120,000
VIP ZONE 1	35,000
EAST STAND, ZONE 8	7,000
EAST STAND, ZONE 7	5,000
EAST STAND, ZONE 6	3,000
WEST STAND, ZONE 22 (FAMILY ZONE)	3,000
SOUTH STAND (FANS)	1,250

PRICE FOR SEASON TICKETS 2007, ROUBLES	
VIP	120,000
VIP ZONE 1	35,000
EAST STAND, ZONE 8	7,500
EAST STAND, ZONE 7	5,500
EAST STAND, ZONE 6	3,500
WEST STAND, ZONE 22 (FAMILY ZONE)	3,000
SOUTH STAND (FANS)	1,300

PRICE FOR SEASON TICKETS 2008, ROUBLES	
VIP	80,000
VIP ZONE 1	30,000
EAST STAND, ZONE 8	7,000
EAST STAND, ZONE 7	5,000
EAST STAND, ZONE 6	3,000
WEST STAND, ZONE 22 (FAMILY ZONE)	3,000
SOUTH STAND (FANS)	1,400

PRICE FOR SEASON TICKETS 2009, ROUBLES	
VIP (DIAMOND CLUB)	80,000
VIP ZONE 1	30,000
EAST STAND, ZONE 8	7,000
EAST STAND, ZONE 7	5,000
EAST STAND, ZONE 6	3,000
WEST STAND, ZONE 22 (FAMILY ZONE)	4,000
SOUTH STAND (FANS)	1,500

PRICE FOR SEASON TICKETS 2012/2013, ROUBLES	
VIP (DIAMOND CLUB)	80,000
VIP ZONE 1	20,000
EAST STAND, ZONE 8	7,000
EAST STAND, ZONE 7	5,000
EAST STAND, ZONE 6	4,000
VIP ZONE 2 (FAMILY ZONE)	8,000
SOUTH STAND (FANS)	1,700

PRICE FOR SEASON TICKETS 2013/2014, ROUBLES	
VIP (DIAMOND CLUB)	90,000
VIP ZONE 1	25,000
EAST STAND, ZONE 8	8,000
EAST STAND, ZONE 7	6,000
EAST STAND, ZONE 6	5,000
VIP ZONE 2 (FAMILY ZONE)	8,000
SOUTH STAND (FANS)	2,500

PRICE FOR SEASON TICKETS 2014/2015, ROUBLES	
VIP (DIAMOND CLUB)	120,000
VIP ZONE 1	45,000
EAST STAND, ZONE 8	15,000
EAST STAND, ZONE 7	12,000
EAST STAND, ZONE 6	10,000
VIP ZONE 2 (FAMILY ZONE)	15,000
SOUTH STAND (FANS)	4,000

ADDENDUM 3

Table 20.2 Price for matchday tickets to FC Lokomotiv matches, roubles

DAY TICKETS. SEASON 2005, ROUBLES			
	1 CATEGORY	2 CATEGORY	3 CATEGORY
VIP	7,000	5,500	4,000
VIP ZONE 1	2,500	2,000	1,500
WEST STAND (ZONE 19,20)	800	650	500
WEST STAND (ZONE 18,21)	600	450	300
WEST STAND (ZONE 17,22)	400	250	200
EAST STAND (ZONE 8,9)	650	500	350
EAST STAND (ZONE 7,10)	450	350	250
EAST STAND (ZONE 6,11)	250	200	150
SOUTH STAND (FANS)	150	100	80

DAY TICKETS. SEASON 2006, ROUBLES			
	1 CATEGORY	2 CATEGORY	3 CATEGORY
VIP	9,000	7,000	5,000
VIP ZONE 1	4,000	3,000	2,000
WEST STAND (ZONE 19,20)	800	650	500
WEST STAND (ZONE 18,21)	600	450	300
WEST STAND (ZONE 17,22)	400	250	200
EAST STAND (ZONE 8,9)	700	550	350
EAST STAND (ZONE 7,10)	500	400	250
EAST STAND (ZONE 6,11)	300	250	150
SOUTH STAND (FANS)	150	100	100

DAY TICKETS. SEASON 2007, ROUBLES			
	1 CATEGORY	2 CATEGORY	3 CATEGORY
VIP	10,000	8,000	6,000
VIP ZONE 1	5,000	4,000	2,500
WEST STAND (ZONE 19,20)	900	700	550
WEST STAND (ZONE 18,21)	700	500	350
WEST STAND (ZONE 17,22)	500	300	250
EAST STAND (ZONE 8,9)	800	600	400
EAST STAND (ZONE 7,10)	600	450	300
EAST STAND (ZONE 6,11)	400	300	200
SOUTH STAND (FANS)	200	150	120

A. Kirichek

DAY TICKETS. SEASON 2008, ROUBLES			
	1 CATEGORY	2 CATEGORY	3 CATEGORY
VIP	10,000	8,000	5,000
VIP ZONE 1	5,000	4,000	2,500
WEST STAND (ZONE 19,20)	1,000	700	500
WEST STAND (ZONE 18,21)	800	550	400
WEST STAND (ZONE 17,22)	600	400	300
EAST STAND (ZONE 8,9)	900	600	400
EAST STAND (ZONE 7,10)	700	450	300
EAST STAND (ZONE 6,11)	500	300	200
SOUTH STAND (FANS)	250	150	100

DAY TICKETS. SEASON 2009, ROUBLES			
	1 CATEGORY	2 CATEGORY	3 CATEGORY
VIP (DIAMOND CLUB)	10,000	8,000	6,000
VIP ZONE 1	5,000	4,000	3,000
WEST STAND (ZONE 19,20)	1,000	700	600
WEST STAND (ZONE 18,21)	800	550	450
WEST STAND (ZONE 17,22)	600	400	300
EAST STAND (ZONE 8,9)	900	600	500
EAST STAND (ZONE 7,10)	700	450	400
EAST STAND (ZONE 6,11)	500	350	250
SOUTH STAND (FANS)	250	200	150

DAY TICKETS. SEASON 2014/2015, ROUBLES			
	1 CATEGORY	2 CATEGORY	3 CATEGORY
VIP (DIAMOND CLUB)	15,000	15,000	15,000
VIP ZONE 1	3,500	3,500	3,500
WEST STAND (ZONE 19,20)	1,000	1,000	1,000
WEST STAND (ZONE 18,21)	800	800	800
WEST STAND (ZONE 17,22)	700	700	700
EAST STAND (ZONE 8,9)	1,000	1,000	1,000
EAST STAND (ZONE 7,10)	800	800	800
EAST STAND (ZONE 6,11)	700	700	700
SOUTH STAND (FANS)	500	500	500

NOTES

1 Information about the operations of FC Lokomotiv during 1922–1991 is taken from https:// ru.wikipedia.org/wiki/Локомотив_(футбольный_клуб,_Москва).
2 Central House of the Soviet Army, the forerunner of FC CSKA.
3 In the German language, the article 'die' indicates the feminine gender of the respective word, in this case 'die Lokomotiv', although the word Lokomotiv is normally masculine in Russian.
4 The CSKA Sports Club has no relation whatever to the CSKA Professional Football Club, except their common name and history, because in the 1990s the football club left the sports club. However, this does not mean much to the fans, who believe that the new president has come from their 'most-hated enemy'.
5 Such additional sources may be articles, books, studies, reports, etc. Use of information from any fan forums available in various data sources is not allowed, as they are often rumours rather than direct quotes.
6 The author was at the match between FC Lokomotiv and the Rostov in August 2014, and he is inclined to think that the actual attendance at the game was a maximum of 6,000 fans, although it was announced that there were 7,014 people present.

RECOMMENDED READING

There are a range of excellent practical resources on the subject of fan engagement including the Fan Engagement Company (http://bradleyprojects.com) and *FC Business Magazine*. In addition, the Birkbeck Sport Business centre has an excellent resource generally, and specifically in regard to Nicole Allison's paper 'Going beyond on-pitch success: Fan engagement as a catalyst for growth' (2013) available at: www. sportbusinesscentre.com/wp-content/uploads/2013/12/Nicole-online-version.pdf (accessed 16 June 2016).

RECOMMENDED WEBSITES

Wikipedia entry about the club (in Russian): https://ru.wikipedia.org/wiki/Локомотив_ (футбольный_клуб,_Москва)
Wikipedia entry about the club (in English): https://en.wikipedia.org/wiki/FC_Lokomotiv_ Moscow
Lokomotiv: www.lokomotiv.info/ or their official website www.fclm.ru
Official Club page in English: www.fclm.ru/en/index.php

A. Kirichek

CASE 21

WHEN SPONSORSHIP TURNS SOUR IN ELITE SPORT

MARIA HOPWOOD AND HAMISH MCLEAN

LEARNING OUTCOMES

Upon completion of this case study, the reader should be able to:

■ analyse the unique dynamics of the relationship between sponsors, fans and elite sporting entities;

■ develop an understanding of the critical issues of sports reputation and relationship management;

■ argue why sports reputation and relationship management is challenging from the perspective of a sponsor when the elite sporting entity is involved in wrong-doing.

OVERVIEW OF THE CASE

Sponsorship is big business in sport, and is driven by the unique opportunity for a sponsor to become part of a tight-knit and supportive 'family'. Fans, who are emotionally engaged to their sporting heroes, will also be drawn to that hero's sponsor, if the 'fit' between sponsor and athlete is compatible and the relationship positive. This in turn creates a fertile marketing advantage for sponsors over their competitors. Given this dynamic environment, this case study examines the questions of:

■ what happens when the relationship turns sour due to sports entity transgressions, and

> ◼ are the bonds that tie fans, players and sponsors sufficient to overcome a reputational crisis?
>
> To find the answers, we draw on two cases studies – those of disgraced cyclist Lance Armstrong and embattled owner of the LA Clippers basketball team Donald Sterling.

CASE STUDY

Sponsorship is defined as 'an investment, in cash or in kind, in an activity, in return for access to the exploitable commercial potential associated with that activity' (Meenaghan, 1991: 36). Colapinto and Benecchi (2014) observe that elite athletes and international competition are of lucrative value to corporate sponsors. Sport enjoys the largest share of global sponsorship (Parker and Fink, 2010), worth an estimated US$53 billion (Meenaghan, 2013). One reason for this may be found in Amis and Slack's (1999: 251) observation that sport sponsorship is 'an effective tool with which to alter and enhance a company's image and reputation'. For the sponsor, the ultimate goal is to become almost synonymous with the party that it is sponsoring.

Sport offers sponsors a valuable, arguably unique, environment to capture the strength of the 'intimate' relationship between athletes and their fans. As Boyle (2013: 95) observes: '[the] sporting discourse is often about emotions and opinions deeply held and readily expressed by athletes and fans.' Sport unifies fans (Osborne and Combs, 2013), who link their social identity to the on-and-off-field performances of athletes and teams (Sanderson and Emmons, 2014). In their examination of the fan–team–sponsor relationship, Parker and Fink (2010) observe that the positive relationship between a team and fans spreads to that with a sponsor; thus a sponsor is able to exploit commercially the emotional engagement of fans.

Amis and Slack (1999) caution, however, that the relationship should not be taken for granted, because the product or service must have value for the market. Sponsorship itself is also evolving. For example, Meenaghan (2013) observes that sponsorship strategies have matured from brand awareness to engagement, with a higher expectation on return of investment and accountability.

Sponsorship arrangements cover teams and clubs, and extend to individual athletes. For example, Amis and Slack (1999) note that sports figures individually enjoy a significant share of endorsements. They elaborate thus:

> There is little reason to doubt that sponsorship deals with sports teams, leagues or other organisations would have a similar positive effect to those with individuals; what is important is that the sponsored entity appeals to the sponsor's target market.
>
> (Amis and Slack, 1999: 254)

Colapinto and Benecchi (2014: 224) also describe individual athletes as marketable commodities: 'his or her looks and fashion choices are assets and they also have a work ethic to preserve.' Sponsors also have a brand to protect. This can be challenging due to the nature of sport. It is an environment which Dimeo argues has a war-like persona, and therefore:

> is fundamentally about winning, hierarchy, elitism and losers get nothing. It encourages people to think of others as enemies. Bias and partisanship are actively promoted. It demarcates the best from the rest. It is all about physical and social superiority. It is a harsh system that is not just intolerant towards failure but explicitly rejects those who fail.
>
> (Dimeo, 2007, cited in Lopez, 2010: 7)

Put succinctly, there are no guarantees on performance, either on or off the field (Amis and Slack, 1999).

There are many instances of where the relationship between the sponsor and the sponsee has irretrievably broken down as a result of a crisis situation in sport. One of the most notable examples of recent times is that of cyclist Lance Armstrong, who in August 2012 was banned for life and stripped of his seven Tour de France titles by the Union Cycliste Internationale (UCI), cycling's ruling body. The move came after a report by the US Anti-Doping Agency (USADA) said that Armstrong engaged in 'serial cheating' and participated in an organised doping ring in the US Postal Services team over several years. All of Armstrong's results from August 1998 have since been expunged from official records.

According to Wood (2012), in any well-drafted sponsorship agreement there will be a standard contractual term – commonly known as a 'moral turpitude' clause – that allows the sponsor to terminate the relationship in the event of the athlete committing an act which fundamentally damages the brand. Doping clearly falls into this category, as does any other form of corruption. The whole purpose of the partnership is for the mutual benefit of athlete and brand – ultimately the sponsor will want to secure the right kind of brand exposure as a result of the agreement and will want to be able to terminate the relationship if the athlete's brand is diminished, as this is also regarded as a breach of contract.

Following the original ban, a number of Armstrong's sponsors stuck by him for some months while he still continued to protest his innocence, which he eventually admitted was all a lie to Oprah Winfrey in January 2013. His various sponsorships with a string of high-profile sponsors including Nike, Oakley and Anheuser-Busch amounted to US$75 million. Armstrong's profile was also indelibly associated with that of the Livestrong Foundation of which he is the founder. It was perhaps Livestrong which had the most to lose from Armstrong's admissions, but his relinquishing of the chairman's role, which he is reported to have described as the most painful moment of his fall from grace, was inevitable, particularly when such statements as 'Lance

Armstrong Killed the Livestrong Bracelet' and the Lance Armstrong memes were starting to appear on social media.

Interestingly, Parker and Fink (2010) examined the relationship from the perspective of a sponsor as a transgressor, rather than the athlete. Once accepted into the relationship, sponsors become part of the tightly knitted fan network. This, in turn, provides a shield during negative events caused by the sponsor. Parker and Fink note that sponsors can be protected against their own transgressions by fans. They explain it thus:

> Sponsoring organisations must understand that being a member of an ingroup (i.e. having a sponsoring relationship with a team) provides a great deal of security for the sponsor when negative events become public. Therefore nurturing the team relationship is essential, and working to remain associated with the team following negative publicity or actions is imperative to the continued support of highly identified fans of the team.
>
> (Parker and Fink, 2010: 201)

In a sports crisis situation such as that of Lance Armstrong, it is evident that sponsors have no choice but to withdraw their support from the fallen entity. The main reason for this is that, increasingly, sponsors are engaging in sponsorship agreements in order to support and strengthen their brand. According to Simon Hart (2012), Nike's association with Armstrong dated back to 1996 and his success in the saddle was instrumental in the company's expansion into cycling. He was the face of numerous marketing campaigns, including a 2001 advertisement featuring footage of him having blood drawn for a drug test and challenging those who accused him of doping. The partnership raised nearly US$50 million through the sale of yellow Livestrong wristbands and the company produced numerous other Livestrong-branded products. Nike has a history of staying loyal to its sponsees – their continuing support of Tiger Woods is testament to this – but they felt that Lance Armstrong had deceived them, and they made this very clear in the concise but powerful statement that the company issued terminating the relationship:

> Due to the seemingly insurmountable evidence that Lance Armstrong participated in doping and misled Nike for more than a decade, it is with great sadness that we have terminated our contract with him. Nike does not condone the use of illegal performance enhancing drugs in any manner.
>
> Nike plans to continue support of the Livestrong initiatives created to unite, inspire and empower people affected by cancer.
>
> (Nike Inc., 2012)

The Lance Armstrong case continues to send shock waves throughout the world of cycling and beyond. A full apology for his transgressions is still awaited, but, as

M. Hopwood, H. McLean

Armstrong acknowledged in his 2013 interview with Oprah Winfrey, his sponsorship agreements are likely to have gone forever – a true fall from grace.

Colapinto and Benecchi (2014) note that a scandal involving an athlete has negative ramifications for the corporate brands of sponsors, which effects are often driven by intense media interest. However, it is not only scandals involving athletes which create problems for sponsors. Our second case example is that of Donald Sterling, the owner of the LA Clippers basketball team. Real estate mogul Donald Sterling gained notoriety due to racist remarks he made in 2014 in relation to the LA Clippers, the NBA team he bought in 1981. In an audiotape leaked to website TMZ in late April, Sterling told his girlfriend, V. Stiviano, not to bring black people to Clippers games. On 29 April NBA Commissioner Adam Silver banned Sterling from the NBA for life and fined him US$2.5 million. The NBA Board of Governors may well decide to force Sterling to sell the team, which Forbes valued at US$575 million but for which one prospective buyer – ex Microsoft CEO Steve Ballmer – is rumoured to be willing to pay US$1.8 billion (Ozanian, 2014). The focus of this case is not on player or athlete transgressions but the recorded 'private' conversations of a renowned American sports organisation owner, which were made publicly available and to which sponsors have responded in devastating fashion. An article in the *Los Angeles Times* states:

> Nearly 20 brands suspended or terminated their sponsorships of the Clippers after the release of a recording in which Sterling, 80, scolded a female friend for associating with black people in public.
>
> (Hsu and Chang, 2014)

Donald Sterling's situation focuses attention on an important perspective of sports public relations and crisis communication management within the context of sponsor relations. Whenever and however today's sport organisation – or its representatives – choose to communicate, the potential for message dissemination to a public audience is very real due to the reach of social media and the 24/7 rolling news agenda. The ease with which the public are now able to create news stories through, for example, recording private conversations and taking photographs on smartphones and then making them public via social media and news organisation websites has serious containment and reputational issues for sports organisations and their employees.

QUESTIONS

1. Describe why sport offers a lucrative and unique marketing opportunity for sponsors.
2. What are the challenges faced by sponsors when elite athletes or sport entities are involved in wrong-doing?
3. Why is an understanding of sports reputation management and relationship management a critical issue for sport management?

CONCLUSIONS

Much like fans, sponsors faced with potential association with a disgraced athlete or sport entity are placed in a position of making a choice – abandon them or continue to support them. Global sports sponsorship continues to grow and shows no signs of abating, and the appetite for a vast range of sponsors to associate themselves with successful sports and athletes is huge. It is increasingly the case, however, that sponsors are considering the reputational and relational dimension of sports sponsorship more carefully than has perhaps previously been the case. As the Bedford Group (2014) observe, scandal and sport sometimes appear to go hand in hand. For this reason, it is important that an organisation thoroughly researches the athlete or team before proceeding with sponsorship negotiations. Nevertheless, even if every precaution is taken to avoid an athlete or team with a scandalous history, negative publicity may arise from a completely unanticipated event such as a recorded private phone conversation. This negative publicity can be detrimental to the company image associated with the athlete/team scandal. The case studies of Lance Armstrong and Donald Sterling illustrate very well the speed with which even long-term, high-profile sponsorship agreements can become own goals in terms of damage limitation.

RECOMMENDED READING

For further reading on the issues raised in the case studies, the following sources are well worth consulting:

- Hopwood, M., Kitchin, P. and Skinner, J. (eds) (2010). *Sport Public Relations and Communication*, Oxford: Butterworth-Heinemann. This is the first book to explore public relations and communications in the sports industry in a global context. It takes the principles of public relations and communications and demonstrates how they can successfully be applied to sport management and marketing issues.
- *Public Relations Review: A Global Journal of Research and Comment*, Volume 34, Issue 2, June 2008 is a Special Edition on Public Relations and Sport edited by Jacquie L'Etang and Maria Hopwood. This edition contains a number of articles which deal with the management of sports reputational issues, player transgressions and similar crises.
- L'Etang, J. (2013). *Sports Public Relations*, London: SAGE Publications Ltd. This book explains how public relations issues arise for sport and sports business and how public relations approaches and thinking may be used to solve them.

BIBLIOGRAPHY

Amis, J. and Slack, T. (1999). 'Sport sponsorship as distinctive competence', *European Journal of Marketing*, 33(3/4), 250–2.

Bedford Group (2014). Avoiding the perils of sport sponsorship, accessed 2 June 2014, http://bedfordgroupconsulting.com/.

Bloxsome, E., Voges, K. and Pope, N. (2011). 'Sport sponsorship: appeal and risks', *Research Journal of Social Sciences & Management*, 1(8), 133–45.

Boyle, R. (2013). 'Reflections on communication and sport: On journalism and digital culture', *Communication & Sport,* 1(2), 88–99.

Colapinto, C. and Benecchi, E. (2014). 'The presentation of celebrity personas in everyday twittering: managing online reputations throughout a communications crisis', *Media, Culture & Society*, 36(2), 219–33.

Hart, S. (2012). Lance Armstrong dropped by sponsors Nike following 'insurmountable evidence' in USADA report that he doped, accessed 25 April 2014, www.telegraph.co.uk/sport/othersports/cycling/9614878/Lance-Armstrong-dropped-by-sponsors-Nike-following-insurmountable-evidence-in-USADA-report-that-he-doped.html.

Hopwood, M., Kitchin, P. and Skinner, J. (eds) (2010). *Sport Public Relations and Communication*, Oxford: Butterworth-Heinemann.

Hsu, T. and Chang, A. (2014). Clippers sponsors slow to return despite NBA ban of Donald Sterling, accessed 10 May 2014, www.latimes.com/business/la-fi-sterling-advertisers-20140510-story.html#page=1.

L'Etang, J. (2013). *Sports Public Relations*, London: SAGE Publications Ltd.

L'Etang, J. and Hopwood, M. (eds) (2008). *Public Relations Review: A Global Journal of Research and Comment*, Special Edition on Public Relations and Sport, 34(2), June.

Lopez, B. (2010). 'Doping as technology: a re-reading of the history of performance-enhancing substance use', *Institute for Culture and Society Occasional Paper Series*, 1(4), 1–17.

Meenaghan, T. (1991). 'Sponsorship – legitimizing the medium', *European Journal of Marketing*, 25(11), 5–10.

Meenaghan, T. (2013). 'Measuring sponsorship performance: challenge and direction', *Psychology and Marketing*, 30(5), 385–93.

Nike Inc. (2012). Nike statement on Lance Armstrong, accessed 25 April 2014, http://nikeinc.com/news/nike-statement-on-lance-armstrong.

Osborne, A. and Coombs, D. (2013). 'Performative sport fandom: an approach to retheorizing sport fans', *Sport in Society: Cultures, Commerce, Media, Politics*, 16(5), 672–81.

Ozanian, M. (2014). Steve Ballmer Said to Offer $1.8 Billion for Los Angeles Clippers, accessed 29 May 2014, www.forbes.com/sites/mikeozanian/2014/05/29/steve-ballmer-said-to-offer-1-8-billion-for-los-angeles-clippers/.

Parker, H. and Fink, J. (2010). 'Negative sponsor behavior, team response and how this impacts fan attitudes', *International Journal of Sports Marketing and Sponsorship*, 1(3), 200–11.

Sanderson, J. (2013), 'From loving the hero to despising the villain: sport fans, Facebook and social identity threats', *Mass Communication and Society*, 16, 487–509.

Sanderson, J. and Emmons, B. (2014). 'Extending and Withholding Forgiveness to Josh Hamilton: Exploring Forgiveness Within Parasocial Interaction', *Communication & Sport*, 2(1), 24–47.

Simpson, C. (2013). Lance Armstrong Killed the Livestrong Bracelet, accessed 25 April 2014, www.thewire.com/business/2013/05/nike-livestrong-lance-armstrong/65646/.

Wood, D. (2012). 'Armstrong scandal highlights the importance of brand protection', *IP & T UK Outlook,* viewed 25 April 2014, www.lexisnexis.com/uk/legal.

RECOMMENDED WEBSITES

IEG: www.sponsorship.com/
Power Sponsorship: http://powersponsorship.com/
PR Week: www.prweek.com/
Sports Business Daily: www.sportsbusinessdaily.com/Journal.aspx

CASE 22

DESIGNING POLICIES AND STRATEGIES TO SAFEGUARD, CONSERVE AND RECLAIM/REUSE WATER RESOURCES AT SPORT FACILITIES

CHERYL MALLEN, CHRIS CHARD, ADEL MANSUROV AND COURTNEY KEOGH

LEARNING OUTCOMES

Upon completion of this case study, the reader should be able to:

- examine the issues of water supply and issues arising from this, and to apply the concepts to sport facilities;
- generate/design a sport facility policy to safeguard water and to develop associated strategies of safeguarding, conserving, and reclaiming/reuse of water resources designed to meet the policy;
- identify current practices in water safeguarding stemming from key resources such as: the Canadian Standards Organization Z2010 Requirements and Guidelines for Organizers of Sustainable Events; the Sustainable Sport Event Toolkit (VANOC, 2010), the Sport Event Environmental Performance Measure (Mallen et al., 2010), and Glavič and Luckman's (2007) foundational principles of environmental performance relating to water.

OVERVIEW OF THE CASE

Canada has vast water resources, but, as in the rest of the world, this water supply is under stress. This case study provides an overview of the water resources Canada needs to protect, the Canadian legislation on safeguarding water, and examples of water issues in Canada. This is followed by a discovery that some key sport facilities in Ontario, Canada do not have water policies to safeguard this resource. Yet examples of sport facilities instituting strategies to safeguard, conserve, and reclaim/reuse water can be found and are presented. Students are then guided to design a water policy for a sport facility. To aid in the development of their conceptual water policy, this case study provides an overview of several key guidelines, including: the Canadian Standards Organization Z2010-10 Requirements and Guidelines for Organizers of Sustainable Events, the Sustainable Sport Event Toolkit (VANOC, 2010), the Sport Event Environmental Performance Measure (Mallen et al., 2010), and Glavič and Luckman's (2007) foundational principles of environmental performance relating to water.

CASE STUDY

Since the beginning of the twenty-first century, most nations worldwide have faced some form of crisis concerning their water resources (World Commission on Water, 2000). This crisis, which has arisen "because of pollution, overuse, and changes in weather patterns, [means that] a consistent supply of clean water everywhere is no longer a sure thing" (Bickford, 2014: 72). Research on water stress and achieving safeguards "is growing at a rate of 9.2% per year" (Frankel, 2015: para. 11). This research has been noted as striving to offer "the potential to help solve the issue" (Frankel, 2015: para. 9). There is limited literature on environmental safeguards in the business of sport (Cachay, 1993; Mallen and Chard, 2012; Spector et al., 2012; Thibault, 2009). In particular, there is a gap in the literature on the safeguarding of water in sport.

Sport is, however, reliant upon water sources. For example, water is necessary to fill indoor pools, to generate ice in venues, to encourage living turf to grow, to clean artificial turf, and to fall as snow for mountain winter sports. Additionally, it has been noted that watering landscaping, such as that around North American sport facilities, accounts for approximately 60 percent of a sport facility's water usage (Bickford, 2014). This, of course, is in addition to that fact that "each person needs 20–50 liters of water a day to ensure their basic needs for drinking, cooking and cleaning" (UN Water, 2012b: para. 1). Safeguarding the world's water resources, or moving to a position of environmental sustainability (ES), is paramount for life and for conducting sport. The United Nations (UN) Brundtland Report (1987: 1) defined sustainability as meeting "the needs of the present generation without compromising the ability of future generations to meet their own needs".

This case study seeks to guide the reader to design policies and strategies aimed at safeguarding, conserving, and reclaiming water resources for sport facilities and events.

What water supplies does Canada have to protect?

Canada has over 243,790 km or 151,480 miles of saltwater shoreline that extends along the Atlantic, Pacific, and Arctic Oceans (Canada's Geography, n.d.; Canadian

Encyclopedia, n.d). Freshwater resources include multiple inland lakes; for instance, "forty percent of Canada's boundary with the United States is composed of water" (Environment Canada, 2014a: para. 2). Many Canadian rivers extend long distances across the country; for example the Mackenzie River traverses over 4,000 km, the Nelson River over 2,500 km, and the Peach, Fraser, North Saskatchewan, Ottawa, Athabasca, Yukon, Liard, and Assiniboine rivers are all over 1,000 km in length (Environment Canada, 2014d). Further, the inland Great Lakes represent "the world's largest freshwater lake system" (Environment Canada, 2014d: para. 2). The atmosphere also holds water vapor and there is interdependency between the surface, air, and groundwater sources (Winter et al., 1998). Canada has surface water in the form of ice and snow, and according to the UN Water (2012a: para. 1), "70 percent [of the world's fresh water] is in the form of ice and permanent snow cover". Furthermore, "a third of the world's fresh water is found underground" (Environment Canada, 2014c: para. 1) and these underground aquifers hold "about 97 percent of all freshwater that is potentially available for human use" (Environment Canada, 2014a: para. 3), and are thus key "in supplying fresh water to meet the needs of Canadians" (Environment Canada, 2014c: para. 1).

Canadian legislation on safeguarding water

The Canada Water Act (1985) outlined how the nation was to manage its water resources. In the spirit of this Act, a Water Charter was developed by the Council of the Federation and was signed by the 10 provincial and 3 territorial Premiers of Canada. This Charter noted that "there is no substitute for water" and that "Canadians recognize our collective obligation to be responsible global water stewards" (Council of the Federation, 2010: 1). Further, Environment Canada (2014d: para. 7) promoted the idea that "water resources must be developed in harmony with the natural ecosystem so that neither the water resource nor the plant and animal life dependent on it are depleted or destroyed for short-term gain and at the expense of future generations".

Water issues in Canada

The World Economic Forum added the worldwide "water supply crises in all its myriad forms to its list of Top 5 global risks" (World Economic Forum, 2012: para. 3). Concern over the safeguarding of Canadian waterways has also increased (World Wildlife Federation Canada, n.d.). The Conference Board of Canada stated that one concern is that there is "excessive water consumption" due to "the lack of widespread water conservation practices, as well as water pricing that does not promote efficiency" (World Wildlife Federation Canada, n.d.). Additionally, Environment Canada (2014d: para. 2) stated that periods of drought in Canada are causing "water shortage[s], and groundwater 'mining' ... (i.e., more water is taken out of the aquifer than is being recharged". Further, many water sources in Canada are stressed. For instance, "the Great Lakes ecosystem is threatened" (Environment Canada 2014b: para. 1). The threats stem from "ongoing biological, physical and chemical stresses, as well as new and emerging challenges like invasive alien species and the impact of climate change" (Environment Canada, 2014b).

Overall, the Conference Board of Canada in their *Water Quality Index* (2012) measured a number of water features such as oxygen levels, acidity levels, and nitrogen and phosphorus levels, and gave Canada a "B" grade and a sixth-place ranking (behind Finland, Sweden, Italy, Norway, and Switzerland) within the comparison of 17 developed countries. This ranking leaves room for improvement, as it would not be advantageous for Canadians, and sport in Canada, if water quality declined further.

Sport facilities and event water policies

Sport facilities and their associated events in Canada are dependent upon the local water resources and, thus, are impacted by water issues, including excessive water consumption, water shortages, and concerns for water quality in Canada. Yet after contacting six managers at key sport facilities in the province of Ontario, it was revealed that although they may have a general sustainability policy, none had established a policy specifically for safeguarding water supplies. The senior managers and event managers at the sport facilities indicated that this lack of policy situation was typical in North America.

Sport facilities and water safeguards

Global examples can be found where sport facilities are instituting strategies to safeguard water resources, including water conservation and reclamation programs. A search revealed a number of such strategies including:

- Sport facility: CenturyLink Field in Seattle, Washington, USA has installed low-flow water fixtures that are saving over 1.4 million gallons (over 5 million liters) of water annually (CenturyLink, n.d.).
- Sport facility: The Melbourne Rectangular Stadium in AAMI Park in Melbourne, Australia utilizes "rainwater collection from the roof" (Davies, 2015) and has a "program to incorporate recycled water from the entire precinct to displace the majority of potable water use", and this reduced "the potable water usage by at least 90 percent" (Business World Magazine, 2011, n.p.).
- Sport facility: Miller Park in Milwaukee, USA has an 8.5 acre [34,398 meters squared] roof and rain falling onto this roof is collected into 3 barrels that can hold 1,500 gallons [5678.11 liters] of storm water for a reclamation program that aims to reduce the use of drinking water for exterior irrigation by 53 percent (Street & Smith's SportsBusiness Journal, 2014).

Sport facility water strategy issues

Interviews with senior managers and event managers at six medium-sized sport facilities in Ontario, Canada indicated that despite the lack of a specific water safeguarding policy, the facilities were making attempts to reduce water usage at their facilities. They offered some statements on issues they have to consider, which they have learned as they have instituted their water strategies, and include the following:

- Each water strategy must be considered based on the return on the investment over time.
- When the temperature setting on the sport facility hot water was reduced, we thought we would have financial savings; however, we found that there is a delicate balance concerning the temperature needed as staff tended to turn on the tap(s) and run the water longer trying to get hot water for their use, negating any potential financial savings.
- Once low-flow water fixtures for the sport facility showers were purchased and installed, we then found that athletes took longer showers to ensure the soap was removed from their skin and this negated the attempt to reduce water consumption.
- We are considering going back to water flush urinals because after an event with high usage, the waterless urinals leave a high concentration of urine in the pipes behind the walls that can smell.

Your task: design a water policy and the associated strategies for a sport facility

To complete the task of designing a water policy and the associated strategy for a sport facility, go to the questions section below and answer the nine questions posed. When answering the questions, use the recommended websites found below as well as the informational aids offered.

Informational aids for completing your task

To aid you in generating your conceptual sport facility water policy and water strategies, an overview from key sources are provided below.

Canadian Standards Association (CSA) Z2010-10 Requirements and Guidelines for Organizers of Sustainable Events (www.csa.ca)

The Canadian Standards Association (CSA) standards, as approved by the Standards Council of Canada (SCC) and outlined in a document titled Z2010-10 Requirements and Guidelines for Organizers of Sustainable Events (CSA, 2010), specifically section 6.3, outlines concerns for water conservation, use, and quality, and includes the following provisions:

> SCC Section 6.3.1 – The event organizer shall conserve water, use water efficiently, and maintain water quality. Water conservation and efficiency can be achieved through:
>
> - use of recognized water-efficient brands of equipment such as washing machines or dishwashers;
> - use of low-flow plumbing fixtures and low-flow toilets;
> - minimizing the use of potable water, where applicable;
> - use of grey water, rainwater, or surface water; and
> - strategic initiatives that enhance or restore watersheds.
>
> SCC Section 6.3.2 – The event organizer shall strive to ensure that waste water or storm water from the event does not negatively impact the environment (e.g., by adversely affecting water quality or contributing to pollution or erosion). This can be achieved through:
>
> - conducting a risk assessment of wastewater and storm water sources and
> - responsible water-management practices including communication and education.
>
> The event organizer shall identify and manage any other water quality issues relevant to the event.
>
> (CSA, 2010: 12–13)

The Sustainable Sport and Event Toolkit (SSET)

The Sustainable Sport and Event Toolkit (SSET) (VANOC, 2010) provides the following recommendations specifically for sport and water resources:

SSET Section 3.4 – Select/build venues with efficient water technologies. Include storm water capture and re-use; low-flow toilets and no-flow urinals; use of grey water; water-saving taps, etc. (p. 11).

SSET Section 4.5 – Implement responsible water and snow management practices. Measure and reduce water usage in your venues and use water from renewable sources. Use snow storage, piling and road salt that avoid negative impacts to local water drainage and natural habitats. Use snow hardening solutions responsibly (p. 13).

SSET Section 6.4 – Provide responsible parking services. Choose parking services that help to ensure clean water drainage and responsible clearing practices (e.g., particularly for snow removal and clearing) (p. 15).

SSET Section 7.1 – Reduce ecological footprint of food ... source from fair-trade, organic, seasonal. Local and regional sources where possible, high percentage of fruits and vegetables and use tap water where appropriate (p. 16).

The Sport Event Environmental Performance Measure

The Sport Event Environmental Performance Measure (SE-EPM) (Mallen et al., 2010) outlined themes and sub-themes specifically on performance water resource sustainability.

The first theme, environmental management performance, encompasses the following sub-themes:

■ water systems including: policies, programs, targets, committees, and funding applications such as auditing and education;
■ implications including: program limitations and perspectives, environmental activities disclosure, environmental relationships, and environmental countermeasures.

The second theme, environmental operational performance, encompasses the following sub-themes:

■ environmental inputs including measuring water usage;
■ environmental outputs including:
　■ measuring waste disposed into water resources;
　■ measuring water drainage;
　■ identifying and measuring pollutants released.

Glavič and Lukman's foundational principles of environmental performance relating to water

Glavič and Lukman (2007: 1876) outlined foundational principles of environmental performance that are organized from preventative action principles to control action principles, including:

- renewable resources;
- resource use minimization;
- source reduction dematerialization (redesigning systems to reduce waste);
- recovery of water;
- reuse of water;
- purification of water;
- end-of-pipe (ensuring purification prior to discharging water);
- degradation of water.

QUESTIONS

1. What water supplies do your community, region, and/or country need to protect?
2. What legislation has been developed for safeguarding water in your community, region, and/or country?
3. What water-related issues impact your community, region, and/or country?
4. Do your local sport facilities have policies to safeguard water resources?
5. What strategies are your local sport facilities using to safeguard water resources?
6. What are the benefits/disadvantages of having/not having a water policy at a sport facility?
7. If you were a sport facility manager, what policy statement would you devise to safeguard water at a sport facility?
8. State the key associated sport facility water strategies that you would institute to meet the aims of the water policy (provide a minimum of four strategies).
9. Consider who could be responsible for instituting the water policy and strategies at a sport facility and the scope of the water safeguards.

CONCLUSIONS

This case study has encouraged the examination of the water supply and related issues as they apply to sport facilities. As part of your conclusions on this task, review your designed water policy and the associated strategies for a sport facility using the following questions:

- What is the scope of the water strategies? Consider the list of items that this responsibility encompasses and consider if they will help to meet the challenge of ensuring water resources for future generations.
- How will the responsible parties measure and report on the water policy and its associated strategies?
- What are the reporting strategy and transparency issues?
- And finally: How is the policy enforceable?

Rate your water policy and associated strategies on the scale of 1 (poor) to 10 (excellent). Now, how can it be improved to ensure water for future generations and what level of priority should these improvements have?

RECOMMENDED READING

International Olympic Committee (IOC) Guide on Sport Environment and Sustainable Development; Section 4.3 Water sports in the natural environment. Available at: www.Olympic.org/Documents/Reports/EN/en_report_1114.pdf.

Mallen, C., Chard, C. and Adams, L. (2013). A water resource sustainability best practice at a sport facility: a case study. *EYQEW*, 1, 1–10.

Mallen, C. and Chard, C. (2011). A framework for debating the future of environmental sustainability in the Sport Academy. *Sport Management Review*, 14, 424–33.

Mallen, C. and Chard, C. (2012). "What could be" in Canadian sport facility environmental sustainability. *Sport Management Review*, 15, 230–43.

Government of Canada. (2010). *Changing currents: Water sustainability and the future of Canada's natural resource sectors*. National Round Table on the Environment and the Economy. Ottawa, Ontario, Canada. ISBN 978-1-100-15877-8.

BIBLIOGRAPHY

Agha, N., Fairley, S. and Gibson, H. (2012). Considering legacy as a multi-dimensional construct: the legacy of the Olympic Games. *Sport Management Review*, 15, 125–39.

Bickford, C. (2014). *Rainwater Harvesting. Energy Smart Homes*. Newtown, CT: The Taunton Press, Inc.

Boiral, O. (2006). Global warming: should companies adopt a proactive strategy? *Long Range Planning*, 39(3), 315–30.

Brundtland Report (1987). 96th Plenary meeting, United Nations General Assembly, Report of the World Commission on the Environment and Development. Our common future. Retrieved from www.un-documents.net/our-common-future.pdf.

Brymer, E., Downey, G. and Gray, T. (2009). Extreme sports as a precursor to environmental sustainability. *Journal of Sport & Tourism*, 14, 193–204.

Business World Magazine (2011). AAMI Park: Building an idea. Retrieved from: www.businessworld-magazine.com/business-profiles-and-featured-articles/infrastructure_articles/aami-park/.

Cachay, K. (1993). Sports and environment sports for everyone – room for everyone? *International Review for the Sociology of Sport*, 28, 311–23.

Canada's Geography (n.d.). Retrieved from www.enchantedlearning.com/school/Canada/Canadamap.shtml.

Canada Water Act (1985). R.S.C 1985, c.C-11. The Department of Justice: Ottawa, Ontario. Retrieved from http://laws-lois.justice.gc.ca/eng/acts/C-11/page-1.html.

Canadian Encyclopedia (n.d.). Coast. Historic-Dominion Institute. Retrieved from http://the-canadianencyclopedia.com/articles/coast.

Canadian Standards Association (CSA) (2010). Z2010-10 Requirements and guidelines for organizers of sustainable events. Toronto, Ontario, Canada. Retrieved from www.csa.ca.

CenturyLink Field (n.d.). Together, we are champions of sustainability. Retrieved from www.centurylinkfield.com/defend-your-turf/.

Chard, C. and Mallen, C. (2012). Examining the linkages between automobile use and carbon impacts of community-based ice hockey. *Sport Management Review*, 15, 476–84.

Costa, C. (2005). The status and future of sport management: a Delphi study. *Journal of Sport Management*, 19, 117–42.

Council of the Federation (2010, August). Water Charter. Retrieved from www.canadaspremiers.ca/phocadownload/publications/water_charter_aug_4_2010.pdf.

Davies, M. (2015). Top 7 sustainable sports stadiums in the world: Section 6, AAMI Park (aka Melbourne Rectangular Stadium). Retrieved from https://humans4sustainablefuture.wordpress.com/2015/11/13/top-7-sustainable-sports-stadiums-in-the-world/.

Dingle, G. (2009). Sustaining the race: a review of literature pertaining to environmental sustainability of motorsport. *International Journal of Sports Marketing and Sponsorship*, 11, 80–96.

Environment Canada (2014a). Great Lakes quickfacts. Retrieved from www.ec.gc.ca/grandslacs-greatlakes/default.asp?lang=En&n=B4E65F6F-1.

Environment Canada (2014b). Great Lakes. Retrieved from www.ec.gc.ca/grandslacs-greatlakes/default.asp?lang=En&n=70283230-1.

Environment Canada (2014c). Water – underground: what is groundwater? Retrieved from www.ec.gc.ca/eau-water/default.asp?lang=En$n=FCE12AAD9-1.

Environment Canada (2014d). Water – in Canada: is Canada a "water-rich" country? Retrieved from www.ec.gc.ca/eau-water/default.asp?lang=en&n=5EA1D86e-1.

Etzion, D. (2007). Research on organizations and the natural environment, 1992–present: a review. *Journal of Management*, 33, 637–64.

Exhibition Place (2011). Exhibition Place leads in waste diversion and reduces energy consumption. Retrieved from www.explace.on.ca/media/press_releases/articles92.php.

Fairley, S., Tyler, D., Kellett, P. and D'Elia, K. (2011). The Formula One Australian Grand Prix: exploring the triple bottom line. *Sport Management Review*, 14, 141–52.

Frankel, T. (2015, 17 June). Nasa data shows the world is running out of water. *Independent News*. Retrieved from: www.independent.co.uk/environment/nasa-data-shows-the-world-is-running-out-of-water-10325188.html.

Gaddenne, D., Kennedy, J. and McKeiver, C. (2009). An empirical study of environmental awareness and practices in SMEs. *Journal of Business Ethics*, 84(1), 45–63.

Glavič, P. and Lukman, R. (2007). Review of sustainability terms and their definitions. *Journal of Cleaner Production*, 15, 1875–85.

Inoue, Y. and Kent, A. (2012). Investigating the role of corporate credibility in corporate social marketing: A case study of environmental initiatives by professional sport organizations. *Sport Management Review*, 15, 330–44.

Jin, L., Zhand, J., Ma, X. and Connaughton, D. (2011). Residents' perceptions of environmental impacts of the 2008 Beijing green Olympic Games. *European Sport Management Quarterly*, 11, 275–300.

Karadakis, K. and Kaplanidou, K. (2012). Legacy perceptions among host and non-host Olympic Games residents: a longitudinal study of the 2010 Vancouver Olympic Games. *European Sport Management Quarterly*, 12, 243–64.

Krippendorff, K. (2004). *Content Analysis: An Introduction to its Methodology* (2nd edn). Thousand Oaks, CA: Sage Publications, Inc.

Lindell, M. and Karagozoglu, N. (2001). Corporate environmental behavior – a comparison between Nordic and US firms. *Business Strategy and the Environment*, 10, 38–52.

Mallen, C. and Chard, C. (2011). A framework for debating the future of environmental sustainability in the Sport Academy. *Sport Management Review*, 14, 424–33.

Mallen, C. and Chard, C. (2012). "What could be" in Canadian sport facility environmental sustainability. *Sport Management Review*, 15, 230–43.

Mallen, C., Adams, L., Stevens, J. and Thompson, L. (2010). Environmental Sustainability in sport facility management: a Delphi study. *European Sport Management Quarterly*, 10, 367–89.

Mallen, C., Chard, C. and Adams, L. (2013). A water resource sustainability best practice at a sport facility: a case study. *EYQEW*, 1, 1–10.

Mallen, C., Stevens, J., Adams, L. and McRoberts, S. (2010). The assessment of the environmental performance of an international multi-sport event. *European Sport Management Quarterly*, 10, 97–122.

Mincyte, D., Casper, M. and Cole, C. (2009). Sports environmentalism, land use, and urban development. *Journal of Sport & Social Issues*, 33, 103–10.

Paquette, J., Stevens, J. and Mallen, C. (2011). The interpretation of environmental sustainability by the International Olympic Committee and Organizing Committees of the Olympic Games from 1994 to 2008. *Sport in Society*, 14, 355–69.

Patton, M. (2002). *Qualitative Research and Evaluation Methods* (3rd edn). London: Sage.

Senge, P., Smith, B., Kruschiwitz, N., Laur, J. and Schley, A. (2008). *The Necessary Revolution: Working Together to Create a Sustainable World*. New York: Broadway Books.

Spector, S., Chard, C., Mallen, C. and Hyatt, C. (2012). Socially constructed environmental issues and sport: a content analysis of ski resort environmental communications. *Sport Management Review*, 15, 416–33.

Stepchenkova, S., Kirilenko, A. and Morrison, A. (2008). Facilitating content analysis in tourism research. *Journal of Travel Research*, 47(4), 454–69.

Street & Smith's SportsBusiness Journal. (2014, January 6–12). Coast to Coast: Milwaukee, p. 22. Retrieved from www.sportsbusinessjournal.com.

Suchorski, A. (2007). A summary of integrated water resources management (IWRM) and its potential in the Caribbean. Montreal: McGill University. Retrieved from: www.mcgill.ca/cariwin/files/cariwin/IWRM_REPORT_MAR2007.pdf.

Thibault, L. (2009). Globalization of sport: an inconvenient truth. *Journal of Sport Management*, 23, 1–20.

UN Water (n.d.a). The volume of freshwater resources on Earth is around 35 million km³. Retrieved from: www.unwater.org/statistics/en/?page=5&ipp=10&tx_dynalist_pi1%5Bpar%5D=YToxOntzOjE6IkwiO3M6MDoiIjt9.

UN Water (n.d.b). A person needs 20–50 litres of water a day for basic needs. Retrieved from: www.unwater.org/statistics/statistics-detail/en/c/211765/.

Vancouver Organizing Committee for the 2010 Olympic and Paralympic Winter Games (VANOC) (2010, April 1). Sustainable sport and event toolkit (SSET). AISTS Mastering Sport. International Academy of Sports Science and Technology, Lausanne, Switzerland. Available at: http://events.whistler.com/downloads/sustainable%20sport%20and%20event%20toolkit.pdf.

Watkins, J. and Cooperride, D. (2000). Appreciative inquiry: A transformative paradigm. *Journal of Organization Development Network*, 32, 6–12.

Welland Recreational Canal Corporation. (2008, June). Welland Recreational Waterway – Master Plan (WRW-MP). Welland, Canada. Retrieved from www.canalcorp.ca/files/WellandRecreationalWaterwayMasterPlanFinal.pdf.

Winter, T., Harvey, J., Franke, O. and Alley, W. (1998). Ground water and surface water: A single resource. US Department of the Interior, Geological Survey Circular 1139. US Government Printing Office: Denver, Colorado.

World Commission on Water (2000). Report on the World Commission on Water. *Water Resources Development*, 16(3), 289–320.

World Economic Forum (2012). Global Risks: An initiative of the Risk Network Response (7th Edition), Geneva, Switzerland. Retrieved from: www3.weforum.org/docs/WEF_GlobalRisks_Report_2012.pdf.

World Wildlife Federation Canada (n.d.). Fresh water: Flowing rivers, healthy watersheds. Retrieved from www.wwf.ca/conservation.

RECOMMENDED WEBSITES

The Horinko Group: www.thehorinkogroup.org/water-resources-policy-sustainable-communities-strategic-design/

CASE 23

THE FOOTBALL WORLD CUP 2014

GERD NUFER

LEARNING OUTCOMES

Upon completion of this case study, the reader should be able to:

■ characterise sports sponsorship in general;
■ understand sports event sponsorship in the framework of a football World Cup;
■ analyse and differentiate various forms of ambush marketing;
■ critically evaluate the phenomenon of ambush marketing from different perspectives.

OVERVIEW OF THE CASE

International sporting events such as the football World Cup constitute the ideal platform for companies to implement their target-group-specific marketing communications. Therefore, sporting event organisers sell exclusive marketing rights for their events to official sponsors. In return, these sponsors acquire exclusive opportunities to utilise the event for their own marketing purposes.

Ambush marketing is the method used by companies that do not actually hold marketing rights to an event, but still use marketing activities in diverse ways to establish a connection to it. The philosophy of ambush marketing consists of achieving conventional marketing objectives using unconventional methods. However, it creates the risk of fines or punishment, since companies that use these strategies even though they do not have sponsorship rights are violating legal requirements.

This case study introduces and analyses the marketing communications tools of sports sponsorship and ambush marketing.

CASE STUDY

Sports sponsorship at the FIFA World Cup

Football World Cups attract more than 30 billion TV viewers worldwide, which makes them the most popular sporting event in the world. The FIFA World Cup 2014 in Brazil involved 20 official sponsors that were divided into three categories: 6 FIFA partners, 8 FIFA World Cup sponsors and 6 national promoters. The six FIFA partners enter into the closest relationship with FIFA, and hence are allowed to advertise within a longer time frame throughout all FIFA competitions. FIFA football World Cup sponsors' rights, on the other hand, are restricted to this event only. Finally, national promoters of the World Cup are local companies having the right to advertise in the event's host country. Altogether, these companies pay more than US$1 billion for all marketing and media rights.

Ambush marketing: an evil attack on sponsorship or innovative marketing?

Ambush marketing is a strategy whereby companies attempt to signal an authorised connection to an event to their direct and indirect audiences, using their own marketing and in particular communication measures. Since the event is sponsored by a third party, however, these companies own no legal (or only lower-privilege) marketing rights for it. Here the line between creative communications policy and the infringement of sponsors' rights is often very fine: official sponsors refer to this ambushing of expensive promotional rights as 'theft' and stress the illegal aspects of ambush marketing. However, there are also advocates of the opposite point of view; they see ambush marketing as a legitimate way to help the sponsoring market become more efficient. That is why ambush marketing is debated as a very controversial topic.

Table 23.1 FIFA's marketing partners in 2014

FIFA partners	FIFA World Cup sponsors	National promoters
Adidas	Budweiser	Apex Brasil
Coca-Cola	Castrol	Centauro
Hyundai-Kiamotors	Continental	Garoto
Emirates	Johnson & Johnson	Itaú
Sony	McDonald's	Liberty Seguros
Visa	Moypark	Wise up
	Oi	
	Yingli Solar	

Source: adapted from http://de.fifa.com/worldcup/organisation/partners (accessed 21 May 2014)

G. Nufer

During the two football World Cups in 2006 and 2010 the beer brand Bavaria, owned by the Dutch brewing company Heineken, attracted great attention.

Before and during the football World Cup 2006 in Germany, Bavaria distributed roughly 250,000 lederhosen imitations in the Netherlands in the national colour of orange, which bore the advertising logo of 'Bavaria'. Their intention was for the Dutch fans to wear these lederhosen during their stay in Germany, the stereotypical 'Lederhosen country', and in particular to display them publicly in the match stadiums.

Figures 23.1 and 23.2 Ambush marketing by Bavaria at the Football World Cup 2006 (Adapted from Nufer, 2013: 44)

At first, this strategy worked out perfectly because thousands of Dutch fans showed up at the group match between Netherlands and Ivory Coast in Stuttgart wearing these lederhosen to – deliberately or not – disseminate the advertisement widely. In order to protect the official sponsors, swift action was required on the part of the organiser. FIFA referred to rule 10 of its ticket trading conditions, which said that 'promotional, commercial, political or religious objects of all kinds, including banners, symbols and flyers … [are] prohibited and … [are] not [allowed] to be brought into the stadiums as long as the organising committee has reason to believe that they are put on display at the stadium'. Therefore, FIFA's rights protection team made sure that all unauthorised Bavaria advertising materials remained outside the stadiums, meaning that over 1,000 Dutch supporters had to take off their lederhosen if they wanted to be admitted to the stadium by FIFA. Although it was ultimately a parried ambushing attempt, the Bavaria campaign aroused massive attention. The fact that over 1,000 people watched a World Cup game at the stadium in their underpants caused great media interest.

During the football World Cup 2010 in South Africa, Bavaria relied on ambush marketing once more and again gained major media attention – this time with the so-called 'beer babes'. At the group match between Netherlands and Denmark in Johannesburg, 36 young women showed up in the audience wearing orange mini dresses. This time, the brand name Bavaria only appeared on a small label in the seam of the dress.

Again, FIFA took drastic action against this campaign, escorting the ladies out of the stadium and even getting them temporarily put under arrest. After this, feelings ran high: the International Football Association filed a lawsuit against the planned campaign and the Dutch embassy provided legal support for the women. Because of the media coverage, the ambushing became public knowledge.

QUESTIONS

1. What are the main goals of sports sponsors in general and what are the specific goals of official World Cup sponsors?
2. What did Bavaria want to achieve with its ambushing activity in 2006? What about its campaign in 2010? In your opinion, are those two methods comparable or completely different? Investigate to see if Bavaria also conducted some ambushing during the World Cup 2014 in Brazil. If it did, describe its methods and evaluate how effective they were.
3. Critically evaluate the pros and cons of ambush marketing. Which position do you take in conclusion? Justify your answer.

CONCLUSIONS

On the one hand, ambush marketing helps non-sponsors to achieve comparable or even greater impact than the official event sponsors. On the other hand, ambushing

Figures 23.3 and 23.4 Ambush marketing by Bavaria at the Football World Cup 2010 (Adapted from Nufer, 2013: 44)

campaigns above all compromise the effectiveness of sponsorship, as official sponsors are forced to share the attention of the target group with additional free-riding advertisers, who are using the theme of the event for their own benefit.

Ambush marketing remains controversial and will continue to be the subject of contentious discussions. From the perspective of the event organisers and sports sponsors it represents an understandable threat, while from the perspective of the ambushers it offers the opportunity to reach the target audience in an attractive environment and at an affordable cost.

RECOMMENDED READING

To begin with, students might find it helpful to read an introductory text on marketing – specifically chapters on marketing communication and sponsorship. A book such as *Principles and Practice of Marketing* by Jobber and Ellis-Chadwick (2013) is an example of such a text. Thereafter, students should consider looking at texts on marketing communications (for example, *Advertising and Promotion. An Integrated Marketing Communications Perspective* by Belch and Belch (2011)) and sponsorship (for example, *Sponsorship: For a Return on Investment* by Masterman (2007)). Nufer's 2013 book on ambush marketing is a helpful insight into the most important aspects of ambush marketing and is worth looking at. Otherwise, Chadwick and Burton's 2011 paper on ambush marketing provides a good introduction to this important and fast-developing phenomenon. Further background reading can also be found in Beech and Chadwick's *The Business of Sport Management* and *The Marketing of Sports*.

BIBLIOGRAPHY

Belch, G. E. and Belch, M. A. (2011). *Advertising and Promotion. An Integrated Marketing Communications Perspective*, 9th edn, McGraw-Hill, Boston, MA.

Bruhn, M. (2010). *Sponsoring. Systematische Planung und integrativer Einsatz*, 5th edn, Gabler, Wiesbaden.

Bühler, A. and Nufer, G. (eds) (2014). *International Sports Marketing. Principles and Perspectives*, Erich Schmidt Verlag, Berlin.

Burton, N. and Chadwick, S. (2009). Ambush marketing in sport: an analysis of sponsorship protection means and counter-ambush measures, *Journal of Sponsorship*, 2(4), 303–15.

Chadwick, S. and Burton, N. (2011). The evolving sophistication of ambush marketing: a typology of strategies, *Thunderbird International Business Review*, 53(6), 709–19.

Jobber, D. and Ellis-Chadwick, F. (2013). *Principles and Practice of Marketing*, 7th edn, McGraw-Hill, London.

McKelvey, S. and Grady, J. (2008). Sponsorship program protection strategies for special sport events: are event organisers outmaneuvering ambush marketers? *Journal of Sport Management*, 22(5), 550–86.

Masterman, G. (2007). *Sponsorship: For a Return on Investment*, Butterworth Heinemann, Oxford.

Nufer, G. (2010). *Ambush Marketing im Sport*. Grundlagen – Strategien – Wirkungen, Erich Schmidt Verlag, Berlin.

Nufer, G. (2013). *Ambush Marketing in Sports. Theory and Practice*, Routledge, London/ New York.

Nufer, G. and Bühler, A. (eds) (2012). *Management im Sport. Betriebswirtschaftliche Grundlagen und Anwendungen der modernen Sportökonomie*, 3rd edn, Erich Schmidt Verlag, Berlin.

Nufer, G. and Bühler, A. (eds) (2013). *Marketing im Sport. Grundlagen und Trends des modernen Sportmarketing*, 3rd edn, Erich Schmidt Verlag, Berlin.

Nufer, G. and Bühler, A. (2015). *Event-Marketing in Sport und Kultur. Konzepte – Fallbeispiele – Trends*, Erich Schmidt Verlag, Berlin.

Pitt, L., Parent, M., Berthon, P. and Steyn, P. G. (2010). Event sponsorship and ambush marketing: lessons from the Beijing Olympics, *Business Horizons*, 53(3), 281–90.

Séguin, B., Lyberger, M., O'Reilly, N. and McCarthy, L. (2005). Internationalising ambush marketing: a comparative study, *International Journal of Sports Marketing and Sponsorship*, 6(4), 216–30.

Shilbury, D., Quick, S. and Westerbeek, H. (2009). *Strategic Sport Marketing*, 3rd edn, Allen & Unwin, Crows Nest.

RECOMMENDED WEBSITES

Fédération Internationale de Football Association (FIFA): www.fifa.com
German Institute for Sports Marketing (DISM): www.sportmarketing-institut.de

CASE 24

'A TALE OF TWO 9'S': THE BUSINESS OF GOLF

RICHARD E. ODDY

LEARNING OUTCOMES

Upon completion of this case study, the reader should be able to:
- identify and explain the landscape of golf globally;
- identify and explain the challenges facing the amateur game;
- compare and contrast measures that are being taken to reverse current trends;
- critically assess the business nature of the professional game;
- highlight future opportunities for the golf industry as a whole.

OVERVIEW OF THE CASE

This case study examines golf as a global business, from both the amateur and professional perspective. The title of this case study portrays the vast difference between the business state of the amateur and professional game. Measures are being put in place to reverse current trends of falling amateur participation, which constitute billions of pounds to economies across the globe. Conversely, the professional game continues to prosper via increased sponsorship deals and growing prize money. Many experts are beginning to suggest that the lifeblood of the sport is being neglected.

CASE STUDY

Background

America continues to be the largest golf market globally, and is thought to contain half of the total number of the world's courses and players. In 2011 estimations concluded that the sport contributed US$70 billion to the economy. However, there is an alarming trend which continues to plague the sport. Participation rates have dropped 18 per cent since 2006 and the US is not alone in seeing this trend. In the UK, the number of people who are members of golf clubs has been steadily declining since 2004, and monthly participation is 25 per cent lower than in 2007. Club membership numbers in Australia have fallen by 20 per cent since 1998 and participation in Japan is down 40 per cent from the mid 1990s.

Conversely, participation rates in China and India are on the increase, with experts suggesting that these countries will start to challenge the traditional golfing hotbeds of the US and UK. Economic growth in these countries has played a major part in this trend, creating a large middle class which is receptive to the game. Should India reach a projected population of 1.5 billion by 2030, a 2.5 per cent participation rate would be equivalent to the golf market in the US (*The Telegraph*, 2014).

Why is the amateur game in decline?

Modern lifestyles seem at loggerheads with the pace and time its takes to play a round of golf. With family dynamics changing towards both parents working, the male majority membership is more likely to be spending weekends as family time, rather than playing a round of golf. In the US, the high rate of divorce is identified as a cause of fewer people playing the game, as weekends are when they have the opportunity to spend time with their children (*The Economist*, 2014).

The game is becoming increasingly harder to play for the average golfer. Technologically enhanced equipment has led golf course designers to build longer and harder courses, thus reducing the game's appeal. The recent economic problems have led many golfers to question the viability of having an expensive yearly club membership.

The professional game – a time of prosperity?

In 2015 the PGA Tour of America smashed many records. TV money hit an annual US$800 million high. The prize money available to the top players rose to US$298 million (an increase of US$20 million from 2008), and charitable donations made by the Tour now equate to US$130 million (Forbes, 2013).

In 2014 a record 97 players won over US$1 million on the PGA Tour. Much of this can be attributed to increased sponsorship, with all 42 tournaments having a title sponsor and the ground-breaking deal with FedEx being extended to 2017. This deal provides US$35 million in prize money for the final four tournaments alone – the FedEx Cup playoffs.

Reversing the trend – innovation

Golf is having to be innovative in order to reverse the current decline. One such innovation is FootGolf, which combines the sports of football and golf in order to broaden golf's appeal. The game is now played internationally and is regulated by the Federation for International FootGolf. Played according to the rules of golf, courses have been created with 21-inch holes into which players aim to kick a football using as few 'shots' as possible. The game is growing rapidly in the UK, US and Australia. In the UK the number of FootGolf courses rose from 10 in 2013 to 75 in 2015. Golf Australia (GA), the national governing body for the sport, is helping to drive the development of the game.

> FootGolf also provides a tremendous opportunity for golf facilities to diversify their revenue streams and to connect with new market segments that help participation. Even better, it's a great way for golf to open its doors and provide an opportunity for new sports participants to enjoy the stunning surroundings of a golf course.
>
> (Cameron Wade, GA's golf development director, Golf Australia, 2014)

Reversing the trend – pricing strategies

Golf clubs are beginning to offer a greater array of flexible memberships and playing packages in order to address the current declining membership figures. Below are two such examples.

Odyssey Golf Club

Odyssey Golf Club is a traditional member's golf course which has experienced a fall in membership over the last ten years. The falling income from these lost memberships has led the club to face financial difficulties. An annual membership costs £849, which has to be paid up front in a one-off payment. The club introduced a 'Try before you join' membership package to give people the opportunity to experience the club and the course before taking out a 12-month membership.

What did they do?
The management of the club decided to create a 3-month membership costing £150 aimed at attracting beginners and those thinking of joining a club. Full playing rights, entry to competitions and a handicap were guaranteed as part of the membership, which was marketed via social media channels.

Results

Seventy-five 3-month memberships were sold, with 30 converting to the full 12-month membership. This increased the membership revenue for the club by £23,779 year-on-year.

It is vital to develop relationships in the local community and businesses, and to take advantage of free online marketing to create awareness of your membership.

General Manager, Odyssey Golf Club,
personal communication

Newpatch Golf Club

Newpatch Golf Club is a local authority-owned club which needed to address lapsed memberships, as people were drifting out of the club because they could not justify paying for full membership (£870) due to restrictions on their leisure time.

What did they do?

The management introduced 'Membership Lite', a cost-efficient way of playing golf and belonging to the club. This cost £249 and equalled 150 'credits' to be used as you play. Full playing rights, entry to competitions and a handicap were guaranteed as part of the membership.

Results

The flexible membership attracted a range of different people to the club from beginners to serious golfers, shift workers and elderly people. Seventy-two 'Membership Lite' packages were sold, increasing membership revenue by £25,000 year-on-year.

Both of these short cases demonstrate that flexible packages can increase participation and memberships. The key question is whether these strategies can be successful in the long term.

QUESTIONS

1. What are the main factors contributing to the current state of amateur golf?
2. Sponsorship and prize money in the professional game continues to grow. Why do you think that is?
3. Critically assess the long-term impact that innovations such as FootGolf could have on the game of golf.
4. What are the future opportunities for golf and how can they best be utilised to reverse the current decline in participation and club membership?

CONCLUSIONS

Golf can no longer be complacent, and there are signs that measures are being put in place to safeguard the lifeblood of the sport. Whilst the professional game continues to generate increasing sponsorship deals and prize money for its top athletes, the amateur game is seeking new and innovative ways to reinvigorate the sport. FootGolf has joined other initiatives such as Golf Xtreme and Speedgolf as a catalyst to do this. There are beacons of light amidst the darkness, with the game growing in Germany and the Czech Republic. Can lessons be learned here? Golf will again become an Olympic sport at the 2016 Olympics in Rio. This global exposure could help to reverse current trends; however, it is the role of the sport's governing bodies to maximise this opportunity for long-term gains.

RECOMMENDED READING

To begin with, students will find it helpful to read *The Marketing of Sport* by Beech and Chadwick (2007), paying specific attention to pricing sports and sports pricing strategies, and managing service quality and innovation in sport. Thereafter, students should consider sport management texts such as *The Business of Sport Management* by Beech and Chadwick (2013). For golf-specific academic work, students can refer to Brooksbank *et al.* (2012), published in the highly ranked *European Sport Management Quarterly* journal.

BIBLIOGRAPHY

Beech, J. and Chadwick, S. (2007). *The Marketing of Sport*. England: Pearson Education Limited.

Beech, J. and Chadwick, S. (2013). *The Business of Sport Management*. 2nd edn. New York: Pearson Education Limited.

Brooksbank, R., Garland, R. and Werder, W. (2012). Strategic marketing practices as drivers of successful business performance in British, Australian and New Zealand golf clubs. *European Sport Management Quarterly*, 12(5), 457–75.

The Economist (2014). Handicapped. [Online] Available from www.economist.com/news/christmas-specials/21636688-though-thriving-parts-asia-golf-struggling-america-and-much-europe (accessed 23 May 2015).

Forbes (2013). The masterful financial state of professional golf: driving for the green. [Online] Available from www.forbes.com/sites/prishe/2013/04/10/the-masterful-financial-state-of-professional-golf-driving-for-the-green/ (accessed 22 May 2015).

Golf Australia (2014). Golf, football unite in landmark FootGolf agreement. [Online] Available from www.golf.org.au/newsdisplay/golf-football-unite-in-landmark-footgolf-agreement/84109 (accessed 21 May 2015).

The Telegraph (2014). Golf on course to be a truly global business. [Online] Available from www.telegraph.co.uk/sponsored/sport/standard-life-ryder-cup/11005876/golf-course-global-business.html (accessed 25 May 2015).

CASE 25

PYEONGCHANG 2018 MARKETING: THE NEW HORIZON FOR THE WINTER OLYMPICS

JIYOON OH AND ALAIN FERRAND

LEARNING OUTCOMES

Upon completion of this case study, the reader should be able to:

- understand the structure of the Olympic Games marketing model;
- analyse the differences between the marketing strategy of the International Olympic Committee and the Organising Committee of the Olympic Games;
- evaluate the effectiveness of the International Olympic Committee marketing strategy;
- apply the Olympic marketing model to engage sponsors for the Organising Committee of the Olympic Games.

OVERVIEW OF THE CASE

This case study examines how the POCOG (The PyeongChang Organizing Committee for the 2018 Olympic & Paralympic Winter Games) is developing a successful marketing programme in collaboration with the International Olympic Committee (IOC), Korean Olympic Committee (KOC), local government and other stakeholders belonging to the Olympic Movement.

CASE STUDY

In July 2011, at the 123rd International Olympic Committee (IOC) Session in Durban, South Africa, the Republic of Korea celebrated the announcement of PyeongChang's successful bid to host the 2018 Olympic Winter Games. The Olympic Games are returning to Korea 30 years after 1988 Seoul Olympics, to a small town in the northeast of South Korea. This also marks the third time that the Winter Olympics have been held in Asia. Korea has successfully hosted many international sports games, such as the 1988 Seoul Olympics, 2002 FIFA World Cup, 2011 IAAF World Championships in Daegu, the 17th Asian Games in Incheon 2014 and the 2015 Gwangju Universiade. Korea's impressive economic advancement in recent years has drastically increased interest in sports. Taking into account Korea's size and population numbers, its performance in international sport competitions has been outstanding.

The Olympic marketing programme involves a large number of stakeholders and requires a value creation process that exploits exclusive marketing properties and rights, which manage strong brands in an international and national environment. This case study examines how, by adopting this model, the PyeongChang Organizing Committee for the 2018 Olympic & Paralympic Winter Games (POCOG) manages its rights in collaboration with the IOC, the Korean Olympic Committee (KOC) as a hosting National Olympic Committee (NOC), local government and other stakeholders belonging to the Olympic Movement to develop a successful marketing programme. The case study will also consider how the POCOG has to create value with all other stakeholders in order to be able to prepare and stage the games successfully.

Case elements

The Olympic marketing model

The Olympic marketing model involves a large number of stakeholders. Ferrand, Chappelet and Séguin (2012) have built a model based on the following dimensions: stakeholders implementing a value creation process exploiting exclusive marketing properties and rights, which manage strong brands in an international and national environment.

The Olympic marketing programme involves a system of stakeholders
According to the Olympic Charter:

> The Olympic Movement is the concerted, organised, universal and permanent action, carried out under the supreme authority of the IOC, of all individuals and entities who are inspired by the values of Olympism. It covers

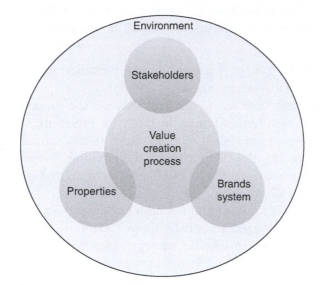

Figure 25.1 Olympic marketing multi-level model

the five continents. It reaches its peak with the bringing together of the world's athletes at the great sports festival, the Olympic Games. Its symbol is five interlaced rings.

(IOC, 2013)

Thus the Olympic Movement encompasses a large number of stakeholders:

- the IOC administration;
- IOC members and organisations;
- the Organising Committees for the Olympic Games (OCOGs);
- NOCs;
- Olympic athletes and their entourages;
- Olympic volunteers and fans;
- International federations;
- the media;
- sponsors;
- recognised sport-related organisations;
- governments;
- other non-governmental organisations;
- the general public;
- professional sport leagues.

These stakeholders form the Olympic system (Chappelet and Kubler-Mabbott, 2008), that is, the network of relationships in which the Olympic marketing programme takes place.

The Olympic marketing strategy is based on the exploitation and protection of exclusive marketing properties and rights

Olympic properties are both numerous and diverse: the modern Olympic Games, Olympic symbol (five interlaced rings, created by Pierre de Coubertin in 1913), Olympic hymn, Olympic medals, Olympic motto (*citius, altius, fortius*), Olympic posters, the Olympic flag, the Olympic oath, the Olympic flame, the Olympic torch relay, the Olympic mascot, Olympic emblems, Olympic pictograms, and still and moving images of the Olympics.

They belong to the IOC. The Olympic Charter sets out the principles under which these properties are managed to benefit these stakeholders. In parallel with the development of the Olympic marketing strategy, since the 1980s the IOC has systematically ensured the protection of Olympic properties. Today, treaties, special laws, trademark registrations and ad hoc contracts ensure these properties are strictly protected for the benefit of the IOC, NOCs and OCOGs.

A brand system linked with the Olympic symbol

The Olympic symbol is one of the strongest brands in the world of sport and an extremely valuable intangible asset, as the IOC sees branding as a top management priority. At the heart of the Olympic brand are three core values: excellence, friendship and respect.

The five interlaced rings are incorporated into the brands of 205 NOCs, OCOGs, Youth Organising Committees of the Olympic Games (YOCOGs) and all candidate cities, in addition to being allied to the brands of numerous sponsors, suppliers, broadcasters, host country governments and other organisations. This complex brand system is based on brand alliances which encompass marketing actions based on the synergy between two or more brands. They are formed to provide a greater return than could be achieved by the two brands working individually.

The Olympic marketing programme involves multiple stakeholders in value creation

In this system, the stakeholder contributes to value co-creation, and the actions of brand alliance impact brand value (Ferrand *et al.*, 2012), as described below:

- Athletes: they are essential for producing brand value and they are the heart of the brand.
- OCOGs: they play an essential role in co-creating value with the Olympic brand. OCOGs have lifespans of seven years, during which time they prepare the Games.
- Local, regional and national governments from around the world: they connect with the Olympic movement by providing funding for athletes and national federations, building sports infrastructure, and so on.

J. Oh, A. Ferrand

- Sponsors: partners in The Olympic Partner Programme (TOP) and domestic sponsors play an active role in creating value through activation programmes, reinforcing Olympic values though advertising/communication programmes and connecting consumers with the Olympic brands.
- Broadcasters: they play an integral role in bringing the Olympics into billions of homes around the world by providing images of the sports and the drama of the competitions, and so on.
- NOCs: they are responsible for protecting and controlling the Olympic brands in their respective countries.

CASE DIAGNOSIS

In order to understand the PyeongChang 2018 marketing strategy, it is important to understand the framework of the Olympic marketing model to be able to analyse the network of stakeholders forming the Olympic system in relation to its marketing rights.

The Olympic marketing programme

The Olympic marketing programme has become the driving force behind the promotion, financial security and stability of the Olympic Movement, which receives most of its funding through the sales of broadcasting rights, the TOP Programme, ticketing and licensing, among other methods.

Founded in 1985, TOP is the worldwide Olympic sponsorship programme that grants to a limited number of companies exclusive worldwide marketing rights to associate themselves with the Olympic Movement, including the IOC, OCOGs and NOCs. It is the highest level of partnership in the Olympic Movement with a four-year cycle that includes one Winter Games, one Summer Games, one Youth Winter Games and one Youth Summer Games. It has worldwide rights to the Olympic marks in the product/service category for the partners of the IOC, the Games, the NOCs and all national Olympic teams.

The most recent programme TOP IX (2017–2020) has 12 partners in the exclusive categories shown in Table 25.1.

Becoming an Olympic partner allows emotional connection with millions of people through one common platform: building brands, increasing sales, connecting with the public, building customer relationships, motivating their employees and enhancing corporate brand reputations. Olympic partners also have exclusive supply rights in a distinct product/service category which allow them to generate revenue through partnership.

While the Olympic partners' activities are coordinated by the IOC, the OCOG is responsible for national programmes, which are conducted on three different levels of sponsorship (usually consisting of three tiers – official partners, sponsors,

Table 25.1 TOP IX (2017–2020)

Partners	Exclusive product or service categories
Coca-Cola	Non-alcoholic beverages
Atos	Information technology services and solutions
Bridgestone	Tyres and rubber products
Dow	Chemicals and raw materials
GE (General Electric)	Energy generation systems, electricity distribution systems, health care, lighting fixtures and systems, etc.
McDonald's	Retail food services
Omega	Timepieces, timing, scoring and on-venue results
Panasonic	Visual and audio-visual equipment
P&G (Procter & Gamble)	Personal and healthcare products
Samsung	Wireless communication equipment, computer equipment
Toyota	Automobiles
Visa	Payment system

suppliers), licensing and ticketing in the host game territory. As regulated by the IOC guidelines in the game hosting country, the OCOG sponsors should not be selected from the TOP partner categories.

The non-Olympic hosting NOC can also have sponsors so long as these sponsors do not come from the TOP partner categories. When the IOC awards the Games to a bidding city, that host city and the host NOC sign the host city contract, which contains all the requirements and obligations for staging the Games under IOC regulations. The Joint Marketing Programme Agreement (JMPA) will only become valid if the games are awarded to the host city. After the OCOG is formed, the IOC and OCOG sign the Marketing Programme Agreement (MPA), which states that the IOC is the ultimate and exclusive owner of all Olympic intellectual property. The OCOG then draws up a marketing plan for the Games in its territory.

POCOG Overview

PyeongChang is hosting the 2018 Olympic and Paralympic Winter Games three decades after the Seoul 1988 Olympic Summer Games. PyeongChang's first and second bids for the 2010 and 2014 Games failed by a narrow margin, but it finally won the bid to host the 2018 Games at the IOC Session at Durban, South Africa on 6 July 2011.

Under the terms of the Olympic Charter, when the final announcement of which city would host the Games was made during the IOC session, the IOC, the Korean Olympic Committee (KOC) as the NOC of the host city, and the governor of Gangwon

Table 25.2 External client groups and relevant organisations

Client Group	Related Organisations/Institutions
Marketing Partner	• TOP Partners • Domestic Sponsors (Tier 1, Tier 2, Tier 3)
IOC/IPC	
KOC/KPC/ Korean NFs	
Government Partners	• Bank of Korea • Korea Mint Corporation • Korea Post • Korea Sports Promotion Foundation
Government	• Central Government • Gangwon Province • Game City (PyeongChang, GanNeung, Jubong city)
Other Partners	• Ticketing Partners • Licensing Partners • Non-commercial Partners • Education Programme Partners
General public, Summer and Winter Olympians	

Province where PyeongChang is located, signed the host city contract. This states that they accept the responsibility to host the PyeongChang 2018 Olympic and Paralympic Winter Games on PyeongChang's behalf. The KOC was responsible for setting up the POCOG, which reports directly to the IOC's Executive Board. Under an accord between the IOC and the International Paralympic Committee (IPC), the POCOG is also responsible for staging the Paralympic Games, inheriting all the legal rights and liabilities of PyeongChang 2018.

Following the host city decision, PyeongChang and the KOC moved swiftly to work on the establishment of the Organising Committee and formed the POCOG, which is composed of 116 members including representatives of the national government, Gangwon Province,[1] PyeongChang and venue cities, Korean IOC members, representatives of the KOC and Korean sports national federations, as well as winter and summer Olympians.

The host city contract and the JMPA allow the POCOG to sell sponsorship on behalf of the Korean Olympic and Paralympic teams (Team Korea) until 2020. The POCOG also has obligations to the KOC and Korean Paralympic Committee (KPC) to protect the marketing rights to the teams. As such the POCOG has a direct role in supporting the Korean teams in the run-up to the 2020 Universiades, which also includes the OCA Asian Games and FISU Universiades.

The POCOG is part of a system of stakeholders who have relationships of influence (e.g. the POCOG's marketing is carried out under the supervision of the IOC)

and dependence (e.g. the POCOG depends on the involvement of the sponsors in its national programme) and whose actions must be carried out in accordance with the rules laid down in the Olympic Charter.

The POCOG has the standing of a legal person under civil law that receives only about 5 per cent of its revenue from the public sector (mostly funding for the Paralympic Games). It has to raise the remaining 95 per cent of its funding privately, mainly through sponsorship, licensing, ticketing, and numismatic and philatelic programmes. In order to maximise sponsorship revenue, it is essential that the association rights granted to sponsors are exclusive. Consequently, in line with the Olympic Charter, the POCOG has been granted special rights under the Special Act on Support for the PyeongChang 2018 Olympic and Paralympic Winter Games.

PyeongChang 2018's vision and strategy

The vision of the POCOG is New Horizons – to open a new horizon for winter sports on a new stage in Asia for the world's younger generations with creative, sustainable legacies in PyeongChang and South Korea. Hosting PyeongChang 2018 was made possible by the Koreans' strong passion and love for winter sports. The third Winter Olympic Games to be held in Asia in 20 years will offer a special experience and instil a sense of confidence into a new generation in Asia, while also sharing the Olympic Spirit with the whole world.

The POCOG has set four core goals under the vision of New Horizon, namely the Olympics of Economy, Culture, Environment and Peace. The POCOG has developed 10 detailed strategies to realise PyeongChang's vision, the interrelated and complementary nature of which will create synergies for their implementation. These strategies are:

1. Construct athlete-oriented and Games-oriented facilities and systems.
2. Minimise cost and maximise benefits.
3. Guarantee completely safe Games.
4. Construct an easily accessible transport network.
5. Maximize convenience for spectators.
6. Develop a successful marketing strategy.
7. Create and leave a sustainable legacy.
8. Develop high-quality and unique cultural/tourism products.
9. Create an atmosphere for nationwide participation.
10. Create the opportunity for possible reconciliation and cooperation between North and South Korea.

POCOG marketing

The POCOG's properties and rights within the system of stakeholders allow it to implement a marketing plan based on national sponsoring, a licensing strategy and a ticket sales strategy. Value co-creation is linked to being associated with the Olympic brand, television coverage, the coordination of the national sponsoring plan and the international TOP programme, public enthusiasm and the involvement of different communities in South Korea.

The POCOG marketing strategy is based on the equity of the PyeongChang 2018 brand. The POCOG, its sponsors and official broadcasters, official merchandise licensees, licensed non-commercial partners, KOC and KPC are the only organisations entitled to use the PyeongChang 2018 brand and the protected Games' marks. Furthermore, as stated in the host city contract and MPA with the IOC, the POCOG has contractual obligations to protect the investment that official broadcasters, sponsors, suppliers and licensees make, and also to protect the integrity of the Games.

Korea in sports

Korea has established a highly advanced commercial sports marketplace by hosting numerous international events and sports games, and has been fortunate to accumulate its vast sport marketing knowledge and expertise from events such as the 1988 Seoul Olympics, the 2002 FIFA World Cup, the 2011 IAAF World Championships in Daegu, the 17th Asian Games in Incheon 2014, the 2015 Gwangju Universiade and others. In addition, there are various global companies which use sports as their marketing platform, such as Samsung, LG, Hyundai, KIA, GS, SK, Doosan, and so on.

Samsung electronics, as the representative Korean company and IOC TOP partner in the wireless telecommunications equipment category, is a global leader in semiconductor, telecommunication, digital media and digital convergence technologies. Samsung started Olympic marketing as a local sponsor of the 1988 Seoul Olympic Games. It has been a TOP partner since the 1998 Nagano Olympic Winter Games and considers its commitment to the Olympic Movement as a key element in its positioning and marketing strategy. It contributes to the success of the Olympic Games, as a result of which the Samsung brand image and its market position is enhanced. Now other Korean companies are considering adopting Samsung's Olympic marketing platform in PyeongChang 2018 to reach a global market.

The ultimate objective of PyeongChang 2018 is to leave a creative and sustainable legacy and provide unique growth potential for PyeongChang and Korea. To ensure successful staging of the Games, POCOG plans to develop marketing strategies that are customer-centred and create value to secure sufficient revenues from various domestic marketing programmes, to protect marketing partners' rights and privileges, and to enhance the Olympic and 2018 Games brand.

QUESTIONS

1. What are the differences between the marketing strategies of the IOC, OCOG and NOC?
2. Will there be any conflict between the host NOC and the OCOG relating to marketing rights?
3. Evaluate whether or not you think the IOC marketing strategy based on the TOP programme and the OCOG marketing strategy is likely to be the most effective one for the development of the Olympic Games.
4. If you were the POCOG marketing manager, what would be your main strategic issues and concerns?
5. From the perspective of a TOP partner, which TOP partner(s) could benefit from the Korean market? And why?

CONCLUSIONS

The Olympic brand is one of the most powerful sport brands worldwide and it is a key element of the success of the IOC marketing strategy, which is based on a corporate brand with two driver brands (Summer and Winter Olympic Games and Youth Olympic Games) and brand alliances with OCOGs, NOCs and sponsors. However, as OCOGs activities are controlled by the IOC and marketing territories are limited, it is important to understand and collaborate with the various stakeholders' objectives. As a result, tensions sometimes arise when it is necessary to choose between different stakeholders' interests in order to find a compromise between societal and functional objectives.

The POCOG signed the JMPA with the IOC in December 2012. The POCOG finalised market analysis of prospective sponsors and initiated sponsorship sales. However, as June 2015, there were only six sponsors (three partners in tier 1 and three suppliers in tier 3) whereas the previous Games had already achieved the target revenue by this stage. The economic depression experienced during this period has prevented the 2018 Games from achieving target revenue, despite the confidence and passion demonstrated in the bid for the Games. The POCOG and all stakeholders are working in close collaboration to maintain an effective interface to deliver one of the most successful Winter Olympic and Paralympic Games in Olympic history.

Guidelines for answering the discussion questions.

1. It is important to understand the structure of the Olympic marketing model and differentiate the marketing rights of the IOC and OCOG.
2. The objective of Questions 3 to 5 is to analyse and think from the perspectives of the IOC, OCOG and sponsors.

NOTE

1 Gangwon Province is building and has ownership of the Olympic stadiums for PyeongChang 2018, while POCOG runs the Games themselves.

BIBLIOGRAPHY

Chappelet, J. L. and Kubler-Mabbott, B. (2008). *The International Olympic Committee and the Olympic System: The Governance of World Sport*. London: Routledge.
Ferrand, A., Chappelet , J.-L. and Séguin, B. (2012). *Olympic Marketing*. London: Routledge.
IOC (2013). *Olympic Charter*. Lausanne: IOC.
POCOG (2013). POCOG Annual Report 2013. Korea.
Séguin, B. and O'Reilly, N. (2011). Olympic Sponsorship and Ambush Marketing. Report presented to the Canadian Olympic Committee. Ottawa.

WEB RESOURCES

IOC
Local Sponsorship Programmes: www.olympic.org/sponsors/local-sponsorship
National Olympic Committees: www.olympic.org/ioc-governance-national-olympic-committees
Olympic Charter: www.olympic.org/documents/olympic_charter_en.pdf
Olympic Marketing Fact File: www.olympic.org/Documents/IOC_Marketing/OLYMPIC_MARKETING_FACT_%20FILE_2014.pdf
Olympic Partner Programme: www.olympic.org/sponsors
The Organisation: www.olympic.org/content/the-ioc/governance/introductionold/

POCOG

About Korea. Economy: www.korea.net/AboutKorea/Economy/The-Miracle-on-The-Hangang
About Korea. How South Korea became a sporting powerhouse: www.korea.net/AboutKorea/Sports/How-South-Korea-Became-Sporting-Powerhouse
Official mascots of PyeongChang 2018: http://pyeongchang2018.com/horizon/eng/index.asp
PyeongChang 2018: www.pyeongchang2018.com/horizon/eng/Olympic_Games/PyeongChang 2018.asp
Samsung: www.samsung.com/global/galaxy/olympics/
Visit Korea, about Korea: http://english.visitkorea.or.kr/enu/1001_About%20Korea.jsp
Seriworld: www.seriworld.org/

GUIDLINE ANSWERS TO DISCUSSION QUESTIONS

1. What are the differences between the marketing strategies of the IOC, OCOG and NOC?

Tutors may wish to begin the discussion by asking students to outline the differences between the three main Olympic stakeholders' marketing frameworks by using the Olympic Marketing Model. It would be interesting to ask students to find examples in previous Games of problems that arose in relation to marketing rights conflicts between the IOC, OCOG and NOC.

NOTE: the question here is focused on non-Olympic hosting NOC

The main differences are as follows:

Territory

The IOC has TOP Programmes that give TOP partners global marketing rights in relation to Olympic intellectual properties (IPs), whereas the OCOGs and NOCs select local sponsors whose rights are limited to their respective territory. The OCOG and NOC sponsors cannot carry out any marketing activation in the territories of other NOCs or OCOGs.

For example, during the London 2012 Olympics, BMW were official Tier 1 sponsors, but since OCOG sponsors only have marketing rights in the OCOG country, BMW Olympic marketing activities in countries other than the UK were illegal.

Intellectual property

IOC – TOP partners have global rights to use the Olympic rings symbol, the emblems of the OCOGs and NOCs, and other IP. See: www.olympic.org/sponsors.

OCOG – Have the right to use the OCOG emblem and its IP and marketing rights only within the OCOG territory www.olympic.org/sponsors/local-sponsorship.

NOC – Have the right to use the NOC emblem and its IP and marketing rights only within the NOC territory.

Exclusive category

IOC – The IOC has TOP partner categories (as of 2015, TOP IV has 12 partners in different categories).

OCOG – The OCOG can select sponsors that do not conflict with the TOP partners' categories.

NOC – The NOC can select sponsors that do not conflict with the TOP partners' categories.

Marketing activations

The TOP partners have priority in any marketing activation. In addition, OCOGs and NOCs must seek approval from the IOC to initiate any marketing activation. Students can share examples from marketing activation carried out by NOCs and OCOGs for previous Games.

2. Will there be any conflict between the host NOC and the OCOG relating to marketing rights?

As the first question is focused on the non-Olympic hosting NOC, this question is focused on the Olympic hosting NOC.

For the Olympic hosting NOC, when the IOC awards the Games to a bidding city, that host city and the host NOC sign the host city contract, which contains all the requirements and obligations for staging the Games under IOC regulations. Therefore, the hosting NOC loses all the marketing rights under the Joint Marketing Programme Agreement (JMPA) which was submitted before the bid and only becomes valid if the games are awarded to the host city.

Because the NOC loses all the marketing rights after seven years and OCOG sponsors spend all the budget to stage the Games, some (or most) of the sponsors do not want to continue to be NOC sponsors after the Games.

In addition, some NOCs also run other events like the FISU (Universiade) and continental games such as the OCA (Asian Games), which affects marketing for the Olympics. It is important to consider this issue before hosting the Olympic Games. The NOC concentrates on winning the bid and the OCOG takes responsibility for delivering the Games for about seven years. The host NOC waives all the marketing rights during this period. The hosting NOC's national federations also have to work within severe restrictions imposed by the Olympic marketing model and guarantee not to use ambush marketing.

It would be interesting to look at China (Beijing 2008), Canada (Vancouver 2010), England (London 2012) and Russia (Sochi 2014) to see how their NOCs operated throughout the Olympic preparation period and how they recommenced marketing after the Games.

3. Evaluate whether or not you think the IOC marketing strategy based on the TOP programme and the OCOG marketing programme is likely to be the most effective one for the development of the Olympic Games

Answers can be very subjective, but this question is asking students to consider the issues from the point of view of the IOC. Since the TOP Programme began in 1985 and has been successful for the Olympic Movement, tutors can ask students to compare it with other sports mega-events such as the FIFA World Cup in regard to branding, financial, marketing, social and other aspects.

4. If you were the POCOG marketing manager, what would be your main strategic issues and concerns?

This question asks students to consider issues surrounding the preparation of the Olympic Games from the OCOG's point of view.

Since the 2018 Winter Olympic Games will be hosted by South Korea, tutors can ask students how they will be different from Games hosted by Western countries, and how the POCOG has to approach the marketing aspects with Korean companies such as Samsung, LG, Hyundai and so on.

5. From the perspective of a TOP partner, which TOP partner(s) could benefit from the Korean market? And why?

This question asks students to consider the Olympic Marketing Model from the TOP partners' point of view. Tutors can ask students to choose from the 10 TOP partners and state reasons why they could be benefit from the Korean market.

It will be helpful to consider the POCOG's vision (New Horizons), its four core goals (the Olympics of Economy, Culture, Environment and Peace) and the 10 detailed strategies to realise PyeongChang's vision, the interrelated and complementary nature of which will create synergies for their implementation.

It is important to consider how the partner's categories and previous marketing activation have been implemented in previous Games. The benefits include the following:

- increasing, deepening and stabilising brand awareness in Korea and Asia;
- improving brand image;
- increasing sales and revenues;
- increasing market share;
- developing B2B opportunities;
- Olympic Legacy and other benefits.

CASE 26

THE NATIONAL FOOTBALL LEAGUE IN LONDON

ADRIAN PRITCHARD

LEARNING OUTCOMES

Upon completion of this case study, the reader should be able to:

- outline the differences between the operation of North American and European sports leagues;
- describe the brand extension strategy of the NFL in overseas markets;
- assess the impact of technology on the manner of NFL consumption since 2000;
- evaluate grass-roots initiatives by sports leagues in overseas markets;
- evaluate the location of a sports team/franchise in another country.

OVERVIEW OF THE CASE

The National Football League (NFL) has tried for a number of years to develop the sport outside North America. This case study examines their commercial operations in the UK, considering the establishment of a franchise based in London.

CASE STUDY

Introduction

That most business organizations grow by developing their markets and trading overseas is well established. In a sporting context the movement into countries outside their teams' home location by professional leagues has been limited. This can be attributed to a number of factors including differences in sporting tastes, logistical difficulties and domestic league commitments. It has proved far easier to stage individual sporting tournaments such as athletics, golf, motor racing and tennis globally than it has team sports.

Most professional team sports now seek to operate in overseas markets to increase the valuation of teams/leagues, aware that domestic markets are mature and have limited growth potential. The growth in the valuation of European football clubs can, to an extent, be attributed to their ability to market their broadcasting and commercial rights on a global basis (Deloitte, 2013). Across the Atlantic Ocean the profit and commercial motives of the North American professional leagues and the teams who play in them is generally acknowledged (Jozsa, 2006).

Financially, the most successful example of a league marketed overseas is probably provided by the National Basketball Association (NBA) in China. Their involvement in this market dates back to 1979, when they started providing free coverage of matches to a local broadcaster, CCTV. Operations in the country developed, and are now managed by a separate company, NBA China, which is owned by the NBA together with a number of Chinese partners. In addition to staging two or three competitive games a season, they market licensing, broadcasting and sponsorship rights. A number of grass-roots initiatives are also undertaken to increase interest in the sport, including exhibition matches and coaching clinics. International sales are estimated to account for about 15 per cent of the league's income and this is rising (Drummond, 2009). The English Premier League (EPL) has talked about adding an additional game to the season, 'the 39th game', that would be played overseas, but has yet to do this. A number of the league's clubs have taken part in pre-season tournaments in North America and Asia. However, these games are harder to market as they are not part of the EPL.

Football, or American Football as it is generally known to the rest of the world, is a sport that has struggled to establish itself professionally outside North America. Attempts were made in the 1980s to gain interest by broadcasting games on Channel 4 in the UK, setting up a European league and NFL teams playing exhibition games in Europe – The American Bowl (UK) series. However, by the end of the twentieth century these initiatives had all ceased. A change in commercial strategy has seen the opening of an office in London to manage operations and the staging of NFL games at Wembley Stadium since 2007. These are played between US-based teams and have attracted high attendances (see Table 26.1). The establishment of a franchise based in

London which would play in the NFL has been discussed and has gathered a great deal of publicity within the sport.

The NFL

Formed in 1920 as the American Professional Football Conference, the league became the National Football League (NFL) in 1922. A number of other leagues operated in North America over the next 40 years, the most notable being the American Football League (AFL), which merged with the NFL in 1966. This led to the first Super Bowl being played in 1967 to decide the league's champion.

The NFL is a non-profit-making organization and is considered a trade association as it is financed by its 32 member teams. Under American law most professional sporting leagues are regarded as cartels and exempt from anti-trust laws, meaning they can control league entry and team location. The teams (with the exception of the Green Bay Packers) are intended to be profit-making businesses. The league, as in other North American team sports, is headed by a Commissioner who is vested with wide-ranging power. Since 2006 the post has been held by Roger Goodell.

Each club, normally referred to within the sports as a franchise, is granted exclusive rights within a given geographical area. There are a few exceptions in areas with a large population concentration, for example New York, where more than one club is allowed. As there is no promotion and relegation system, entry to the league is based on financial criteria. The Dallas Cowboys at US$2.1 billion are the most valuable sports franchise and all clubs rank among the top 50 most valuable sports teams in the world (Forbes, 2013). This league structure, together with the need for most franchises to be profitable, ensures that there is always likely to be demand for a team to be sited in geographical regions where no team is currently based.

Games are played on Sunday afternoons and Monday and Thursday evenings. The Super Bowl is always held on a Sunday. All games are broadcast live provided they are sold out; if this does not happen, there is a blackout on broadcasting in the local area. Television rights are split between four television stations: CBS, ESPN, Fox and NBC. The combined value of these contracts is estimated to be nearly US$5 billion per annum (Forbes, 2013).

League and season structure

The NFL has consisted of 32 teams since 2002. The strategy of placing franchises in large population areas and the limited number of games played have helped it to attract the highest average attendance of any sports league in the world, at over 65,000 per match (Forbes, 2013). The franchises are split into two conferences, with each having four divisions of four clubs. North American leagues differ from most European team leagues in terms of match scheduling. In the latter format most teams play each other both at home and away once. The structure in most North American sporting leagues is also more complex, as teams play some games against clubs who are not in the same division.

The season can be split into three sections:

- **Pre-season.** A four-week period consisting of four games; two at home and two away; these are exhibition games and do not count towards league standings.
- **Regular season.** A 17-week, 256-game season running from September until the week after Christmas, in which each team plays 16 games.
- **Post-season.** A knock-out tournament starting in January, consisting of the top 12 teams, which culminates in the Super Bowl. In 2015 this was held on the first Sunday in February.

NFL in Europe prior to 2000

Initial attempts to gain interest in the sport saw the newly created Channel 4 starting UK coverage with an hour-long highlights show. This was later increased to include live coverage of the post-season and the Super Bowl in 1983. In the late 1980s average audiences were nearly 3 million, peaking at 3.7 million in the 1987/8 season. The channel was supported by the purchase of advertising slots in commercial breaks by a number of American corporations. Most prominently, Anheuser-Busch promoted a link between their beer Budweiser and the sport. The increased interest also led to the emergence of specialist NFL magazines and coverage in newspapers. A number of merchandizing deals were also signed with food and drink producers (Maguire, 1991). Interest in the sport wavered during the 1990s and Channel 4 ceased coverage in 1998, though it recommenced in 2013.

Further attempts were made by the NFL to capitalize on interest by setting up a European league. The World League of American Football (WLAF) was the first venture in 1991 but only lasted two years. Of the ten teams only three were based in Europe. The other seven were in North America. The league was relaunched in 1995 as NFL Europe, an exclusively European league consisting of the three original teams – Barcelona, Frankfurt and London – together with teams based in Amsterdam, Dusseldorf and Edinburgh. The league was not a great commercial success; average gates never exceeded 20,000 and most of the franchises were moved to German cities. By 2005 five of the six teams were located there, with the other based in the Netherlands. In late 2006 it was officially branded as NFL Europa; this league only ran for a season before ceasing operations.

The London Monarchs competed in both the WLAF and NFL Europe, playing their last season as England Monarchs. In total they played 60 games in 6 seasons (10 games per season – no games were played in 1993 and 1994). Their first season was the most successful in terms of gates, with an average attendance of over 40,000 for games played at the then 80,000 capacity Wembley stadium. When the league resumed in 1995, attendances fell to 16,000 as they moved to White Hart Lane, the home of Tottenham Hotspur football club. The new ground caused a problem as the pitch was too small, and special dispensation had to be obtained from the NFL to play there. They then moved to Stamford Bridge, home of Chelsea football club, in 1997, were rebranded as England Monarchs for 1997, and enjoyed a nomadic existence playing in smaller venues in London, Birmingham and Bristol. Average attendances dropped to below 6,000 and at the end of 1998 the franchise was shut down and relocated to Berlin (World League of American Football, 2013).

The NFL in London in the 2000s

Wembley Stadium was redeveloped by its owners the Football Association, reopening in 2007 as a 90,000 capacity venue. Although it is most well known for staging international (Association) football matches and Cup Finals, it needs to stage other events in order to be economically viable. For example, the pop group Take That played eight sell-out concerts there in 2011.

The manner of operation of the NFL London games is that a franchise moves one of its eight home games from the regular season to London (see Table 26.1). Crowds have been good, and the initial schedule of one game per year was increased to two in 2012, and three from 2014. It has been mooted that the stadium could be used to host a franchise (Conway, 2013).

Like most leagues, the NFL extends its brand by offering more than just a match. A number of events have been held as part of the build-up to the regular-season London games. The inaugural NFL Fan Rally was held in Trafalgar Square,

Table 26.1 NFL matches at Wembley Stadium since 2007

Year	Date (all on a Sunday)	Designated Visitors	Designated Home	Crowd
2007	October 28	New York Giants	Miami Dolphins	81,176
2008	October 26	San Diego Chargers	New Orleans Saints	83,226
2009	October 25	New England Patriots	Tampa Bay Buccaneers	84,254
2010	October 31	Denver Broncos	San Francisco 49ers	83,941
2011	October 23	Chicago Bears	Tampa Bay Buccaneers	76,981
2012	October 28	New England Patriots	St. Louis Rams	84,004
2013	September 29	Pittsburgh Steelers	Minnesota Vikings	83,518
	October 27	San Francisco 49ers	Jacksonville Jaguars	83,559
2014	September 28	Miami Dolphins	Oakland Raiders	83,436
	October 26	Detroit Lions	Atlanta Falcons	83,532
	November 9	Dallas Cowboys	Jacksonville Jaguars	83,603

Source: NFL (2015)

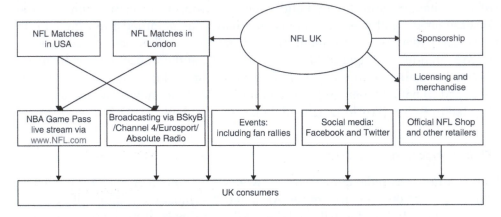

Figure 26.1 The distribution of NFL products and services in the UK

London in 2010, and repeated in 2011 and 2012. In 2013 it was held in Regent Street for the Vikings vs. Steelers game, and Trafalgar Square for the Jaguars vs. Cowboys game. Estimates are that hundreds of thousands of people attended the 2013 events. These seek to showcase the sport by providing themed activities including meeting players, video games, cheerleader displays and the sale of merchandise (Frenette, 2013).

Commercial operations are managed by NFL UK, the London office of the organization, whose activities include negotiating broadcasting and sponsorship deals. Broadcasting contracts are held by Absolute Radio, BSkyB, Channel 4 and Eurosport. NFL UK estimated combined audiences to be 4.3 million in February 2013. A further viewing option is the NFL Game Pass that can be purchased to allow all regular games to be viewed via the web (nfluk.com, 2013). The range of products/services offered is illustrated in Figure 26.1.

Jacksonville Jaguars

This is considered to be the franchise that would be most likely to move to London. It is located in one of the smallest catchment areas – Jacksonville, Florida; the Oakland Raiders are the only team to be valued at less than the Jaguars (Forbes, 2013). Since being formed in 1995, they have had limited success; they have never been in a Super Bowl, and have only qualified for the post-season play-offs five times, their last appearance being in 2007/8.

The franchise has a number of links with London, team owner Shahid Khan having bought the EPL club Fulham in 2013 (although they have since been relegated). The Jaguars have also signed up to play a regular home game at Wembley for four consecutive seasons, commencing in 2013. This means that in each of these four seasons only seven regular season games will be staged at their normal home stadium,

EverBank Field. The loss of a game has led to a number of Jaguar fans complaining about the reduction in matches.

QUESTIONS

1. Evaluate the setting-up of an NFL franchise in London, discussing the issues of broadcasting, logistics and time differences.
2. Describe the benefits of commercial association with the NFL for companies marketing in the UK.
3. Discuss how the advent of technology has impacted on the product/serving offering of the NFL since the 1990s. To what extent can it be used to help in marketing the sport?
4. Explain why grass-roots initiatives to develop interest in American Football are important.
5. Compare London with Los Angeles as a location for an NFL franchise.

CONCLUSIONS

The most successful sports leagues and the teams that play within them are constantly seeking to expand. Many believe their domestic markets are saturated or have limited growth potential, and that there is a great deal of potential in overseas markets. Examples of expansion are provided in this case study, amongst others by English football teams in Asia and the NBA in China. The ability to harness internet-based technology, the greater commercial focus of clubs, increasing interest from overseas sponsors and the increase in foreign ownership of teams are all factors that are likely to lead to increased attempts to penetrate foreign markets. The portfolio of products/services offered by teams/leagues is constantly evolving in both home and overseas markets in line with technological developments.

RECOMMENDED READING

For a history of the development of the NFL and other American leagues including the franchise movement, see Jozsa (2006), who examines the expansions and mergers of leagues in the USA since the latter part of the nineteenth century. A number of authors have contrasted the operation of leagues in North America and Europe, most concisely Sloane (2006) and Pritchard (2011). For a description of the strategy of the NBA in China see Drummond (2009); at the time of writing the author was a senior NBA employee. Apostolopoulou (2002) categorizes the range of products/services offered by North American sports teams.

BIBLIOGRAPHY

Apostolopoulou, A. (2002). 'Brand extensions by U.S. professional sport teams: motivations and keys to success', *Sport Marketing Quarterly*, 11(4), 205–14.

Conway, R. (2013). 'Why the NFL matters to Wembley Stadium's financial future'. 24 September. Accessed 3 April 2015 from www.bbc.co.uk/sport/0/american-football/24227296.

Deloitte (2013). Captains of Industry: Football Money League, Sport Business Group at Deloitte. Accessed 3 April 2015 from www.deloitte.com/view/en_GB/uk/industries/sports-businessgroup/sports/football/deloitte-football-money-league/c0d0cc64dac5c310VgnVC-M3000003456f70aRCRD.htm.

Drummond, E. (2009). 'Entrepreneurship a good play for NBA in China', *Institute for International Business – Global Forum Report*, Winter, 14–15.

Forbes (2013). NFL team values: The business of Football. Accessed 3 April 2015 from www.forbes.com/nfl-valuations/.

Frenette, G. (2013). 'NFL team in London? Not crazy', 26 October, *The Florida Times-Union*. Accessed 3 April 2015 from http://members.jacksonville.com/opinion/premium/blog/400565/gene-frenette/2013-10-26/gene-frenette-nfl-team-london-not-crazy.

Jozsa, F. P. (2006). *Big Sports, Big Business. A Century Of League Expansions, Mergers and Reorganizations*. Praeger: Westport.

Maguire, J. (1991). 'The media–sport production complex: the case of American Football in Western European societies', *European Journal of Communication*, 6, 315–35.

Nfluk.com (2014). NFL communications. Accessed 3 April 2015 from http://nflcommunications.com/2013/10/24/2014-international-series-games-confirmed/.

Ozanian, M. (2013). 'The most valuable NFL teams', *Forbes*, 14 August. Accessed 3 April 2015 from www.forbes.com/sites/mikeozanian/2013/08/14/the-most-valuable-nfl-teams/.

Pritchard, A. (2011). 'Between a base and a footplace', *International Journal of Sports Marketing and Sponsorship*, 12(2), 153–66.

Sloane, P. J. (2006) 'The European model of sport' in W. Andreff, and S. Szymanski (eds) *Handbook on the Economics of Sport*. Edward Elgar: Cheltenham.

World League of American Football (2013). Accessed 3 April 2015 from www.worldleagueofamericanfootball.com/index.html.

RECOMMENDED WEBSITES

Official website of the NFL: www.nfl.com.

Official UK website of the NFL: www.nfluk.com.

Forbes – The Business of Football: www.Forbes.com/nfl. Forbes provides useful information about financial aspects of the NFL and the incomes and profitability of the franchises that play in it.

The World League of American Football: www.worldleagueofamericanfootball.com/. This site provides a background to the history of the NFL outside North America. It provides some useful information on the teams who have competed in the various league guises.

VIDEO LINKS

A range of material is available at YouTube.com. The following are recommended:

Rise of the NFL in the UK / International series at Wembley (2014) Guardian Sport: www.youtube.com/watch?v=iXhAj5j-6Lk(8.04 minutes) Examines the NFL's expansion into the UK.

Is a NFL team headed to London? (2013): www.youtube.com/watch?v=vgtY_MvMF_4 (1.51 minutes) CBS.

NFL London Franchise 2013? (2013): www.youtube.com/watch?v=QdOmiQtyKXw (5.31 minutes) TYT. The above two clips both discuss the setting up a franchise in London. The second has some industrial language!

London, L.A. May Be Options if Jaguars Leave Jacksonville (1.48 minutes) Bloomberg www.youtube.com/watch?v=3fbYp8JT9fc. This considers the movement of the franchise to either Los Angeles or London.

CASE 27

'WE DON'T DO WALKING AWAY'[1]

BALWANT SAMRA, STEPHEN CASTLE AND GAYE BEBEK

LEARNING OUTCOMES

Upon completion of this case study, the reader should be able to:

- relate marketing theories of segmentation, targeting and positioning to the sports fan as consumer;
- understand different motivators for fans, and be able to relate that motivation to marketing theory;
- assess the benefits that fan engagement brings to clubs;
- critically evaluate management decisions that impact fan loyalty and engagement.

OVERVIEW OF THE CASE

This case study considers fan loyalty and can be read in conjunction with other case studies within this book. As with all consumers, fans are a mixed bunch; they all have different backgrounds and motivations. There are differing degrees of loyalty that fan-customers show to 'their brand'. It is not all about winning either. Some fans stay with their brand through thick and thin (even being relegated four divisions in the case of football club Glasgow Rangers), whilst others show only little brand loyalty. If it is a simple repeat purchase, fine – but if they have to make an effort such as travelling 35 miles for home games – that is a different matter. This case study considers fans' motivation, fan loyalty and marketing theory to engage with the various fan types or segments.

CASE STUDY

Glasgow Rangers launched their 2014–15 season ticket campaign by announcing a price increase of between 15 and 25 per cent (Sky Sports, 2014). This was a bold test of the loyalty of the fans – fans who had already been boldly tested for years. Finances continued to be in the bin, with a recently announced £3.5 million loss for the six-month period to 31 December 2013 (BBC, 2014a). However, the fans have continued to support their team through the difficult times. Remember, this is the celebrated Scottish Premier League team that went into administration and dropped four – yes four – divisions in 2012 (Tribalfootball, 2012). For the seasons 2012–13 and 2013–14 more than 72,000 season tickets were sold, and in 2013–14 season ticket sales generated nearly £7 million, and accounted for nearly half of Rangers' annual revenues (Finnerty, 2014). The club stated:

> The last two campaigns have seen a 33% decrease and a subsequent freeze in season ticket prices. This season as the club prepares to return to the top flight, challenge and re-establish Rangers at the top of Scottish football, we must invest further in all areas across the Club. An increase in season ticket prices is therefore necessary.
>
> (Rangers, 2014a)

Rangers are now used to facing financial problems. They had been struggling for cash in 2011–12. In July 2012 the club had reportedly sold only 250 season tickets, a major decline from the previous year's total of 40,000 (*Daily Record*, 2012). Later the same month they went into administration, and they became another example of 'franchised football' when Sevco Scotland Ltd bought the club. To top it off, the Scottish Football League decided that the new Rangers club should start from the bottom of the league (CNN, 2012). After going into administration, it was estimated that Rangers would sell between 25,000 and 50,000 tickets for the following year (McConville, 2012). The fans showed their full support, and sales picked up – from only 250 season ticket sales in 2012, they achieved 38,014 sales in the 2012–13 season. Only Manchester United, Arsenal and Newcastle United had reportedly sold more (Grahame, 2013).

Rangers fans had shown exemplary support for their team through the bad days of financial struggle, administration and starting from the bottom of the league. Now their loyalty was being tested again. Once again, the team was facing financial difficulties and the club resorted to fan support. Luckily they do have a loyal fan base. Rangers fans 'don't do walking away'; they were, are and continue to be fans. The new ticket campaign for Rangers emphasised that the club is more than just football; it is heritage: 'This is not just your seat. You are keeping it warm for the generations to come' (Rangers, 2014b).

'We don't do walking away'

Portsmouth FC is another club that has had a rocky ride, starting in the 2009–10 season. The club went into administration before the season ended, and it was relegated from the Premier League to the Championship. During that year the club sold 9,700 season tickets for 2010–11(Partridge, 2011). The team barely stayed in the Championship that year, following which financial problems became apparent again, and the club went into administration for the second time. When new season tickets were released for sale, despite the club's financial issues and being relegated twice, there was an £18 increase (4.5 per cent) from the previous season's price of £400. Questions arose as to whether the fans would still fully support the club. A research survey conducted with 1,515 Portsmouth FC fans reported that 39 per cent of the respondents were inclined to renew their season tickets for 2011–12, while 5 per cent of respondents would not renew at all, even if the ticket prices were frozen. The rest were undecided whether to renew or not, and at least 1 in 4 fans in this group would possibly opt not to renew (Partridge, 2011).

Uncertainty regarding the finances and the unsuccessful run of the club was putting the fans' loyalty to the test once more. The actual season ticket sales were estimated to be 8,519, a decrease from the previous season (Partridge, 2011). Despite the series of unsuccessful seasons, the fans were still supporting their club. Yet, at the end of the 2011–12 season, Portsmouth still could not pick up their game and they were relegated to League One. This time, the club did not want to risk the loyalty of their fans, and the season ticket prices were reduced by up to 70 per cent for the 2012–13 season (Portsmouth Vital Football, 2012). The result was successful. An attendance analysis showed that during the 2012–13 season Portsmouth FC had the second highest attendance level in League One, behind Sheffield United (Football League, 2013). However, much to the fans' despair the team was once again relegated, to League Two, at the end of the 2012–13 season (Cartright, 2013). In April 2013 Portsmouth became the largest fan-owned football club in the country (BBC, 2013).

In contrast to Rangers and Portsmouth, Coventry tries the patience of its fans for a different reason, giving a new descriptor to 'home games'. In July 2013 the Football League approved Coventry City's move from the Coventry Ricoh Arena to the Sixfields Stadium in Northampton. This move was requested by the club's hedge-fund owner Sisu. The Ricoh Arena had been Coventry City's home for eight years, until the dispute between Sisu and the Arena landlords resulted in a 35-mile move for home games. The fans were furious and blamed Sisu. They showed their feelings by threatening to boycott the 'home' games (Percy, 2013). And they backed up their words with action. For the second 2013–14 fixture fewer than 2,000 fans were present at Sixfields – and the majority of them were watching the game from the surrounding hills and not in the stadium(!) (Rouge, 2013) – quite a difference to the average of 21,000 fans attending the Ricoh Arena in 2005–06

B. Samra, S. Castle, G. Bebek

(BBC, 2014b). In the 2013–14 season the average home gate at Sixfields was 2,169 (BBC, 2014b) – and remember, these are not just Coventry fans. In contrast there were between 439 and 3,406 fans travelling to away matches (BBC, 2014b), topped by 7,000 City fans travelling to Stadium MK – nearly 50 per cent of the crowd (BBC, 2014b). The fans formed the 'Not a Penny More' group, which campaigned to force Sisu out of the club (Gilbert, 2013). The current owners are Otium (BBC, 2014b).

The fans are taking a very clear stand here. They continue to be the team's supporters, but they simply do not want to tolerate and compensate the owners, who have torn the team out of their home only to reduce their costs. This was most evident when 10,000 fans opted to attend the Coventry Legends (former club players) vs Midland Allstars game at the old home Ricoh Arena, while only 1,000 tickets were sold for a home game at Sixfields during the same week (Sanghani, 2013). The number of fans attending the Ricoh Arena was never huge, but this change of 'home' is estimated to have affected season ticket sales, with a decrease of some 5,000 to 15,000 season ticket sales and less than 1,000 fans showing up at Sixfields (Rouge, 2013). The club say that they fully intend to return to Coventry in three to five years and that they made an agreement with the Football League to this effect, with a £1 million penalty if they fail to return. However, the fans very understandably fear that they may never return (*Coventry Telegraph*, 2013) – after all, there is the example of Wimbledon's relocation to Milton Keynes. Yet this is surely a reaction to the club's abandonment of the fans. When Coventry City FC was relegated to League One at the end of season 2011–12, even though the fans were not happy, they still supported the club. For the 2012–13 season they had the third-highest fan attendance numbers of League One clubs (Football League, 2013).

Fans seem to be quite forgiving and loyal if their club is in financial trouble, becomes a franchise or is even relegated. They keep supporting their teams no matter what. However, when a club moves away from its fans, or abandons its fans, quite understandably they feel forced out. As much as financial stability and success is important, surely a football club without its fans would not mean much. Unfortunately, the owners of Coventry FC seem to be disregarding that risk.

QUESTIONS

1. Describe fan loyalty. Why is it important for a football club to have loyal fans?
2. What are the different fan motivations that can be seen within this case study? Divide the fans into discrete groups (or segments). How should the club management engage with these different groups?
3. Speculate on the reasons why fans would continue to support the team through rough times (i.e. financial problems, poor performance, etc.).

'We don't do walking away'

4. What lessons can be learned from this case study in relation to customer/brand loyalty?
5. What lessons can you learn from this case study when making difficult management decisions?

CONCLUSIONS

This case study demonstrates that sports fans are classic consumers/customers. Fans behave according to classic consumer marketing theory – and equally management can engage with their customers according to classic marketing theory. It is just as with any other service: the 'product' is mostly intangible. It is important within the sports business that clubs and managers recognise this and engage with the fans according to marketing theory and practice.

RECOMMENDED READING

To begin with, a general marketing book will be of benefit to the reader (for instance Jobber and Ellis-Chadwick (2013) or Masterson and Pickton (2014). Fill's review of marketing communication is also recommended (Fill, 2013). Considering research on fans more specifically, the reader is drawn to *Sports Marketing* (Mullin *et al.*, 2000). Also there are general research articles in the *International Journal of Sports Management and Marketing* and *International Journal of Sports Marketing and Sponsorship*. For specific papers on fans, see Backman and Crompton (1991), Bristow and Sebastian (2001), Ferrand and Pages (1996), Funk and Pastore (2000), Jacoby and Kyner (1973), Oliver (1999) or McAlexander *et al.* (2002).

NOTE

1 Rangers fan's shirt slogan (Grahame, 2013).

BIBLIOGRAPHY

Backman, S. J. and Crompton, J. L. (1991). Using loyalty matrix to differentiate between high, spurious, latent and loyal participants in two leisure services. *Journal of Park and Recreation Administration*, 9, 1–17.
BBC (2013). Portsmouth FC begin new era as football league starts, accessed 7 May 2014 from www.bbc.co.uk/newsbeat/23527669.
BBC (2014a). Rangers interim accounts show £3.5m losses amid ticket warning, accessed 7 May 2014 from www.bbc.co.uk/sport/0/football/26763952.
BBC (2014b). Coventry City: Why Sky Blues are taking 7,000 to MK Dons, accessed 7 May 2014 from www.bbc.co.uk/sport/0/football/25089406.

Bristow, D. N. and Sebastian R. J. (2001). Holy Cow! Wait 'til next year! A closer look at the brand loyalty of Chicago Cubs baseball fans. *Journal of Consumer Marketing*, 18(3), 256–75.

Cartright, P. (2013). Matt Smith's header ensured Lee Johnson's Oldham beat father Gary's Yeovil and condemned both Hartlepool and Portsmouth to relegation, accessed 7 May 2014 from www.bbc.co.uk/sport/0/football/22075591.

CNN (2012). New Rangers must start in bottom tier of Scottish football, clubs decide, accessed 7 May 2014 from http://edition.cnn.com/2012/07/13/sport/football/football-rangers-third-division-barclays/#cnn-disqus-area.

Coventry Telegraph (2013). Coventry City fans' group fears club will never return after Sixfields move, accessed 7 May 2014 from www.coventrytelegraph.net/sport/football/football-news/coventry-city-fans-group-fears-5105983.

Daily Record (2012). Rangers in crisis: Charles Green faces £15m black hole after just 250 season tickets are sold, accessed 7 May 2014 from www.dailyrecord.co.uk/sport/football/rangers-in-crisis-charles-green-faces-1166134.

Ferrand, A. and Pages, M. (1996). Football supporter involvement: explaining football match loyalty. *European Journal for Sports Management*, 3(10), 7–20.

Fill, C. (2013). *Marketing Communications: Brands, Experiences and Participation,* 6th edn. Pearson, Harlow.

Finnerty, A. (2014). Glasgow Rangers put on a brave face despite yet another financial crisis, accessed 7 May 2014 from http://soccerly.com/article/finnal/glasgow-rangers-put-on-a-brave-face-despite-yet-another-financial-crisis.

Football League (2013). Attendance Analysis 2012/13, accessed 7 May 2014 from www.efl.com/news/article/attendance-analysis-201213-1742544.aspx.

Funk, D. C. and Pastore, D. L. (2000). Equating attitudes to allegiance: the usefulness of selected attitudinal information in segmenting loyalty to professional sports teams. *Sports Marketing Quarterly*, 9(4), 175–84.

Gilbert, S. (2013). Coventry City fans plan protest picnic at Sixfields, accessed 7 May 2014 from www.coventrytelegraph.net/sport/football/football-news/coventry-city-fans-plan-protest-5831949.

Grahame, E. (2013). Rangers' season tickets – only Manchester United, Arsenal and Newcastle United have sold more, accessed 7 May 2014 from www.telegraph.co.uk/sport/football/teams/rangers/9806862/Rangers-season-tickets-only-Manchester-United-Arsenal-and-Newcastle-Unted-have-sold-more.html.

Jacoby, J. S. and Kyner, D. B. (1973). Brand loyalty vs. repeat purchasing behaviour. *Journal of Marketing Research*, 10, 1–9.

Jobber, D. and Ellis-Chadwick, F. (2013). *Principles and Practice of Marketing*, 7th edn. McGraw-Hill, Maidenhead.

McAlexander, J. H., Schouten, J. W. and Koenig, H. F. (2002). Building brand community. *Journal of Marketing*, 66, 38–54.

McConville, P. (2012). Rangers FC in 2012–2013: could it survive financially, accessed 7 May 2014 from http://scotslawthoughts.wordpress.com/2012/07/27/rangers-fc-in-2012-2013-could-it-survive-financially/.

Masterson, R. and Pickton, D. (2014). *Marketing: An Introduction,* 3rd edn. Sage, London.

Mullin, B. J., Hardy, S. and Sutton, W. A. (2000). *Sport Marketing*, 2nd edn. Human Kinetics, Champaign, IL.

Oliver, R .L. (1999). Whence consumer loyalty? *Journal of Marketing*, 63, 33–44.

Partridge, M. (2011). Season ticket survey: the results, accessed 7 May 2014 from www.portsmouth.vitalfootball.co.uk/article.asp?a=237892.

'We don't do walking away'

Percy, J. (2013). Coventry City will play their home games at Northampton's Sixfields Stadium for the next three seasons, accessed 7 May 2014 from www.telegraph.co.uk/sport/football/teams/coventry-city/10167458/Coventry-City-will-play-their-home-games-at-Northamptons-Sixfields-Stadium-for-the-next-three-seasons.html.

Portsmouth Vital Football (2012). Up to 70% off season tickets, accessed 7 May 2014 from www.portsmouth.vitalfootball.co.uk/article.asp?a=283775.

Rangers (2014a). Season ticket renewals begin, accessed 7 May 2014 from www.rangers.co.uk/news/headlines/item/6720-season-ticket-renewals-underway.

Rangers (2014b). Season tickets 2014–15, accessed 7 May 2014 from www.rangers.co.uk/tickets/season-tickets.

Rouge, L. (2013). Eye witness assessment: Coventry City and sorry Sixfields, accessed 7 May 2014 from http://thetwounfortunates.com/eye-witness-assessment-coventry-city-and-sorry-sixfields/.

Sanghani, R. (2013). Coventry City fans boycott club's move to Sixfields Stadium in Northampton, accessed 7 May 2014 from www.telegraph.co.uk/sport/football/teams/coventry-city/10234320/Coventry-City-fans-boycott-clubs-move-to-Sixfields-Stadium-in-Northampton.html.

Sky Sports (2014). Scottish Football: Rangers have announced an increase in season-ticket prices, accessed 7 May 2014 from www1.skysports.com/football/news/11788/9257467/scottish-football-rangers-have-announced-an-increase-in-season-ticket-prices.

Tribalfootball (2012). Rangers drop down to Scottish third division, accessed 7 May 2014 from www.tribalfootball.com/articles/rangers-drop-down-scottish-third-division-3349371#.U2pViq1dXZU.

RECOMMENDED WEBSITES

BBC Football: www.bbc.co.uk/sport/0/football/. This website is a useful resource for following the fortunes of clubs such as Rangers, Portsmouth and Coventry. The bibliography above provides examples of newspapers which report off-pitch developments at football clubs.

Vital Football: www.vitalfootball.co.uk/. This site is recommended to obtain a fan perspective.

APPENDIX: Questions and Answers

1. DESCRIBE FAN LOYALTY. WHY IS IT IMPORTANT FOR A FOOTBALL CLUB TO HAVE LOYAL FANS?

Discussion can focus on the ability of a club to attract, develop and retain fans. Loyalty is important because it helps to protect a brand from competition and allows a chance to charge increased prices, thus creating a higher revenue stream (Aaker, 1994). Loyalty can be illustrated by the things consumers do (behavioural loyalty) as well as consumers' perceptions and attitudes towards a brand (attitudinal loyalty).

B. Samra, S. Castle, G. Bebek

In the sports context, behavioural loyalty is demonstrated through fans attending team games, their purchase of team merchandise and the length of their loyalty to a particular team (Gladden and Funk, 2002). Attitudinal loyalty, on the other hand, involves fans' commitment to and affiliation with their favourite team, as well as willingness to follow that team (Gladden and Funk, 2002). Both types of loyalty are necessary in order to maintain a steady stream of loyal fans and revenue.

Loyalty of sports fans is fascinating because loyalty is important to the fan in a way that is not seen with consumers in most sectors (how many shoppers will sing 'loyal customers' as they make their weekly trip to the supermarket?) (Tapp, 2004: 204). Therefore, loyalty to a team is a highly meaningful concept for sports fans. While Parker and Stuart (1997) point out that exclusive loyalty to a team is the norm and that loyalty is not affected by team success at all, other authors state that loyalty of sports fans cannot be taken for granted. They emphasise that different types of sports fans show different types of loyalty and different behaviour depending on the team's success (Tapp, 2004). Based on the work of Dick and Basu (1994), Tapp (2004) found a number of football supporter categories based on their attitudinal and behavioural loyalty to a team. At one end of the spectrum there are fanatics and at the other end are supporters who attend only occasionally. Whereas fanatics will still be loyal to a team even when it is not successful, casual supporters might cease to watch the games in such a situation. These different reactions are described by Cialdini *et al.* (1976) as BIRGing (Basking in Reflected Glory) and CORFing (Cutting Off Reflected Failure) behaviour. Several researchers have found that BIRGing and CORFing tendencies vary across different types of sports fans (Madgrial, 1995; Sloan, 1989). Wann and Branscombe (1990) found that individuals high in team identification were more likely to BIRG after a victory and less likely to CORF after defeat. Those fans are likely to support their team even when it drops down a league, and their loyalty is not linked to satisfaction with the outcome of a game (Tapp, 2004).

Sports marketers can enhance fans' loyalty by gearing towards increasing both behavioural and attitudinal loyalty as well as increasing satisfaction levels. Promotional and communication tactics should be implemented to encourage fans to follow their favourite team by attending games, watching broadcasts or reading about the team. Efforts to provide a superb experience at the game through excellent service, entertaining product delivery, perks and fan appreciation initiatives, and quality of concessions and other value-related aspects could increase fans' satisfaction and encourage them to repeatedly attend games. In addition, access to the team through opportunities for fans to interact directly with coaches and players could significantly strengthen fans' identification with the club, leading to increased loyalty.

2. WHAT ARE THE DIFFERENT FAN MOTIVATIONS THAT CAN BE SEEN WITHIN THIS CASE STUDY? DIVIDE THE FANS INTO DISCRETE GROUPS (OR SEGMENTS). HOW SHOULD THE CLUB MANAGEMENT ENGAGE WITH THESE DIFFERENT GROUPS?

The focus here is to discuss various motivations and different types of fans.

Sports consumption motives

Below we consider eight different motives for sports consumption that fall into one of three categories: (1) social motives, (2) psychological motives and (3) personal motives.

Social motives

Family. Sport consumption can be part of a family ritual, whether it is direct consumption (i.e., attending events) or indirect consumption, such as watching games on TV. Interest in a sport or team often begins with exposure at an early age due to the influence of family members.

Group affiliation. Becoming part of a community of people who share an affinity for the same sport, team or player is another socially based motive. Group affiliation motives can be met by direct consumption at sporting events or indirectly through such activities as participation in online message boards or membership in social networking groups.

Psychological motives

Self-esteem. The decision to become a fan or follower through sports consumption may be influenced by the impact it has on one's personal identity. A person's beliefs about how he or she is perceived by other people can be enhanced through sports consumption, and the benefits of group affiliation can have a positive impact on self-esteem.

Escape. One form of hedonic consumption motives that sports can meet is to provide an escape from everyday life. Problems, stress and other conditions can be left behind for a period of time while participating in sports or consuming as a spectator.

Personal motives

Aesthetic. This motive relates to one's interest in the sport itself – the strategy of baseball, the aggressiveness of football and the skill of Kobe Bryant are examples of the aesthetics of a sport influencing sports consumption. Marketing a sports product to people motivated by aesthetics may represent the 'low hanging fruit' of an audience easy to persuade. However, they are usually insufficient in number to be the only type of consumer in the target market.

Entertainment. In contrast to an aesthetic motive, people motivated to consume sports for its entertainment value seek benefits from the total experience of sports consumption. Sports properties respond to consumers' entertainment motives by designing interactivity and multisensory environments into their experiences. Examples of this include pre-game or post-game concerts, in-game contests and giveaways.

Sensory stimulation. This is related to the entertainment motive. Some consumers seek to experience sensory stimulation through sports. For spectator sporting events, the game is a production – literally! Entertainment elements like music, video and graphics are scripted into game production, and timed to occur at specific points during the event. And the event itself can be a source of sensory stimulation – speed, violence and other aspects of action are ways to elicit sensory responses.

Economic. The economic motive is linked to monetary gain or benefits that people may enjoy from sports. People who gamble on sports may follow a particular sport or teams to gain an advantage when wagering on sports. On a broader scale, fantasy sports players may be attracted to participate by an economic motive. The prospect of winning cash or merchandise prizes in a fantasy football league, for example, may prompt some players to invest time and money in an effort to improve their chances of winning.

Fan segments

Fans can be divided into three segments, as discussed below.

Temporary fan

The more strongly an individual identifies himself or herself as a 'fan', the more the individual uses this specific identification with regard to other people and also internally, to discern himself or herself. However, being a fan is not something that is used by the temporary fan for self-identification (i.e. being a fan is not central to the temporary fan's self-concept). The temporary fan's interest in the phenomenon is time-constrained. After the phenomenon of interest is over, the fan is no longer motivated to exhibit behaviour related to the sports object, but rather to return to normal behaviour.

This time boundary is the primary factor that differentiates the temporary fan from other sports fans. What might explain a temporary fan's motives and behaviour? Cialdini *et al.* (1976) suggested the BIRG theory as a way to understand fans. It involves the tendency for an individual to attempt to internalise the success of others.

Devoted fan

The devoted fan remains loyal to their team or player, even if either the specific short-term event that captivated their temporary attention has ended or if they are removed from the context of the original geographical location. According to Ball and Tasaki (1992), a person is attached to a particular object to the degree that the object is used to maintain his or her self-concept. The more an object constitutes part of a consumer's identity, the more the consumer exhibits protective behaviour toward the object, and the greater the effort the consumer spends on maintaining the object, the greater is the consumer's emotional difficulty in accepting deterioration or loss of the object. Thus neither BIRGing nor CORFing explain the motives and behaviours of the devoted fan. The devoted fan possesses an attitude of 'my team, right or wrong', or 'we don't do walking away'. The devoted fan uses being a fan as an important part of self-identification, yet not the most critical or central self-definition in their life.

Fanatical fan

Early explorations of social psychology theories currently adopted in sport sociology research of fan loyalty provide preliminary insights that help to increase our understanding of the development of fanaticism and this unique form of intense loyalty. For example, the concept of socialisation provided explanations that can explain the process by which individuals are introduced to the brand that later becomes the object of fanaticism; for example, socialising agents such as family, peers, school and community attract or draw individuals and teach them to accept the values, goals, beliefs, attitudes and norms of the fan culture (James 1997; Huffman *et al.*, 2000; Wann *et al.* 2001). Consumer fanaticism is a unique form of loyalty characterised by strong and intense levels of commitment, allegiance, devotion, passion, emotional attachment, enthusiasm and involvement (Bristow and Sebastian, 2001; Cova and Cova, 2002; Funk and James, 2001; Muniz and O'Guinn, 2001; Oliver, 1999; Redden and Steiener, 2000; and McAlexander et al. 2002). Fans are unique consumers because their interest in a brand is self-sustaining (Pimental and Reynolds 2004). They voluntarily engage in behaviours beneficial to protecting the brand and ensuring the brand's continued existence and legacy (Doss, 1999; Fournier, 1998; Fournier and Yao, 1997; Pimental and Reynolds, 2004; Rozanski et al., 1999). Fanatical consumers exhibit a deep love for the brand and remain loyal despite poor brand performances (Hugenberg, 2002; Hunt *et al.*, 1999; Rifkin, 1999; Whang *et al.*, 2004). They display a true admiration for the brand, and their devotion, passion and enthusiasm are often considered infectious in attracting new customers and fellow followers (Belk, 2004; Pimental and Reynolds, 2004; Rifkin, 1999).

Fanatics are valuable customers of a brand and attractive to marketers for a variety of reasons. For example, some fanatics have extreme consumption drives, which imply heavy usage and purchase patterns (Hoffman *et al.*, 2000). They act as opinion leaders to bring the attention of others to the brand and attract new customers on behalf of the company (Rifkin, 1999). Fanatics go to great personal and financial lengths to support the brand, such as by joining and actively participating in brand communities (Funk, 1998; Muniz and O'Guinn, 2001). Their support is consistent, persistent and resistant to any attempts at reducing this attachment, which includes the active disregard of marketing messages from competitor brands (James, 1997). Hugenberg (2002) explains that organisations become wealthy as a result of fan loyalty.

The fanatical fan is similar to the devoted fan in that the fanatical fan is not bounded by time or distance and defines 'self' through attachment with the sports consumptive object. The fanatical fan uses being a fan as a very important part of self-identification. The fanatical fan engages in behaviour that is beyond that of the normal devoted fan – a greater level of knowledge, a greater level of anxiety and greater arousal when watching their team compete (Branscombe and Wann, 1991; Wann *et al.*, 1999). Yet this behaviour is accepted by significant others (family, friends, other fans) because it is considered supportive of the team, player or sport. Devoted fans may go to games. The fanatical fan may go to the game and paint their body with colours of the team, or go in costume, or in some way exhibit behaviour that is different from the devoted fan. Interaction with the club is highly valued. Supporters engage in website discussions and email commentaries, are keen to join supporter groups, and actively seek out and subscribe to newsletters and fanzines.

Why segment audiences for sports?

Market segmentation is not an option; it is a decision that sports marketers must be prepared to make. Limited resource availability for marketing, and greater accountability for demonstrating that marketing expenditure delivers a return on investment are reasons for evaluating a market and determining how to divide or segment it into groups that represent the most likely buyers (target consumers). The terms market segmentation and target market are highly interrelated concepts. Segmentation is the process used to analyse a population to determine the group or groups best suited to serve. The target market is the output of market segmentation, a description of the customer group(s) around which a marketing mix will be developed.

But what is market segmentation? While the definition of market segmentation provides an answer to the question 'what is market segmentation?', a deeper examination reveals what segmentation actually is. Specifically, market segmentation is described as having three characteristics: (1) it is a default strategy, (2) it is an adaptive strategy and (3) it is a creative process. Market segmentation is a default strategy because not everyone in a population will want what you have to sell. This fact is particularly applicable to the sports industry, as a majority of Americans do not consider themselves to be sports fans, for instance. So if you are selling sports, it is evident that segmentation is necessary to focus marketing efforts on those people with at least some interest in sports or your team.

A purchase decision is usually made because of what the product or service will do for the consumer. Maslow's (1943) hierarchy of needs is presented as an explanation

'We don't do walking away'

for why people might consume sports. Specifically, meeting needs at higher levels in the hierarchy including social needs, esteem needs and self-actualisation needs are often the motivations for engaging in sports consumption. Understanding why people buy can assist sports marketers not only in making targeting decisions but subsequently with how to tailor the marketing mix to appeal to motivations to satisfy unmet needs.

Benefits sought are not restricted to the needs described in Maslow's hierarchy. More practical considerations such as low price or convenience may be the benefits sought. Regardless of the framework used for asking this question (utilitarian vs. hedonic consumption; Maslow's hierarchy of needs), the purpose is the same – gain an understanding of why people buy and segment customers based on similarities of benefits sought.

Learning about descriptive characteristics tells us more about *who* customers are. Learning about benefits sought from purchases explains *why* customers buy. Learning about customer behaviours gives insight into *what* they do. Using customer behaviours as a segmentation basis, this can be considered in two different ways. First, behaviour in terms of psychographic characteristics such as interests, values or hobbies enables us to segment consumers based on how they live out their lives. Under Armour is an example of a brand that has effectively segmented using psychographic characteristics. The brand appeals to athletes who seek to perform at high levels.

Another way that customer behaviours can feed into market segmentation is by learning more about buyers' product usage rate. Frequency of purchase or dollars spent can be criteria for usage rate segmentation. Usage rate figures prominently in segmentation strategies for sports properties that sell tickets. Season ticket holders represent high usage segments. Other segments might include occasional attendees (multi-game attendee), infrequent attendees (single-game ticket buyer) and non-attendees. Marketing needs will differ for each of these segments.

3. SPECULATE ON THE REASONS WHY FANS WOULD CONTINUE TO SUPPORT THE TEAM THROUGH ROUGH TIMES (I.E. FINANCIAL PROBLEMS, POOR PERFORMANCE, ETC.).

This question enables students to think about fan identity, affiliation and community pride. Fan identification is defined as the personal commitment and emotional involvement fans have with a sports organisation.

Affiliation characteristics refer to the sense of community that a fan builds as a result of a team. The community affiliation component is defined as the 'kinship, bond or connection the fan has to a team. Community affiliation is derived from common symbols, shared goals, history, and a fan's need to belong' (Sutton *et al.*,

1997: 15–22). The sports team provides fans with a way to feel connected to the community and fulfils the need for affiliation. In addition, the more a fan's reference group (family and friends) favour going to games, the more the individual identifies with the team.

4. WHAT LESSONS CAN BE LEARNED FROM THIS CASE STUDY IN RELATION TO CUSTOMER/BRAND LOYALTY?

Fans behave as loyal consumers who exhibit several loyalty behaviours, such as repeating their purchase or patronage, or insisting on staying in the relationship between brands or products. Regular and repeated consumption is the clearest indicator of a particular emotional investment by the fan. Brooker and Jermyn (2003) and Harrington and Bielby (1995) identify the relationship between repeated consumption and the emotional commitment of these fans. Sandvoss (2005) observes that most of those who label themselves as fans, point to their repeated consumption patterns. He defines fandom on the basis of repeated consumption and emotional bond with the fanatic objects, and his description of the fan equates with consumer loyalty behaviour. Such loyal behaviour is a composite blend of brand, an attitude and behaviour with indexes that measure the degree to which the consumer favours and purchases a brand repeatedly (Day, 1969; Pritchard *et al.*, 1999).

The aim for the sports organisation is to have a large base of fans who show a long-term commitment to the team, player or sport. These vested fans recruit other fans, follow the team loyally and view the team as a vital part of the community. They exhibit a number of concrete behavioural characteristics and are most likely to return to sporting events, attend home and away games, and invest more financially.

5. WHAT LESSONS CAN YOU LEARN FROM THIS CASE STUDY WHEN MAKING DIFFICULT MANAGEMENT DECISIONS?

This question is intended to make students think how the dynamic between the fans and the club makes it necessary to modify the rules that apply to other business and management situations. An important prompting question would be: 'Can a sports club/team exist without any fans/supporters?' The focus here is that it is vital that organisations build a loyal base of fans who invest not only financially in the organisation in terms of buying merchandise and so on, but also emotionally by attending the games and giving moral support throughout defeats and other difficult times. If the clubs lose this fan base, then the results are poor season and match-day ticket sales, leading to poor turnover and long-term financial instability.

BIBLIOGRAPHY

Aaker. D. (1994). Building a brand: the Saturn story. *California Management Review*, 36(2) 114–33.

Ball, A. D. and Tasaki, L. H. (1992). The role and measurement of attachment in consumer behaviour. *Journal of Consumer Psychology*, 1(2), 155–72.

Belk, R. W. (2004). Men and Their machines. *Advances in Consumer Research* 31, 273–8.

Branscombe, N. R. and Wann, D. L., (1991). The positive social and self-concept consequences of sports team identification. *Journal of Sports and Social Issues*, 15, 115–27.

Bristow, D. N. and Sebastian R. J. (2001). Holy Cow! Wait 'til next year! A closer look at the brand loyalty of Chicago Cubs baseball fans. *Journal of Consumer Marketing*, 18(3), 256–75.

Brooker, W. and Jermyn, D. (eds) (2003). *The Audience Studies Reader*. Routledge, Abingdon.

Cialdini, R. B., Borden, R. J., Thirne, A., Walker, M. R., Freeman, S. and Sloan, L. R. (1976). Basking in reflected glory: three (football) field studies. *Journal of Personality and Social Psychology*, 34, 366–75.

Cova, B. and Cova, V. (2002). Tribal marketing: the tribalisation of society and its impact on the conduct of marketing. *European Journal of Marketing*, 36(5/6), 595–620.

Dick, A. S. and Basu, K. (1994). Customer loyalty: towards an integrated conceptual framework. *Journal of the Academy of Marketing Science*, 22(2), 99–113.

Doss, E. L. (1999). *Elvis Culture: Fans, Faith & Image*. University Press of Kansas, Kansas.

Fournier, S. (1998). Consumers and their brands: developing relationship theory in consumer research. *Journal of Consumer Research*, 22, 343–73.

Fournier, S. and Yao, J. L. (1997). Reviving brand loyalty: A reconceptualization within the framework of consumer–brand relationships. *International Journal of Research in Marketing*, 14, 451–72.

Funk D.C. (1998). Fan Loyalty: The Structure and Stability of an Individual's Loyalty toward an Athletic Team. Unpublished Doctoral Dissertation. Columbus: Ohio State University.

Funk, D. C. and James, J. D. (2001). The psychological continuum model: a conceptual framework for understanding an individual's psychological connection to sport. *Sport Management Review*, 4, 119–50.

Gladden, J. M. and Funk, D. C. (2002). Developing an understanding of brand associations in the team sport: empirical evidence from consumers of professional sport. *Journal of Sport Management*, 16(1), 54–81.

Harrington, C. and Bielby, D. (1995). *Soap Fans: Pursuing Pleasures and Making Meaning in Everyday Life*, Temple University Press, Philadelphia.

Huffman, C., Ratneshwar, S. and Mick, D. G. (2000). Consumer goal structures and gold-determination processes: an integrative framework, in S. Ratneshwar, D. G. Mick and, C. Huffman (eds), *The Why of Consumption: Contemporary Perspectives on Consumer Motives, Goals, and Desires*. Routledge, London.

Hugenberg, B. (2002). Communicatively Constructed Stakeholder Identity: A Critical Ethnography of Cleveland Browns Fan Culture. Unpublished Doctoral Dissertation. Bowling Green: Bowling Green State University.

Hunt, K. A., Bristol, T. and Bashaw, E. R. (1999). A conceptual approach to classifying sports fans. *Journal of Services Marketing*, 13(6), 439–52.

James, J. D. (1997). Becoming a sports fan: understanding cognitive development and socialization in the development of fan loyalty. Unpublished Doctoral Dissertation. Columbus: The Ohio State University.

McAlexander, J. H., Schouten, J. W. and Koenig, H. F. (2002). Building brand community. *Journal of Marketing*, 66, 38–54.

Madrigal, R. (1995). Cognitive and affective determinants of fan satisfaction with sporting event attendance. *Journal of Leisure Research*, 27, 205–27.

Maslow, A. H. (1943). A theory of human motivation. *Psychological Review*, 50, 370–96.

Muniz, A. and O'Guinn, T. C. (2001). Brand community. *Journal of Consumer Research*, 27 (March), 412–32.

Oliver, R. L. (1999). Whence consumer loyalty? *Journal of Marketing*, 63, 33–44.

Parker, K. and Stewart, T. (1997). "The West Ham Syndrome," *Journal of the Market Research Society*, 39 (July), 509–17.

Pimental, R. W. and Reynolds, K. W. (2004). A model for consumer devotion: affective commitment with proactive sustaining behaviour. *Academy of Marketing Science Review*, 5, 1–45.

Pritchard, M. P., Havitz, M. E., and Howard, D. R. (1999). Analyzing the commitment–loyalty link in service contexts. *Journal of the Academy of Marketing Science*, 27, 333–48.

Redden, J. and Steiner, C. J. (2000). Fanatical consumers: towards a framework for research. *Journal of Consumer Marketing*, 17(4), 322–37.

Rifkin, G. (1999). How the Red Sox touch all the branding bases. *Strategy and Business*, 17, 75–83.

Rozanski, H. D., Baum A. G. and Wolfsen, B. T. (1999). Brand zealots: realizing the full value of emotional brand loyalty. *Strategy and Business*, 17, 51–62.

Sandvoss, C. (2005). *Fans: The Mirror of Consumption*. Polity, Malden, MA.

Sloan, L. R. (1989). The motive of sports fans, in J. D Goldstein (ed.), *Sports, Games and Play: Social and Psychosocial Viewpoints*, 2nd edn. Lawrence Erlbaum Associates, Hillsdale, NJ.

Sutton, W. A., McDonald, M. A., Milne, G. R. and Cimperman, J. (1997). Creating and fostering fan identification in professional sports. *Sports Marketing Quarterly*, 6(91), 15–22.

Tapp, A. J. (2004). 'Loyalty of Football fans – We'll Support You Evermore'. *Database Marketing and Customer Strategy Management*, 11(3), 203–25.

Tapp, A. and Clowes, J. (2000). From "carefree casuals" to "professional wanderers" segmentation possibilities for football supporters. *European Journal of Marketing*, 36(11–12), 45–59.

Wann, D. L. and Branscombe, N. R. (1990). Die-hard and fair-weather fans: effects of identification on BIRGing and CORFing tendencies. *Journal of Sport and Social Issues*, 14(2), 103–17.

Wann, D. L., Melinick, M. J., Russell, G. W. and Pease, D. G. (2001). *Sport Fans: The Psychology and Social Impact of Spectators*. Routledge, New York.

Wann, D. L., Tucker, K. and Schrader, M. (1996). An exploratory examination of the factors influencing the origination, continuation and cessation of identification with sports teams. *Perceptual and Motor Skills*, 82, 995–1001.

Wann, D. L., Schrader, M. P. and Wilson, A. M. (1999). Sport fan motivation: Questionnaire validation, comparison by sport, and relationship to athletic motivation. *Journal of Sport Behaviour*, 22, 114–39.

Whang, Y. O., Allen, J., Sahoury, N. and Zhang, H. (2004). Falling in love with a product: the structure of a romantic consumer–product relationship. *Advances in Consumer Research*, 31, 320–7.

'We don't do walking away'

CASE 28

RED BULL IN ENERGY DRINKS AND FOOTBALL

STEN SÖDERMAN

LEARNING OUTCOMES

Upon completion of this case study, the reader should be able to:

- structure Red Bull's marketing strategy and tactics;
- define what is a football industry;
- identify and describe factors of importance when taking big decisions like purchasing a football club.

OVERVIEW OF THE CASE

This case study attempts to identify some possible motives for how sports can function as a tool for marketing and act as content for marketing campaigns by examining the history of Red Bull. The issues surrounding the purchase of a football club and the challenges of managing a fan base are elaborated.

Spring 2014 – purchasing a soccer team in the UK

The sport director of Red Bull Salzburg, Rolf Rangnick, shouts before he slams the door and leaves the board meeting:

> Red Bull needs a team which can compete in Champion's League; the only market that we have not reached. The best is if we can purchase a team in the London area, but both Everton and Liverpool are of interest. I have looked at the Championship, but there we can spend a fortune without coming any-where. Look at Charlton, which reached the Premier League in Spring 2014. Its new owner Roland Duchatelet did it again. He has simultaneously man-aged to get his top team Standard to win the Belgian league. He understands the economies of scale in managing sport.

For most of its existence Red Bull has focused heavily on marketing and branding, which has enabled it to sell its drinks at a much higher price point than other soft drinks. Its aim has always been to be on the edge, whether through being condoned and sought after by influential DJs in hip New York nightclubs, or by being used by famous extreme sports practitioners. Red Bull is no ordinary soft drink; it is infused with more caffeine than most caffeinated soft drinks and also includes taurine and other supposedly uplifting ingredients. As such, it is a drink that if it actually has the positive effect on mental and physical alertness and vigour that it is marketed to have, it would very well suit the night owls and life extremists who are used to brand it.

So why would Red Bull consider buying a football club from the Premier League? It already owns other sports teams, including in football, Formula One, baseball and other sports. But why is it specifically attracted to the Premier League, and what are some of the perspectives that can be applied when attempting to understand the implications of such an acquisition?

This case study will attempt to clarify some of the possible reasons why sports can function as a tool for marketing and as content for marketing campaigns by examin-ing the history of Red Bull.

History of Red Bull

Red Bull GmbH is an Austrian company founded in 1984 by an Austrian (Dietrich Mateschitz) who, while visiting Thailand in 1982, met a Thai businessman (Chaleo Yoovidhya) who worked for a pharmaceutical company. In Thailand, Dietrich found an energy drink named Krating Daeng that supposedly alleviated his jet lag (*The*

Economist, 2002). This energy drink was developed by Chaleo's company, which prompted Dietrich to join forces with Chaleo and start a new company in order to bring the drink to Europe under the name Red Bull.

Sponsoring – exposure

The main reason for Red Bull to invest in (and own) a top football club is most likely not to make profit from the club itself. Its reasons are rather the indirect gains that come from anchoring and strengthening its brand. This is of course expected to generate profits in the long term through generating sales and being able to keep charging premium prices for its product. These are similar or the same reasons most sponsors have for sponsoring.

Marketing – five perspectives

Symbolism – Red Bull gives you wings

The management of Red Bull (GmbH) seems to be very aware of the symbolisms of their brand and how to control and use them for the best effect. The slogan 'Red Bull gives you wings' is closely connected to the reasons customers have for buying Red Bull. One can assume their customers do not primarily buy Red Bull for its great taste or for quenching their thirst, but rather for the extra 'lift' of energy that the metaphorical 'wings' of the drink supposedly gives the consumer.

It can be speculated that the target for their marketing efforts is the wider general audience of the sponsored or purchased sports teams or events. This should be true for almost any of Red Bull's sports-related endeavours, whether it is sponsoring Felix Baumgartner's record-breaking parachute jump from the stratosphere, the acquiring and ownership of Formula One teams or the prospective acquisition of a Premier League team. The purpose is not to reach only the specific team's or person's immediate fans, but rather to reach the much wider spectra of potential consumers – everyone from the core fans to the casual spectator.

When Red Bull acquired the Austrian football team today named FC Red Bull Salzburg, the fans of the team were more or less ignored, even as they protested at the changes Red Bull forced upon the team. The hard-core fans opposed a change in the team's name, logo and colours. Red Bull was not bothered by the core fans of the team, but was instead interested in the wider audience to which a football team is exposed through competitions, through which a football team can carry and convey symbolic meanings that resonate with the Red Bull product. In short, through buying a football team Red Bull isn't trying to create satisfied customers – fans of the particular team – but rather to reach and be exposed to customers who are looking for something extra. In the case of Red Bull, the 'extras' provided are the exciting ingredients caffeine and taurine.

Strategies

What is Red Bull's strategy? Red Bull sells 4 billion cans of energy drink each year and earned almost €5 billion in revenue in 2012, which is remarkable considering the company was only founded 25 years ago (Pangarkar and Agarwal, 2013). But what industry does it consider itself to be in? Red Bull's businesses span many different fields and its participation in areas from ownerships to sponsorships is just as expansive. Conglomerates are usually not well received by financiers and Red Bull is clearly involved in different branches of entertainment (different sports and events) apart from energy drinks.

Structure

A third perspective is that Red Bull is not driven by customers or strategy but by its organization/structure. It is said that a strategy theory is important, but that it has no value unless it is put into practice. In the case of Red Bull, a structure is clearly visible as it is a conglomerate that is involved in many different areas in order to leverage its sales of its energy drink. Its management can't know everything, but they seem to have a clear understanding of the symbols they use and a good enough appreciation of the potential of those symbols to enable Red Bull to become hugely successful in its line of business.

Could this be an example of an emerging trend of new kinds of structures where football teams in the future will be part of conglomerates? Red Bull today owns arenas and teams in different sports, and is involved in culture projects all around the world. It already owns several football teams, but is this multiple ownership problematic for Red Bull, as well as for the teams and the leagues and associations arranging the competitions in which the teams participate?

Governance

As mentioned earlier, the ownership of football teams can be motivated by different reasons, not only for direct, or as in the case of Red Bull, indirect financial gain. Paris Saint-Germain, for example, is currently owned by the Qatar Tourism Authority and Qatar Airways, who are sponsors of both Barcelona and Paris Saint-Germain. The motives for owning foreign companies are many. For example, it is likely that Roman Abramovich, the Russian owner of Chelsea FC, gains a special position and a kind of legitimacy or even political protection from his ownership of a Western football team.

Also, the distinction between sponsors and owners are increasingly diminishing, and as a result of this, new types of ownership seem to be emerging, complicating things even more.

Some teams are more likely than others to be acquired, depending on who the owner or owners are and what are their present reasons for ownership. Tottenham Hotspur FC, for example, is owned by ENIC International Limited, a part of the

ENIC Group, a UK-based investment company. Any team could likely be bought if the price was right, but a team owned by an investment company is probably easier to buy since the ownership is primarily a business investment with the intention to bring in profit for the company, as opposed to an investment that has a heavier emphasis on creating status or a personal connection for the owner. In that latter case, selling the team to Red Bull would probably be a difficult thing, even if the price was really good. This is especially true looking at Red Bull's track record in team acquisition. When Red Bull bought Salzburg FC, it completely ignored the fans' protests and changed the team's name, logo and colours; Red Bull seems to have added insult to injury by being completely insensitive to the fact that it stepped in to a world filled with emotion and passion, as expressed by a football culture commentator:

> The violet and white colours of Austria Salzburg were replaced with a kit more suitable for the marketing of 'the brand', with supporters' protests completely ignored by the clubs hierarchy. Also gone was the clubs traditional badge, once again replaced by a tawdry Red Bull infected logo without a shred of pride or passion. As supporters protested furiously for the return of Austria Salzburg's soul, Red Bull's [*sic*] offered a so-called compromise. 'If colours are so important to the supporters, the goalkeeper can wear violet socks' said Red Bull.
>
> (Dudley, 2013)

Any owner who is also a lifelong fan of a football club would most likely think twice before selling their team to Red Bull, considering it has this kind of reputation amongst people who are not even necessarily fans of Salzburg FC but of the sport itself, even if Red Bull offered to pay a lot more than the team could be considered to be worth in monetary terms. As Tottenham Hotspur is owned mainly by an investment company, this team is probably more at risk of being sold to a change-oriented company like Red Bull. However, FC Red Bull Salzburg reached much higher levels of success in competitions with the new financial backing and investment from Red Bull.

> There was opposition to the Salzburg idea from fans, some of whom set up their own club in opposition, but it still went through and the newly named operation has, domestically at least, enjoyed its most trophy-laden era.
>
> (Edwards, 2013)

Liverpool is another team that could possibly be interesting to Red Bull as it has American owners and is very popular internationally. However, the international fans of Liverpool might be just as, or even more protective of their club as the local fans were of Salzburg, and any mistakes on the part of Red Bull could prove to be fatal for its brand, since Liverpool is a much larger team with many more fans.

Efficiency

Marketing is the main focus of Red Bull, while the other parts of its business, such as production and distribution, have been outsourced. Cheap production and distribution have enabled it to invest heavily in marketing, which in turn allows for its product to be priced at a premium. Red Bull's marketing has led not just to the success of the company, but also to the company being recognized as a world leader and declared the 'most innovative sponsor over the past 20 years' (IMR Sports Marketing, 2013). This stands in stark contrast to the view of the people opposing what Red Bull did to FC Salzburg. Perhaps this divergence suggests that the management of Red Bull has an overall good idea of what is good for their brand, but that there is a hint of hubris in their aggressive expansions, where some sports and teams require greater sensitivity to their culture and history. Not all publicity is good publicity, but where should the line be drawn and will Red Bull know if and when it has crossed that line? If Red Bull had not changed the logo and colours of FC Salzburg so drastically and had listened more to the Salzburg fans, would it have gained more credibility and goodwill from football fans in general, and would that have led to better sales of its energy drink?

Autumn 2014 – more contacts

In the light of this history and these perspectives, what are the possible outcomes – possibilities and risks – if Red Bull buys a Premier League football team and makes it a platform for communicating its brand name?

The speculations in the press continue. At the beginning of November 2014 *The Telegraph* reported that Leeds FC, a Championship club, was in talks with Red Bull through an agent. But the new owner of Leeds, Massimo Cellino, asserted that he would not sell the club. According to the same source, Red Bull had had discussions in Spring 2014 with the Premier League club Newcastle, but did not accept the high price of 300 million euros asked by Newcastle. Red Bull is said to estimate the value of Leeds FC to be 70 to 90 million euro (Edwards, 2014). Speculations continue in 2016.

Possibilities

Red Bull already owns several football teams in Europe, the USA and Brazil, in addition to teams in other sports, so why is it now considering investing even more in football by buying a team in the Premier League? There could be several reasons. Even though Red Bull already owns other football teams in other countries, it is still arguably mostly known from its connection to extreme sports and Formula One teams. Owning a team in the Premier League would increase not only its reach but also its frequency of exposure, especially if the team was a top team in that league, and a team with the possibility of reaching Champions League or the top of that league. Therefore, by buying a Premier League team, Red Bull has the possibility of reaching a lot of new potential customers and anchoring its brand name with new as well as old segments and customers. Focusing more on a 'regular' sport such as football rather than extreme sports could also render it more 'accessible' than can be achieved with extreme sports. In a sense, what is communicated when a football team carries the Red Bull brand is that you don't have to do something extreme to have a reason to drink Red Bull. It could be argued that the consumer can more easily identify with a (professional) football player than with someone participating in a more extreme sport.

Football is the world's largest sport and the Premier League is the world's largest sports league. It reaches 600 million homes in 202 different countries. This reach is enormous and is not only confined to reaching millions of TV viewers around the world. It also sends ripples through news sites and social media where pictures, articles and video clips are posted and discussed. This communication is fuelled by the passion and interest of the millions of fans of the league. This means even more attention and exposure on top of the TV exposure. Add some of the league's more famous players to this equation and the brand is connected with them as well (mostly for the better, but also possibly with negative repercussions). According to a source of *The Mirror*, Red Bull wants a team that has the possibility of reaching the Champions League, since if it succeeded in doing so, it would generate even greater public interest and increase their attention even more, especially if it was Red Bull that brought the team to Champions League. This would mean an even wider reach and increased frequency for the exposure of Red Bull. The source told *The Mirror* (2013) that:

> Red Bull wants a team to take into the Champions League. It is the only market they have not reached yet. Ideally this would be in the London area, but both Everton and Liverpool interest them too because it would not take much to get them to that level.

However, the boss of the Red Bull Formula One team, Christian Horner, does not believe Red Bull is about to make such an acquisition, stating to BBC Radio Five Live that:

> They have got their own team in Salzburg, they have another one in Germany, so I am not sure they would want to take another one on at the moment, but with Red Bull, you never know.

(Kent, 2013)

Horner's analysis of the situation may be as good as anyone's; but he probably doesn't wish for Red Bull to invest heavily elsewhere, since that could divert funds from his Formula One team. In addition, any possible resulting controversies could lead to a high-level branding failure with a massive backlash amongst fans in the world of football that could trickle over to Formula One and make his team look bad – and make other sponsors lose interest.

QUESTIONS

1. Is Red Bull's involvement in sports good or bad?
2. What types of sponsorship exist?
3. Is it a good idea for Red Bull to invest in the Premier League? Examine the pros and cons of such an investment.
4. Would the scenario where only a few actors each owned several top football clubs be viable?
5. What strategies do you recommend to a club owner for managing the club's fan base?

CONCLUSIONS

Buying and sponsoring sports is always an endeavour with higher risks than other types of marketing, due to a variety of uncontrollable factors. This is true even if the sponsor does not plan to make any large encroachments into the team culture and history, as has been the case with Red Bull and their acquisitions. The success (or rather lack thereof) of the sponsored or bought team can be a real problem when calculating whether it is a good idea or not to invest in it, if it turns out that the team doesn't do well or if it does worse than before being acquired, for example. Other more general conditions such as the weather during important games might also lower the quality of the game, meaning fewer viewers than expected, and so on. Also of course, sponsored teams or individuals can create controversies on their own, which may cast shadows over the sponsors or owners.

One of the most difficult problems directly related to the management of the team is the pre-existing supporter culture and history that is part of most teams. When Red Bull bought the Austrian team then named SV Austria Salzburg, now named FC Red Bull Salzburg, the fans were completely ignored as they resisted the name change and fiercely protested the team's change of logo and colours. This made Red Bull unpopular with the fans of the very team they bought, most likely resulting in fewer cans of Red Bull being sold to that specific group of consumers. Still, one can imagine that Red Bull came out on top financially after calculating the costs of buying and keeping the team and the possible loss of sales to those fans who disliked what Red Bull did to their team, versus the value of the greater reach of their brand outside of the group with whom they became unpopular. And if the dissatisfaction of the fans remains a local question and does not extend to the general audience of the entire league, the problem is minimized.

When buying a more expensive and famous team, though, it can be expected that the fan base is even more conservative and sensitive to this kind of intrusion. There is a worry amongst some, especially in Europe where people are not used to thinking of sports as a business (read entertainment business), that a lot of professional sports are becoming more commercialized as more and more money is involved. Renaming arenas and teams after large, wealthy companies is often viewed as an unsavoury expression of this commercialization, and that through this commercialization the authenticity of the teams and the entire sport is lost.

> This is the world we live in. This is the commercialization of sport. This is football. Too many innovations, too many gimmicks, too much money, too many who believe change is always for the best ... I don't think our national sport is in a better state now than it was when I was a child. It is bigger, more popular, better covered, maybe even more exciting as a result, but it is not better.
>
> (Edwards, 2013)

If Red Bull were to buy a Premier League team with a long-standing history and fan club, changing that team's visual profile (colours, logo etc.) could create a larger outcry than Red Bull expects from fans and from others who are fans of the sport or league, albeit not of the specific team. In that case, the positive of having great reach thanks to great public interest could turn into something very negative – not least in the social media. Then there is a risk that the discussions about the competition in all media in general, and in the social media in particular, start focusing on how Red Bull is ruining the sport by destroying its spirit and authenticity. In this way, owning or sponsoring, and by extension altering, teams that have a long history is very different from sponsoring one-off or exceptional events. The 'space jump' from the stratosphere by Felix Baumgartner was made possible thanks to Red Bull; at least that is how it can be perceived. Therefore, Red Bull was celebrated by many for having made the jump possible. In sponsoring such an event there is no history Red Bull could possibly trample over.

The criticisms regarding the bad influence of money in football comes from many directions and is not only aimed at owners and sponsors. Hamburg economics professor Henning Vöpel is very critical of UEFA rules and how UEFA disposes of its revenue from media rights, favouring the big clubs while making it very difficult for smaller clubs to take loans to make one-time investments in players.

UEFA dishes out huge sums to the big, successful clubs, which then in turn use the money for buying players, attracting them with huge salaries, and the stars then help them strengthen their position ... UEFA has a monopoly on the Champions League and can afford to push through its interests and ideas and ignore the fans' preferences. And the clubs are all in favor of the lucrative group stage, which simply means more revenue from marketing media rights. So you could say UEFA has really commercialized football, he told Deutsche Welle.

(Kaufmann, 2013)

So far 'multiple ownership', where two teams with the same owner play against each other in the same competition, are not allowed according to UEFA rules, but the limits for what is possible could change as different types of owners create different kinds of collaborations. And if it is true that UEFA are more interested in profits than in the sport, no one knows what the future may hold.

RECOMMENDED READING

Beech, J. and Chadwick, S. (2013). *The Business of Sport Management*, Pearson, New York.
Demir, R. and Söderman, S. (2015). Strategic sponsoring in professional sport: a review and conceptualization, *European Sport Management Quarterly*, 15(3), 271–300.
Gorse, S., Chadwick, S. and Burton, N. (2010). Entrepreneurship through sports marketing: a case analysis of Red Bull in sport, *Journal of Sponsorship*, 3(4), 348–57.
Söderman, S. (2013). *Football and Management*, Palgrave Macmillan, Basingstoke.
Söderman, S. and Dolles, H. (eds) (2013). *Handbook of Research on Sport and Business*, Edward Elgar, Cheltenham.

BIBLIOGRAPHY

Dudley, B. (2013). Against Red Bull Football. [Blog] *Supporters Not Customers*. Available at: http://supportersnotcustomers.com/2013/06/11/against-red-bull-football/ (accessed 9 May 2014).
The Economist (2002). Selling energy. [online] Available at: www.economist.com/node/1120373 (accessed 7 May 2014).
Edwards, L. (2013). Red Bull putting their name to a Premier League team would be another step in commercialising the sport. *The Telegraph*. [online] Available at: www.telegraph.co.uk/sport/football/10459627/Red-Bull-putting-their-name-to-a-Premier-League-team-would-be-another-step-in-commercialising-the-sport.html (accessed 9 May 2014).
Edwards, L. (2014). Leeds United in talks with Red Bull about investment in the club. *The Telegraph*. [online] Available at: www.telegraph.co.uk/sport/football/teams/leeds-united/11205123/Leeds-United-in-talks-with-Red-Bull-about-investment-in-the-club.html (accessed 2 May 2014).

IMR Sports Marketing (2013). Red Bull voted best sponsor. [online] Available at: www.imr-publications.com/newsdetails.aspx?nid=48 (accessed 10 May 2014).

Kaufmann, D. (2013). UEFA has commercialized football. *Deutsche Welle*. [online] Available at: www.dw.de/uefa-has-commercialized-football/a-17095173 (accessed 10 May 2014).

Kent, D. (2013). Red Bull's Premier League takeover not likely to have wings any time soon, says energy drink giant's F1 chief Horner. *Mail Online*. [online] Available at: www.dailymail.co.uk/sport/football/article-2457450/Red-Bull-Racings-Christian-Horner-says-Red-Bull-Premier-League-franchise-likely-happen-soon.html (accessed 4 May 2014).

Mirror (2013). Red Bull looking to buy English football club and take them into the Champions League. Available at: www.mirror.co.uk/sport/football/news/red-bull-looking-buy-english-2366075 (accessed 8 November 2016).

Pangarkar, N. and Agarwal, M. (2013). The Wind Behind Red Bull's Wings. *Forbes*. [online] Available at: www.forbes.com/sites/forbesasia/2013/06/24/the-wind-behind-red-bulls-wings/ (accessed 7 May 2014).

The Telegraph (2014). Leeds United in talks with Red Bull about investment in the club, 3 November. Accessed from www.telegraph.co.uk/sport/football/teams/leeds-united/11205123/Leeds-United-in-talks-with-Red-Bull-about-investment-in-the-club.html (accessed 22 June 2016).

RECOMMENDED WEBSITES

Newcastle United: www.nufc.co.uk/page/Welcome/
Premier League: www.premierleague.com/en-gb.html
Red Bull: www.redbull.com/
Red Bull Salzburg: www.redbulls.com/en

DEVELOPMENT OF A PROFESSIONAL FOOTBALL LEAGUE IN SINGAPORE: A SINKING OR SUCCESSFUL LEAGUE?

DONNA WONG

LEARNING OUTCOMES

Upon completion of this case study, the reader should be able to:

- understand the football industry in Singapore;
- understand the unique characteristics of football in Asia;
- recognise some of the determining factors in managing a professional football league;
- recognise and understand the impact European football can have on Asian football development;
- appreciate the challenges Asian countries face in trying to develop their local football leagues.

OVERVIEW OF THE CASE

This case study looks at the development of the first professional football league in Singapore – the S-League. Since its inception in 1996, attendance at league matches has for some years been on a downward spiral, and linked to failures in numerous respects – ineffectual management, waning interest and the mediocre standard of football clubs. This case study aims to analyse the barriers Singapore is facing on the development of the domestic football league in the face of the enormous popularity of the various manifestations of European football.

CASE STUDY

> With this move, we hope to relive the glory days.
>
> (Football Association Malaysia Deputy President Tengku
> Abdullah Sultan Ahmad Shah, cited in Lee, 2011)

The above comment, made in reference to the announcement of the return of Singapore football team to the Malaysia Cup, sums up the current state of domestic football in Singapore. A flurry of interest (in the press and online) followed this announcement (Little, 2013). Given the popularity of the sport in Singapore, this reception might not seem unusual had it been coverage of European football, such as the English Premier League (EPL), Germany's Bundesliga or even Spain's La Liga. However, such attention on domestic football has been unprecedented for more than a decade, as it has been struggling to capture both the public imagination and the attention of much of the mainstream media. Over the years, the malaise in the performance and quality of Singapore's football has been witnessed by its FIFA ranking, which fell from its highest level of 92 in 1996 to its lowest level at 171 in 2016 (FIFA, 2016).

This case study aims to look at the causes of Singapore's steadily diminishing stature in the domestic and regional football arena. The early development of football in Singapore has been dealt with in previous works (see for instance Aplin, 2013; Aplin and Quek, 2002; Horton, 2001). Here we seek to consider the contemporary development, shedding light on the governance and management of football in Singapore which has led to its regression in quality and performance levels over the last two decades. This case study aims to analyse the significant barriers domestic football in Singapore is facing with its (lack of) developmental agenda, in the face of the enormous popularity of manifestations of European football, in particular the EPL. Before delving into Singapore's struggle with its league development, it is pertinent to take a brief look at football development in Singapore in recent years. These episodes of development set the background for the discussions to follow.

S-League

The underlying sporting traditions in Singapore have been inherited from British imperial values and social systems, which have prevailed since the colonisation of Singapore in 1819. Meant initially for British and other European settlers, organised football arrived in Singapore with the establishment of the Singapore Amateur Football Association (SAFA) in 1892. As a sport that transcends language barriers, football quickly gained a following within the different communities in Singapore and became a national sport. Inter-state competition with Malaysia (then known as Malaya) started with the Malaya Cup (later to become Malaysia Cup) in 1921. Participation in the Malaya Cup provided the vibrancy needed by the local football scene. SAFA was subsequently renamed the Football Association of Singapore (FAS) in 1952. In 1995, as a result of social and political tensions, Singapore withdrew from the Malaysia Cup and league tournaments. This created the opportunity for the FAS to develop its own national league – the Singapore League (S-League). Modelled on Japan's J-League, the new S-League was launched in 1996, the professional football league in Singapore starting with eight professional football clubs (FAS, 2014).

Governance and developments

The determination of the league to create its own football framework started off well and drew reasonable support from the community. The novelty of a local league attracted close to 5,000 spectators per match during its first season. However, local football interests proved difficult to sustain in subsequent seasons. Two years after its inception, the number of league spectators was halved to an average of 2,239 per match (Little, 2013). In a series of attempts to revive interest in domestic football, legalised football betting ('SCORE') was introduced in 1999. This opened up a revenue source for the S-League, which also helped to fund local football development programmes (FAS, 2014). However, whether the move has brought in more spectators (or punters) to the stadium remains debatable. Several clubs struggled, with the withdrawal of two clubs and the merger of two others by 2003.

Concerns were expressed by the league's governing body over its ability to maintain a high standard of competition in a country with a small population and limited player base. The FAS's withdrawal from the Malaysia Cup limited participation opportunities and restricted the development of local talent on and off the field. In a move to grow its talent pool and attract more spectators through the raising of football standards, the FAS adopted the Foreign Sports Talent (FST) Scheme in 2000. The FST is a scheme introduced in Singapore in 1993, used predominantly by sports associations and organisations to scout for and facilitate the migration of non-Singaporeans deemed to possess sports talent to play and represent Singapore in sporting events. It aimed at boosting local sporting standards through the import of sporting expertise. The FST scheme was initially limited to talent-scouting for the Singapore national football team. The scheme was revised in 2007 to allow the recruitment of foreign players to play in the S-League and the national team after being granted Singaporean citizenship.

In its continual effort to address diminishing interest in the S-League, the FAS made the decision to invite foreign clubs to expand the league in order to raise the level of competitiveness and profile of the league. Sinchi Football Club, composed of Chinese players, became the first foreign club to participate in 2003. Although the admittance of foreign teams arguably helped to develop the league in Singapore, the decision by the FAS to pull out of the Asian Champions League, Asia's biggest football competition, polarised opinions among the locals. In 2010 the Asian Football Confederation (AFC) declared that it would not allow teams from leagues that include non-domestic squads to participate in the 2011–12 Champions League competition. The presence of foreign teams in the domestic competition contravened AFC criteria for entry to the region's top club competition. The FAS concluded that the presence of foreign clubs offered a channel to increase interest in the domestic league through generating fan excitement and improving the standard of play. More crucially, foreign clubs helped the S-League financially by attracting new sponsors, providing regional publicity and home country support for the league. Although the need to increase support at home, outweighing the opportunity to participate in the Champions League, has prompted self-imposed exile, the all-domestic-club rule is not the only AFC provision that the S-League failed to meet. The AFC also requires an average attendance of 5,000 per match, whereas the S-League matches were drawing an average of fewer than 2,000 per match (Drew, 2010).

In the wake of the withdrawal from the Champions League, supporters for domestic teams expressed their disappointment, citing the limitation of playing opportunities for local footballers. Local teams were thought to have benefitted from playing in Asia's premium tournament (Davidson, 2010). The deprivation of this participation opportunity may compromise the growth of the game in Singapore. At the same time, local supporters argued that with the limited funding the S-League is receiving from the government, funding for foreign players should be cut back and invested in local football to ensure a sustainable development of local talent (Goh, 2013).

Adding to the thorny issue of inclusion of foreign clubs in the S-League are the constant misadventures of some of these foreign clubs, which basked in the limelight for the wrong reasons. These ranged from disciplinary issues over under-par performances to fielding substandard players (Chia, 2011). Brawls started to become commonplace in the S-League matches, involving both foreign and local clubs. While struggling to revive local interests in the game, the S-League is also plagued by match-fixing and corruption scandals. In 2006 Sporting Afrique, an African club (now defunct) which had been invited to play in the S-League, came under investigation for corruption. The club was also involved in a salary dispute which had drawn international attention of the wrong kind earlier in the year (BBC, 2006). More match-fixing cases started to surface in 2008 when Liaoning Guangyuan Football Club, a Chinese club, was embroiled in one of the worst match-fixing cases in Singapore. Seven players were jailed, while the team manager, who was facing similar charges, fled the country (see Humphreys, 2010 for more details of match-fixing cases within the league). The integrity of the league and the game came under further attack when the ringleader of the 'world's largest and most aggressive match-fixing syndicate' (Interpol Secretary-General Ronald Noble, cited in *South China Morning Post*, 2013) was arrested in late 2013 in Singapore. The Singapore-based betting syndicate was headed by Dan Tan, whose match-fixing activities were linked to players, referees and officials across the world (*South China Morning Post*, 2013). Although the S-League has not been implicated in Tan's arrest, this incident has indirectly tarnished the integrity and value proposition of the S-League. Coupling this with dwindling attendances, finding sponsors for the league became a yearly challenge for the league's management (Tan, 2009).

Local private companies were not too convinced of the league as a viable product. With a low return on their sponsorship investment, major sponsors like Tiger Beer (Asia Pacific Breweries), which has been involved (initially as title sponsor) in the league's inception stages, began switching their loyalty to overseas football, particularly the EPL, as local interest in this grew (Little and Naughright, 2009). The twin drivers of pay-TV and increasing economic prosperity made Singapore an ideal target for the expansionary strategies of profit-seeking EPL clubs (Gilmour and Rowe, 2012). This happened at the very same time as Singapore set up its own professional football league. With the increasing popularity of the EPL, along with the Champions League and other European football competitions (e.g. Spanish La Liga, Italian Serie A and German Bundesliga), this further weakened public interest in the local league. Local clubs struggled to compete against this global phenomenon, losing spectators and sponsors to their global rivals. In fact, within the first year of being set up, S-League matches were rescheduled from their regular evening kick-off time to early afternoon in order to avoid a clash of fixtures with an EPL match at the weekends (Little, 2013).

The manifestation of the EPL and other European football is highly visible through local media coverage. The *Straits Times*, the main English broadsheet in Singapore, does not cover the S-League on a sustained basis. Its sports pages are dominated by the EPL and other prominent international sports. *TODAY*, a free tabloid, is the only English media that reports consistently on the S-League, and even that is on the back of an agreed advertising deal between *TODAY* and the FAS. While games are televised once a week on the local public service broadcaster *MediaCorp*, this telecast is funded primarily by the FAS with negligible viewership (Tan, 2009). Nevertheless, the FAS managed to secure a deal with a local pay-TV provider StarHub in 2012, where live coverage of one match per week is broadcast across its pay-TV, online and mobile platforms in Singapore (Long, 2012).

The intrusion of the EPL and its European counterparts is not unique to Singapore; this pattern is symptomatic of a wider trend within the majority of countries within the region such as Malaysia and Indonesia (Gilmour and Rowe, 2012; Little, 2013). Although the saturation of European football has also impeded football development in these countries, the Indonesian and Malaysian football leagues are not affected as much as the S-League owing to Singapore's population levels. As one of the smallest countries in Asia with a population of only five million, there is a lack of critical mass in Singapore to sustain the S-League. With the younger generation of football fans weaned on a diet of European football and the lack of familiarity with home players (partly as a result of the introduction of foreign players and foreign clubs), the S-League fails to make an emotional connection with Singaporeans.

The fact that the league functions as a stand-alone series where the continued participation of teams is based on the discretion of the FAS does nothing to improve support for the league. Participating teams are selected based on several criteria including, but not limited to, financial sustainability and management capability. Several teams have exited the league in the 18 years it has existed, having failed to meet acceptable standards. The fluidity of participating teams has rendered the establishment of a fan base, let alone club loyalty, a challenge. Without a relegation or promotion system, a 33-game season seems overly long and supporters potentially lose interest even before the season is over. The competition format and the lack of competitiveness has resulted in further regression of fan interest in the S-League. The average attendance for the 2013 season dropped further to a dismal 932[1] (Chin, 2014), despite match tickets costing only a maximum of S\$7 (£3.50).

Faced with the enormous challenge of overseas football and the stagnant state of the local league, a discourse was initiated as early as 2005 within the FAS exploring its return to the Malaysia Cup (Little, 2013). Although not the sole factor, Singapore's absence from the Malaysian league significantly weakened public interest in local football in both countries at the very time it was facing its biggest challenges from European football. The plight of football in Singapore mirrors a similar predicament in Malaysian football. Despite efforts to revitalise the Malaysian League, interest in their domestic football was waning as well (see Gilmour and Rowe, 2012). Touted as 'an experiment to pull in the crowds' (*TODAY*, 2010), an agreement was reached between FAS and the Football Association of Malaysia (FAM) in 2011 for Singapore's return to the Malaysia Cup from 2012. Under this agreement, a team – Singapore LionsXII – comprising five senior national players, a complement of foreign players and national players under the age of 23 (U23) from Singapore participate in the Malaysian Super League and Malaysia Cup. This partnership also saw the Malaysian U23 squad, the Harimau Muda (Young Tigers), joining the S-League.

Although sceptics have argued that the return to the Malaysia Cup is a regressive step with the local league being marginalised as a result, the bid to revive the glory days of football and boost dwindling attendances in Singapore appears to have breathed some life into local football. The LionsXII were crowned the 2013 Malaysian Super League Champions, the first Malaysian league title since 1994. Home matches have been well attended, averaging attendance of 6,200 for the 2013 season (Chin, 2014). With the return to the Malaysia Cup still in its early stages of development, the early success of the LionsXII may not be indicative of a similar fortune for the S-League. There is no certainty that interest in the S-League can be automatically generated among locals via the 'trickledown effect' from the Malaysia Cup. The proposition that the engagement with the Malaysia Cup can be channelled into passion for the local league misunderstands the dynamics of the historical links between Singapore and Malaysia. As emphasised by the FAS President Zainudin, 'There is always a special romance between Singapore and Malaysian football' (FAS, 2011). Patriotism comes into play when Singapore plays against the Malaysian team in the Malaysia Cup. With the constant change and influx of foreign teams, the S-League simply does not resonate with most Singaporeans. There is a lack of emotional connection between spectators and teams or players. With a third of the league's matches played at a neutral venue, this has also impacted on the clubs' ability to engage with their local communities.

QUESTIONS

1. What are the reasons for the overall poor performance of the S-League?
2. What effect does the popularity of European leagues (e.g. EPL, La Liga etc.) have on a league such as the S-League?
3. Suggest a strategy that could be used to improve the viability of the S-League in both the short and long term.
4. Gambling is a major problem in sport worldwide. Suggest a range of measures that organisations could take to alleviate some of the bad effects of this practice.

CONCLUSIONS – WHERE TO NOW?

Reflecting on the current state of football in Singapore, there is no lack of interest in local football, as can be seen in the recent reaction to the LionsXII and their winning of the Malaysia League Championship. Yet football in Singapore has for some years been on a downward spiral, failing in numerous aspects – there is waning interest in the domestic league, the standard of football clubs is at best mediocre and the current FIFA ranking of the national team is disappointingly low (171 as at November 2016).[2] The popularity and performance of the league is undeniably also being undermined by numerous weaknesses, including poor management of clubs and ongoing concerns regarding match-fixing. All these factors combine to generate a vicious circle – poor playing and management standards lead to a drop in the number of spectators, which in turn leads to reduced revenue from gate receipts and even less media interest, which impacts on sales of broadcasting rights and sponsorship. The perpetuation of the vicious circle dovetails with the increased availability of European football on television, which largely satisfies local appetite for the sport and overshadows the domestic football league.

There will be no easy answers or short-term fixes to all these woes. The move to return to the Malaysia Cup may just be the latest in a long line of pronouncements and initiatives to revamp the floundering S-League. Scholars (Coalter, 2004; Hindson et al., 1994) have warned about the dangers in depending on a 'trickledown effect', where reliance is placed solely on presumed support without embedding initiatives in any systematic programmes of development. It raises expectations which cannot be fulfilled and may possibly further alienate support within the wider football community. Unless these initiatives are embedded in a long-term developmental strategy, the S-League is very unlikely to see any improvements and general impact on attendances. With the generation of public interest through Singapore's return to the

Malaysia Cup, it remains critical for the FAS to harness the momentum generated and channel it into action plans to build a sustainable local league. However, there remains no guarantee that this interest will continue; until a strategy is implemented, there is still a probability that the league will continue to struggle and decline, despite these recent encouraging developments. Empty stadiums, sponsor indifference, brawling players, poor facilities and staid matches will continue to be a norm for the S-League.

NOTES

1 The average seating capacity of an S-League stadium is 4,500 (Sport Singapore, 2014).
2 Compared to 75 when the FIFA ranking started in 1993 (FIFA, 2016).

RECOMMENDED READING

Aplin, N. and Quek, J. J. (2002). Celestials in touch: sport and the Chinese in colonial Singapore. In J. A. Mangan and F. Hong (eds), *Sport in Asian Society: Past and Present* (pp. 65–98).
Gilmour, C. and Rowe, D. (2012). Sport in Malaysia: national imperatives and western seductions. *Sociology of Sport Journal*, 29(4), 485–505.
Horton, P. (2001). Complex creolization: the evolution of modern sport in Singapore. In J. A. Mangan (ed.), *Europe, Sport, World: Shaping Global Societies*. London: Frank Class (pp. 77–104).
Humphreys, N. (2010). *Match Fixer*. Singapore: Marshall Cavendish.
Little, C. (2013). 'Hamlet without the prince': understanding Singapore–Malaysian relations through football. *Soccer and Society*, 14(5), 635–51.

BIBLIOGRAPHY

Aplin, N. (2013). The slow contagion of Scottish example: Association football in nineteenth-century colonial Singapore. *Soccer and Society*, 14(5), 588–602.
Aplin, N. and Quek, J. J. (2002). Celestials in touch: sport and the Chinese in colonial Singapore. In J. A. Mangan and F. Hong (eds), *Sport in Asian Society: Past and Present* (pp. 65–98).
British Broadcasting Corporation (2006). Hopes dashed in Singapore. *BBC* [Online], 14 June. Available from: http://news.bbc.co.uk/sport1/hi/football/africa/5079434.stm (accessed on 1 March 2014).
Chia, H. K. (2011). High time for S-League revamp. *Asia One* [Online], 25 May. Available from: http://news.asiaone.com/News/Latest+News/Sports/Story/A1Story20110525-280499.html (accessed on 15 July 2013).
Chin, D. G. (2014). Balestier hope ex-Dinamo star Ljubojevic can help improve poor S-League attendances. *TODAY* [Online], 11 February. Available from: www.todayonline.com/sports/balestier-hope-ex-dinamo-star-ljubojevic-can-help-improve-poor-s-league-attendances (accessed 1 May 2014).

Coalter, F. (2004). Stuck in the blocks? A sustainable sporting legacy. In A. Vigor, M. Mean and C. Timms (eds.), *After the Gold Rush: A Sustainable Olympics for London*. London: IPPR/ Demos (pp. 91–108).

Davidson, J. (2010). How Europe is killing Singaporean football. *CNN* [Online], 20 October. Available from: http://yoursdp.org/news/how_europe_is_killing_s_porean_football/2010-10-21-2114 (accessed 10 January 2013).

Drew, K. (2010). Why can't Singapore play in Asian league? *New York Times* [Online], 15 October. Available from: www.nytimes.com/2010/10/16/sports/soccer/16iht-SOCCER.html?_r=0 (accessed 1 April 2014).

Fédération Internationale de Football Association (FIFA) (2016). FIFA/Coca-Cola World Ranking – Singapore. *FIFA* [Online], 20 October. Available from: www.fifa.com/associa-tions/association=sin/ranking/gender=m/ (accessed 14 November 2016).

Football Association of Singapore (2011). Memorandum of understanding between Football Association of Singapore and Football Association of Malaysia. *FAS* [Online], 12 July. Available from: www.fas.org.sg/news/memorandum-understanding-between-football-asso-ciation-singapore-and-football-association-malays (accessed 8 May 2014).

Football Association of Singapore (2014). History of football. *FAS* [Online]. Available from: www.fas.org.sg/fas/history-singapore-football (accessed 30 March 2014).

Gilmour, C. and Rowe, D. (2012). Sport in Malaysia: national imperatives and western seduc-tions. *Sociology of Sport Journal*, 29(4), 485–505.

Goh, I. (2013). Local football needs more rivalry, funds to develop talent. *TODAY* [Online], 14 November. Available from: www.todayonline.com/sports/local-football-needs-more-rivalry-funds-develop-talent (accessed on 2 March 2014).

Hindson, A., Gidlow, B. and Peebles, C. (1994). The 'trickle-down' effect of top level sport: myth or reality? A case study of the Olympics. *Australian Leisure and Recreation*, 4(1), 16–24.

Horton, P. (2001). Complex creolization: the evolution of modern sport in Singapore. In J. A. Mangan (ed.), *Europe, Sport, World: Shaping Global Societies*. London: Frank Class (pp. 77–104).

Humphreys, N. (2010). *Match Fixer*. Singapore: Marshall Cavendish.

Lee, M. K. (2011). Singapore is back in the Malaysia Cup. *Straits Times Indonesia* [Online], 13 July. Available from: www.thejakartaglobe.com/archive/singapore-is-back-in-the-malaysia-cup/ (accessed 28 April 2014).

Little, C. (2013). 'Hamlet without the prince': understanding Singapore–Malaysian relations through football. *Soccer and Society*, 14(5), 635–51.

Little, C. and Nauright, J. (2009). Globalization and development in sport: perspectives from South East Asia. In D. Nault (ed.), *Development in Asia: Interdisciplinary, Post-neoliberal and Transnational Perspectives*. Boca Raton: Walker Press (pp. 195–214).

Lee, K. Y. (1973). Speech by Prime Minister Lee Kuan Yew at the opening of National Stadium. *National Heritage Board* [Online]. Available from: www.nas.gov.sg/archive-sonline/speeches/record-details/7359f206-115d-11e3-83d5-0050568939ad (accessed 18 December 2010).

Long, M. (2012). StarHub and ESPN Star Sports on board with the S.League. *Sports Pro* [Online], 9 February. Available at: www.sportspromedia.com/news/starhub_and_espn_star_sports_on_board_with_the_s.league/ (accessed 16 March 2014).

South China Morning Post (2013). Singapore match-fixing ring was world's biggest: Interpol. *South China Morning Post* [Online], 25 September. Available from: www.scmp.com/sport/soccer/article/1316987/singapore-match-fixing-ring-was-worlds-biggest-interpol (accessed 8 May 2014).

Sport Singapore (2014). Sports Centres. *Sport Singapore* [Online]. Available from: www.myac-tivesg.com/facilities (accessed 6 May 2014).

Tan, L. (2009). S.League sponsorship – a good marketing play or national service? *Red Sports* [Online], 17 February. Available from: www.redsports.sg/2009/02/17/sleague-sponsorship-football/ (accessed 28 February 2014).

TODAY (2010). An experiment to draw in the crowd. *TODAY* [Online], 17 December. Available from: www.todayonline.com/Sports/EDC101217-0000268/An-experiment-to-pull-in-the-crowds (accessed 8 November 2013).

INDEX

Page numbers in **bold** refer to figures in the text.